PRAIRIE CITY, IOWA

Prairie City, Iowa

Three Seasons at Home

Douglas Bauer

G. P. PUTNAM'S SONS
NEW YORK

Library of Congress Cataloging in Publication Data

Bauer, Douglas.
    Prairie City, Iowa: three seasons at home.

    1. Bauer, Douglas. 2. Prairie City, Iowa—
Biography. 3. Prairie City, Iowa—Social life and
customs. I. Title.
F629.P75B38   977.7'594   79-10314
ISBN 0-399-12359-8

Printed in the United States of America

Notes and Acknowledgments

Most of all, I would like to thank John Wapner, and also Cindy Bobseine, who accommodated me in ways that give new definition to friendship. Also, at various important times, Laurie Cray, Barbara Gaines, and Guy Motanky cared more for me, and for the work, than the evidence seemed to warrant.

Over the course of the writing, three editors helped greatly. John Dodds initially encouraged it. Hugh Howard saw it through a mid-life crisis. Judy Wederholt found what was actually there, and what was, as Conrad warned, "a love of one's words—that is a form of self-love, a fatal love which leads a young writer to excesses."

I'm grateful to Arlene Bouras, a vigilant sentry of the printed word, whose affection for language is always evident.

From the day we met, nearly ten years ago, Mary Frances Fisher has been to me a figure of inspiration and subtly directive encouragement, and at the same time an easy, most accessible friend.

There must be special acknowledgment of the people of Prairie City, those not included as well as those whose lives are visited—some of whom, the reader should note, have been given new names, ages, shapes, and even in one passing case, gender. Everyone in so intimate a place will most probably recognize himself, and perhaps all others futilely disguised. It is hoped, nevertheless, that for anyone who wishes anonymity, the descriptions are sufficiently misleading.

For my parents, who brought me to this book,
and for Kate, who brought it home

Once in his life a man ought to concentrate his mind upon the remembered earth, I believe. He ought to give himself up to a particular landscape in his experience, to look at it from as many angles as he can, to wonder about it, to dwell upon it.

—N. Scott Momaday,
The Way to Rainy Mountain

PROLOGUE

LEAVING

In the high September sun, Ruby Conley surgically prunes her hedge. She guides her heavy clippers above the thick row at the front of her lawn, a twisting green fence against the highway that runs past her house and on through Prairie City, west to east, eight neat blocks, bisecting the town as quickly as a butcher's stroke. Ruby deftly evens her bushes, moving about her work as surely as she did twenty years ago, when she came periodically to our farmhouse with rolls of new wallpaper and buckets of thick, sweet-smelling paste, to redo our kitchen or a bedroom.

I remember her, strong and imperviously aged to my ten-year-old eyes, slapping her wide dripping brush along an awkward length of paper, then swiftly sealing it to the wall. She brought with her not only a clattering, cheerful efficiency but also the almost spiritual power of transformation—turning beige rooms powder blue, ever improving. Also, she brought a freeing chaos. The ladders and sawhorses, her accidental collages of paste and fallen paper scraps, provided one of the rare occasions when my mother, as militant a housekeeper as lives on this earth, was forced to surrender for a few days to spectacular disorder.

Now, two decades later, she cuts her hedge with the same unhesitating strokes. She looks remarkably unchanged, her hair full and white, her body large and strong. She has informed her solicitous neighbors in the southwest corner of town not to worry as she lifts and trims and tugs, explaining that she hopes for nothing more than that death will claim her suddenly, painlessly, as she's bending in her back yard for a resisting weed.

Prairie City lasts no more than a few blocks in any direction before the fields resume. Crop rows run to the edge of town, crowding it all around, like an ocean eating resolutely at its shore. Immaculate frame houses fill the city blocks, laid out in a strict grid of straight, flat streets, and there is an overwhelming dominance of sky, swooping down, uninterrupted by trees or buildings, to the horizon. Clean winds blow freely across the lawns, carrying no dust from tar-and-pebbled streets. Behind modest ranch houses, painted in pastels, stand huge wooden garages, awkward and incongruous. The garages were built as stables—behind houses that have since been replaced—and are still used for cars.

There's a trailer court, crowded to city standards, at the northwest edge of the town; new streets and new homes at the north; a short stretch of broad lawns and old homes at the south; a fence row of plain frames in treeless yards at the east, against the fields.

Nearly 1200 people live here, about 350 more than when I left, 12 years ago, though it's hard to see the growth. Most of the new people have Des Moines jobs and find Prairie City, just twenty miles away, the gentlest sort of suburb. Some people who've always been here complain that they no longer recognize every face on the street.

The highway runs without stoplights past Ruby Conley's hedge, past the P.C. Drive In, Casey's 7-Eleven, and the Prairie House apartments, one of those cheaply styled mansard-roofed buildings that have spread over the land like kudzu on a Southern roadbed.

The Tower Cafe, once the only bar in town, stands empty and the town's public drinking is done in newer surroundings, at the Cardinal Inn, one block farther east. When I was growing up here, the Tower was owned by Everett Shutt and his wife, Katherine. Shutt was a huge man who spoke in a brusque, raspy voice and he may well have owned something other than the white-cotton T-shirts I always saw him wear. He catered to a thirsty clientele who boldly parked their cars in the Tower's lot, for all the town to notice. Everett, however, was no fool to the mores of a small, self-scrutinizing place, so he also kept well-stocked coolers of beer next to his back door, which could be entered from the town's darkest alley. Even if just two or three cars were parked in front, Everett was more than likely doing good business out back. The Shutts lived in a small and dingy apartment above the bar. They are gone now, both dead.

Jim Billingsley owns both the Tower and the Cardinal. Indeed, he owns much of the town—a gas station, a drive-in and two bars on 163, more buildings on the square one block north. He kept both the Tower and the Cardinal open for a while, staggering their hours so that the bars did simultaneous business from four to six. It seemed a fine idea—doubling the population of taverns for two hours in the late afternoon—but he found that those who began at the Tower resisted the notion of interrupting card games and a happily growing numbness to get up at six o'clock and move one block to the Cardinal to start again. So he closed the Tower altogether and rented the upstairs apartment to a young cement-plant worker who presides over the silent bar and the locked back door, and who sweeps the dust from his floor through an open register, down onto the memories below.

The highway lifts, then settles, past more gas stations and Howard Cook's auto-body shop, thickly shaded on three sides. For years, Cookie enjoyed a totally enveloping shade, until he lost a tremendous elm on the west side of the building. He said, when he first saw death on the tree, that he would leave the shop when the elm fell, but he didn't.

At the edge of town, the road seems to come alive again, curving and rising. It winds past the baseball field, home of the Prairie City Lions, serving as its short and dangerous right-field fence. Generations of outfielders have cursed the ditch, the steep, grassy incline, then the highway at their backs, as a towering fly ball drifted fatefully toward the road and they pedaled gracelessly back, fighting to keep the ball in sight while watching and listening for traffic.

A few miles farther out, the highway meets a narrower road—County F62. Before it was paved and straightened and given institutional numbers, this was a rolling gravel strip where horses raced. It was known then as the Diamond Trail, but no longer deserves so lyrical a name.

Left on F62. Second house on the right. A big, sprawling farmhouse, additions extending eccentrically up and out, a pillared porch wrapping around two sides. My grandfather came to these 140 acres in 1937 from an inferior farm nearby, paying the Depression price of $119 an acre for its rich ridge of soil, house and buildings included. He farmed it, first alone and then with my father, and they farmed an adjoining 80 acres belonging to Miss Byrdie Rush, a reclusive old maid with a spare mouthful of witches' teeth, who kept a snarling pack of chow dogs that leaped from her neglected grass at anyone who approached the house.

For forty years, Bauers have farmed here. My parents and I used the upstairs rooms as an apartment for a time and in 1950 took over the entire house when my grandparents, following a timeless tribal ritual, built a small house in town and moved there to finish their lives. From the house in town, Grandpa drove daily to the farm, helping with field work and finding an endless variety of small tasks around the barnyard. He moved slowly from shed to barn, dragging a leg that had healed stiff as iron in his youth after he'd failed to cleanly hurdle a high board fence. Driving a tractor, he stood all day at rigid attention next to the seat and balanced himself with instinctual grace.

What in my grandfather was an affinity for the soil became, in my father, a strong, methodical competence. It did not survive at all into the third generation; I have neither the talent nor the temperament for farming. We all saw this early, as tractors I drove would leap with a will of their own out of deep furrows; as sharp cultivator blades would leave weeds untouched and head, instead, for rows of new beans. My father sometimes kept chickens, but very little other livestock, so I had few dawn and evening chores, a fact that rendered me indolent in the eyes of friends. There gradually evolved a compromise between farming and me. I was used intermittently in the fields for simple jobs—harrowing, disking, hoeing—when my mistakes would not literally threaten the crops. When more delicate work—plowing, planting, picking—was being done, I was assigned marginal duties or excused altogether. This arrangement suited me, though I enjoyed the fields, the roaring solitude atop a tractor. Sometimes I stood, imitating my grandfather's posture, the steering wheel jerking in my hands, feeling the ferocious sun and the engine's strength. But I was aware of no satisfying identity with farming and my only moments of passing regret came when I was unable to quote the latest tractor-model numbers in conversation with classmates, and when my skin remained, after spring planting, incriminatingly pale.

I was awkward with soil and with machines. But neither was I from *town*, with parents who were merchants or factory workers, and I never knew a childhood in the village—friends next door, paper routes, bicycling to DeWit's for a small sack of groceries. All this I glimpsed briefly on rare overnight visits with town friends.

But I was happy in Prairie City. Like many farm children, I was able to retreat into fantasies. By myself, I played entire baseball games, every position, announced them, too, to an imaginary audience. I led regiments of cavalry from the saddle of my mother's kitchen broom. I moved through school, accumulating awards and high marks. I belonged to every group, led many, spelled perfectly, attended regularly, sang beautifully, arrived punctually. I found easy competition among my twenty-seven classmates and, from a few of them, good friendship.

There were moments, nevertheless, when I felt an unarticulated sense of exile. It caused me no concern; it was simply there, an unshaped presence at the distant suburbs of awareness, and the only clarity it ever assumed was a growing certainty that I would leave the farm, leave Prairie City, and not return. I had no idea where I was going, or why, and I assumed it would not be far. No drive for fame, no wanderlust had me, and I was never fed at our dinner table broadening notions of a larger, deeper culture. Certainly, my lack of talent with the land helped separate me and perhaps I knew viscerally even then that whatever I became in life would not depend upon the mute, hard-bitten impulses of central Iowa.

I left Prairie City in the fall of 1963, dressed in tie and sports jacket, sweltering in a full September heat, for the beckoning uncertainty of higher education. I was tremulous with fear, sensing as I rode with my parents away from the farm, chauffeured like a mourner in the back seat, that all my days in Prairie City had prepared me for nothing more than the narrow continuation of life as I'd known it on this remote piece of earth. Throughout my final year of high school, I'd considered colleges, but even at the beginning of the term, with the reality of leaving still months distant, I could not imagine a campus more than a hundred miles away. The University of Iowa was out there, to the east, but its size suggested a swarming, impenetrable population and I dismissed it. Leaving the state for school was an alternative I did not consider even in passing.

My cowardice was aided by Prairie City's location in the smooth center of Iowa. For 150 miles in every direction, there was nothing but more of Iowa. No nearby borders afforded quick trips into another state. No matter that Iowa's neighbors only duplicated its inexorable prairie; at the state line, there would have been at least a crossing into a place with another name, provably different.

Not so in Prairie City, where everyone endured a geographic quarantine. I did not leave Iowa at all until I was sixteen years old, when, with fellow Young Methodists, I rode a chartered bus east to view the vistas and tombstones of Washington. In a tightly scheduled week, our group paid ten minutes of homage to every conceivable spot of patriotic interest. And what impressed me most were those spectrally lighted pedestrian tunnels that transported us magically from one side of the Pennsylvania Turnpike—traffic whispering violently overhead as we scurried through—to a Howard Johnson's restaurant on the other, where one could order sandwiches filled with something other than beef, costing nearly a dollar.

So the world was vague and dangerous and I instinctively reduced its radius. Drake University, where I finally enrolled, was in Des Moines, twenty miles away, at the edge of the earth. As I rode that day toward college, my parents chatting aimlessly to try to ease my silent gloom in the back seat, there rose in me a seizing desire to *stay;* stay forever in the strong grip of this clean and certain life, asking no more from the rest of my days than its unelaborate demands.

An entire life appeared to me: I'd work at the grain elevator on the highway west of town, soon managing all its operations. After all, the owner of the elevator had asked my father the previous spring what I'd planned after high school; obviously, he had notions for my future. People would greet me with big smiles on the streets and after I'd passed, they'd nod their heads appreciatively at the idea of one so young bearing so much responsibility.

For a feverish moment, it all seemed ideal, a life so uncluttered that I could stand at one end of it and envision it whole. The promise of such a life seemed all any mortal could ask.

Then our car passed the softball field, brown-grassed from the summer, and the gas stations and highway homes, closed against the Devil's Sabbath-day seductions. The town felt that day, as it feels on Sundays now, a place swiftly evacuated after some threat of natural devastation. In a moment, we were out of Prairie City, taking the steeply banked curve that wraps around DeRaads' farm and turns the road straight west, and the land moved behind us, drawing like a curtain, closing on the scattered homes at the city limits, the arching outline of trees that gave shade and a sense of proportion to the town. Out of the curve, my father accelerated as the highway dropped with the hillside, leaving on the shifting, dipping landscape not a sign of Prairie City.

Although Des Moines, and Drake, were geographically close, I might as well have crossed mountain ranges and seas; and within weeks it seemed as if I had. I found myself with students from Kansas City, Milwaukee, and Chicago, all of whom had graduated with more people than lived in Prairie City. From my roommate, who lived in New Paltz, New York, I heard stories of New York City and its unimaginable pleasures.

In return, I entertained my city friends with the small sums of my own youth: the size of my graduating class, of our football squad and the fact that we fell three members short of the number required for a scrimmage. I showed them the *Prairie City News* and they howled with disbelief at headlines announcing births, deaths, and barn fires. My home-town stories, filled with quaint customs and vivid simplicities, earned me a reputation I did not contest as the shit-kicking farmer who'd taken well to city cloth.

At Drake, I simply repeated my high school career, joining every group and collecting sufficient hours for a degree. I was acquainted with some of the brighter students on campus—poets and editors and soft-voiced activists who wore sandals and rode bicycles about campus—and I liked them, reluctantly. But I believed that they played their lonelier roles on a highly social campus only after having first been rejected by the prevailing tastemakers; they could not have willingly chosen their student lives.

Others whose roots are deep in country towns, notably Willie Morris in *North Toward Home*, have written of their university days as the time of an outlandish awakening to the presence of ideas, to life's illimitable variety. I made no such discoveries, and the angry currents of the '60s—which may or may not have gotten my attention—were not moving in the air at Drake.

When I graduated, a ceramic left knee keeping me from the draft, I took an advertising-copywriting job in Des Moines, refusing an offer from the *Chicago Tribune* that would have confronted me with a strange and sprawling city.

For more than a year, I wrote junk mail for *Better Homes and Gardens* magazine, offering millions of people all over the country the opportunity to receive two years of *Better Homes* for the price of one. I intimately began my letters, "Dear friend," detailed the wonders awaiting them in the pages of the magazine and signed the whole package with my nom de plume, Barbara Joyce. For decades, the magazine had signed its promotional letters Barbara Joyce and each year, at Christmas, she received dozens of cards from pathetic souls who wished her happy holidays and expressed their pleasure at having heard from her once again.

I thought it was the best job in the world. I had an office, shared a secretary, and I saw my own words in print. I was a writer. The vast majority of *Better Homes and Gardens* employees had nothing to do with the content of the magazine. Neither did I, but as a "writer," I received the nervous deference they awarded to anyone who wrote or drew or took pictures for a living.

In late summer, on my birthday, I got married, and then made my first professional mistake. I accepted a promotion. Giving up my status of writer, I took more money, a title, an office, and the job of program head, which brought with it a calculator and a responsibility for budgets, inventories, and percent-return forecasts. For nearly two years, I sat hunched over that contemptible calculator, watching in spiteful awe as it jumped and chewed at a miraculous rate the numbers I gave it. And when I'd finally had all of it I could bear, I went to the editors of *Better Homes and Gardens*, clutching my more impressive junk mail, and asked for work as an editor. But they refused me. I had, they said, conceivable potential, but, buried deep beneath Barbara Joyce's gurgling voice, it remained purely that—potential, conceivably.

That fall, I scattered résumés like handbills across the country, and about two weeks after I'd bundled up a scrapbook of Barbara Joyce's prose and mailed it off to Chicago, I answered my office phone to hear an efficient young woman's voice inviting me to *Playboy*'s offices for an interview. I set the phone gently into its cradle, as if the slightest noise at my end might jar the lady's eardrums and she'd ring me back angrily to tell me the whole thing was off.

The next day, I flew to Chicago and arrived at the offices of *Playboy*, more the youth at his first carnival strip show than the serious job applicant. Guided by the cheerful personnel woman who'd phoned me, I was led down hallways of rich paneling and artfully sweeping pebble plaster.

My first interview was with an editor, introduced as the man who wrote a good deal of the magazine's fashion copy. He wore loud plaid pants, a green shirt that was not so much wrinkled as crumpled, and a sports coat of another, equally brilliant plaid. Next, for what seemed like several weeks, I listened to an editor who leaned imperiously over his travertine-topped desk and spoke with a kind of tired outrage on everything from food to cars to the rising cost of psychotherapy, all the while moving his mouth in the faintly quivering way of a beached trout. He, in turn, led me to an editor (newly arrived and very important, I was told) who chatted in a sort of staccato English accent, speaking at a tremendous speed some form of language fully incomprehensible to my Midwest ears. He smiled and smoked furiously, rattling on like an Oxford-educated chipmunk. Whatever I may have been prepared for that day—perhaps squadrons of Bunnies serving trays of Pepsis, or a voyeuristic glimpse of a photo session in progress—these antic characters took me completely by surprise. They had collectively outflanked my expectations because, like the rest of America, I'd presumed the editors of *Playboy* would animate the propaganda of their magazine, would step forth and greet me, impeccably dressed and urbanely mannered, with gliding jazz rhythms playing in the background like a movie score, while they casually tapped their pipes and rang their secretaries to make lunch reservations at The Club. Instead, I'd seen a formidable assortment of men, their personalities dangling like loose threads, as if each of them had worked in front of a mirror at home, to perfect a unique, inimitable neurosis.

At the end of my interviews, I was led to a small office, given an old issue of *Playboy* with certain copy blocks carefully scissored out, and was asked to compose my own copy for the pictures on the page. I sat for a while, watched the Chicago sky darken, then wrote my copy, a scrambled essay on autumn fashion trends filled with the winking *entendres* I assumed all *Playboy* copy required. At five o'clock, I handed the "fashion" editor my pages and talked briefly with him once again. He laughed macabrely at my résumé and asked whether my "Methodist sensibility" (the application had asked for "religious preference") would tolerate the editorial irreverence to which I'd be subjected.

In another hour, I was flying back to the calm of Des Moines, a place that would never again look to me as it had at eight o'clock that morning, and that night I related to my wife in fine detail what had happened. I described the opulence, the editors, the great breadth of gray, clangorous city—the same city I'd resisted after college.

"You've got to take it if they offer you the job," my wife said soberly.

"Sure, sure," I said, then reached for my emotional cane: "but I don't have a chance."

Naturally, I wanted the job desperately. Also, more than anything, I hoped they'd turn me down.

At noon the following day, the editor with the quivering trout's mouth called, offering a job. He said they'd been fairly impressed and that, while my fashion copy had been hopelessly confusing, I'd nevertheless managed some nice turns of phrase, particularly one having to do with zippers.

I worked four years for *Playboy* and met in that time an assortment of young writers who seemed to have been hired according to quota, and I wondered every now and then if I'd been accepted in order to fill the vacant "farmer's" slot. I was welcomed by a Californian who worshiped dope, a Southerner who worshiped Faulkner, a Boston Catholic trying not to worship at all. I met Bronx Jews, Manhattan Jews, Brooklyn Jews. There was also another Midwesterner, or at least he was considered Midwestern by the others, though he was from Cleveland.

At *Playboy*, I watched each of these bright and talented

people enact his locale with a devotion to form that grew at times into caricature. The tenth floor often resembled an imaginative costume party, with editors in cowboy hats, editors barefoot and wearing rock-star T-shirts, editors in crocheted leather jump suits. The shows offered more than entertainment; they provided a kind of theatrical travelogue of our diverse origins and eventually provoked in me a new consideration. Had I been inclined toward such public costuming, what would I have worn? Beneath the straw hat and overalls, what were the subtler spiritual garments of the rural Midwest? Whenever I tried to reach back and bring up the peculiar realities of Prairie City, I found that I hadn't the slightest notion of them.

Until then, my close friends had been only other Midwesterners, but in Chicago I met a graduate student from Tennessee, a *Playboy* employee living through her first winter outside California, and a black woman, schooled in Japan, whose Air Force father had taken his family over a good deal of the globe. Not only did these friends display their own ethnicity but they also delightedly pointed out mine—underlining for me moments when my emotions flared suddenly, then instinctively drew back; imitating the accent I knew I didn't have.

In my office, one of them often dropped in and asked, like a child postponing bedtime, to be told a "farmer story." I'd put down my magazine or switch off my typewriter, swing my chair around and select from my repertoire. Normally, I chose one that had as its theme my surpassing hatred for chickens, and my voice rose in a half-serious evangelical fever.

"Chickens are so dumb they'll peck themselves to death!" I'd say, and described hens craning their necks to inflict further damage to ass ends already bald and bloody. "A chicken is so stupid," I would continue, "that if it sees you driving a tractor straight toward it, it'll stop dead in its tracks, squat down where it stands, and just *wait!"*

Then I'd recall the story of an afternoon with my cousin Jim, from Colfax. My father had a long, loop-ended wire with which he would hook a hen by the neck for dinner. Jim and I took the wire and made up a game that lasted an entire afternoon. Each of us got ten minutes alone in the closed chicken house. The object of the game, in that space of time, was to hook a chicken by the neck with the wire. One point for a hen, because there were so many of them, two points for a rooster. Whoever was not inside sat in the sun on top of our tractor with the official watch. In order for a point to count, the timekeeper had to be shown a chicken at the end of the wire, flapping in a pantomime of flight.

"We played all day," I'd say. "Jim won, I think. But you cannot imagine the panic of those chickens being chased around inside a closed house. No place in the world for them to hide. It's amazing none of them died. Finally, the air was so thick with feathers and dust we quit.

"Not an hour later, my father, who had no idea what had happened, innocently opened the chicken-house door! My God—" And any final description of the flock of chickens, shrieking and mad wth fright, beating the choking air and slamming headlong into windows and walls, was covered by laughter. I'd laugh along, and say finally, "I do hate chickens. I think that's why I love to eat chicken so much. It's some perverse knowledge that there's one fewer of them out there to make life miserable for a farm kid." With that, my friend would rise, spirits renewed, and thank me for the tale.

It was fun. And after she'd left, I'd pause to look around at the walls, at the original art hanging in every nook, and out my windows across Walton Street to the

Drake Hotel and the great slow curve of the North Shore. And without actually enunciating the thought, I could feel the phrase, whole: How far you've come.

It took much longer than it should have to see that my memories, polished and comedically accomplished after many retellings, were small lies, implying that I'd left home much more a farmer than I'd ever been in fact. It took even longer for me to recognize the condescension in them, that whenever someone asked a more serious question about Prairie City and the farm, I had no answers of substance or insight. When pressed for descriptions, I'd speak of the overwhelming flatness, the enveloping power of the land's alternating colors: white, brown, black, green, gold, back to white.

But what's it like out there?

I spoke of wide, flat streets without cars or stop lights.

How was it, growing up by yourself, out there on a farm? How did it feel?

I used to help in the fields. Harrowed and disked, mostly.

But what does it do to a person, seeing the same faces every day in town? Knowing everyone you meet?

God, I hated chickens, still do. Have I ever told you about the day my cousin Jim and I. . . .

In May, 1975, my mother had called me in Chicago to tell me that Grandmother Bauer, my last living grandparent, had died, and I flew to Iowa the following morning. For nearly four years, she had lain, peacefully dying, in the nursing home, but I'd not seen her since a long visit in her home after the first small stroke that started her decline.

Travis Walters' funeral home stands just behind the

railroad tracks that run east and west through Prairie City. We parked on the street next to the home and entered, into the long front room and the heavy, humid quiet. Distant relatives sat in overstuffed chairs along the walls, and rose to greet my parents and me, finding that compromise of hearty sadness that people use when a funeral brings them together for the first time in years. After a moment, I walked alone into a smaller room, too small for my grandmother's coffin and all the flowers.

For some time, my eyes searched the tiny body for signs of her. She'd lost half her weight, her big breasts were gone, and she looked as if she'd found great relief, as if a violent racking had passed. I looked at her mouth, a thin line, trying to hear her high, hoarse giggle. Only her nose, large and proud, disproportionate on her death face, seemed to be something of her. The rest was bird-like and strange and told me how long I'd been gone.

After her funeral, I stayed for a few days. It was spring, the fields showing new green rows faintly striping the black. I'd nearly decided, before Mother's phone call, to come back for as long as I needed to, and to write my way back to this place. So I patiently observed Prairie City, watched the movements of the town, leisurely but patterned, and felt its genuine life. I spoke with Mel Wicker, who'd driven my school bus, at the Co-op gas station, and he seemed pleased to see me. So did the banker and the widow of the most brilliant teacher I'd ever known, and so did several women from the Methodist Church who served lunch after my grandmother's funeral.

I had left *Playboy* nine months before, after coming to the clear recognition that the magazine had done for me all it could, and that I was no longer doing what I could for *it*. Increasingly, I'd wanted simply to write my pieces, and the few administrative details of the job, or rather my outsized resentment of them (I imagined at any moment the reincarnation of the living, breathing calculator), began to take all my working energy. So, accepting the farewell present of an article assignment, I began the transient life of a magazine writer, traveling around the country from one assignment to the next, like an itinerant fieldworker moving to his harvests.

My private life had assumed an equally scattered geography. My marriage had ended about the same time I quit the magazine; in the length of a summer I was, both emotionally and professionally, loose in a life without formal pattern. It was deeply frightening for one whose life steps had been small and mostly tested. And the fear was exhilarating, a fuel.

Now I saw Prairie City with two kinds of curiosity, a native's and a stranger's, and I felt the two grow and converge into a mutant inquiry—nostalgic and assessing. I flew back to Chicago after a week and spent the summer there, tying off that life and organizing my move.

Two highways pass through Prairie City, quartering it. 163, the busier of the two, is the road that runs east and west, from Des Moines. 117 runs north and south, and has become increasingly popular with its link to Interstate 80, a dozen miles north. Several times a month now, usually late at night, out-of-state cars wander helplessly through town, their drivers searching for the turn they missed.

On that same highway, with its loud and laboring traffic of trucks and cycles and local tractors pulling grain wagons, I've rented a small white frame house with green shutters. In front, there's a miniature porch, roofed, but its air is too public and too noisy—just a short, open lawn from the highway—for the languid ease one seeks on porches. The house is fringed with yard ferns and in back, there's a steep hump of ground, a cave, with a clay-pipe chimney coming out of the earth like a periscope. Once, meat was hung inside the cave, but it now holds scrap piles of wood and sheet paneling left from an ambitious repair of the house.

Here, in the gathering momentum of a rural autumn, I have settled for a time.

AUTUMN

When these skies are cold and dark, as they are today, the town seems to lose a finishing dimension, some depth or adornment it normally has, is entitled to have. The absence is visible, as if an artist had left Prairie City incomplete on his canvas.

This is a purely private aesthetic, but everyone in Prairie City has his ideas about the skies. They drop low and close and hold the future; approaching weather is in the skies, and Prairie City's crops, Prairie City's economy, rely on properly timed weather. There's a particularly constant burden on farmers and their merchants, seeing their situation in the skies. There's no escaping them, and if the skies stay clear when water is needed, or if they refuse to break after drowning rains, they are everywhere, *hanging*, reminding. Over generations, these people seem to have developed an extraordinary pessimism about nature. They will look up scornfully into ideal weather, then squint into the west, inspecting the horizon like a cavalry scout in a '50s Western looking to the earth's edge for that inevitable forming line of Apaches.

Moving into the cold, gray skies, the newest Co-op

grain silos are nearly finished, nearly as high as they'll be. It takes only ten days to build a silo, the work never stopping once it has begun. A silo is, elementally, a hollow cylinder of concrete several stories high and the concrete, once poured, must not be allowed to dry. If it did—if work stopped at the end of a day and resumed the following morning—a seam would form where the day's fresh batter met yesterday's, letting air into the silo. Air and moisture do nothing good to stored grain. So up and up the silos go, methodically, undetectably, growing as a crop grows, and every foot of growth adds space enough for one thousand bushels of grain.

The day crew leaves the circular wooden scaffolding as new workers ride up in a bucket, and flood lamps maintain a rising halo of daylight. People from town come in the evening to watch the work, but not with the awe they felt when the first new towers were built, several years ago. This kind of construction has become an almost annual event, with the increasing yields, and the sense of spectacle has worn off. Nevertheless, there is something optically magical in watching the silos rise—silently and with no signs of strain—especially at night, when the workers are lit up in the black sky of the sleeping town. Their words and comradely laughter float down and they seem celebrities up there, floodlit and watched from below. They drew crowds years ago, when I was twelve or thirteen and came with my father to watch them. Now they get a few couples, for a minute or two, and head cranings from passing car windows. The magic has gone and the town views these growing silos with the same ennui that the rest of the country feels about seeing men in space.

After its shift, the day crew heads directly across the highway for cases of beer at Jim Billingsley's Cardinal Inn. They are mostly young men, with the shaggy heads, and beards of the new blue-collar worker, and they move with an almost parodistic muscularity. They look like members of a motorcycle gang, and they create a kind of compressed tension whenever they come down from their work and rub against the town. It's a more complicated matter than their appearance, though that's some of it. They possess an unaccommodating boldness that clashes with the settled tempo and they're not the least apologetic for it. They stride into the Cardinal with authority, suggesting the tension between an occupying army and its provincial village.

The Cardinal has a far wider clientele than its predecessor, the boarded-up Tower Cafe. It's new and clean and serves deep fried food. On weekends, it also serves steaks and families drive from all over Jasper County for dinner. In fact, much of the weekend business comes from a distance, for, although the Cardinal offers a good deal more than liquor, it's nevertheless a "tavern" to those in Prairie City who don't drink and won't enter a place where people do. Other people would rather welcome the weekend in the next town, where they can have a chance at anonymity, where local judgment is less likely to find them. So there are families from Pleasantville and Newton and Colfax at the Cardinal, and families from Prairie City in Pleasantville and Newton and Colfax.

But these rearrangements come on weekends. Monday through Thursday, the Cardinal fills with local couples, young and old, and with those men who've followed the bar all over town through the years, wherever it was and whoever owned it—Bing Miller on the square; Everett Shutt at the Tower; Jim Billingsley here. Their loyalty is simply to drinking some beer at night. Every few weeks, one of them asks Billingsley to open the Tower again, so they can sit on a barstool with men of similar purpose and without couples and children eating tenderloins and French fries behind them.

The construction workers move among the tables, the

day's dust on their clothes and powdering their hair, and the conversation in the room drops, then comes slowly back. After the noise resumes, nearly everyone continues to stare without discretion at the workers. When they move, heads move with them in seemingly rehearsed precision. A small-town stare can be humbling, for it violates the assumed rhythms of human exchange, staying on you hard, and demanding all kinds of explanations, long after you've met it and moved on. It's then, after you'd thought it was over, that you feel the stare and, glancing again, realize that it's been watching you all the time and is in no hurry. There's a deep defensiveness in it, at a level below the rudeness, a reactionary drawing of lines and taking of stands.

But the construction workers have been in this sort of company many times and they know that it's best to break up the stares and pick them off singly. The biggest of the workers begins to move toward the bathroom, his blue-denim shirt open to his waist and long days of physical labor bunched in his chest and coming out of the V. He selects an old couple and returns their stare with one of his own, as strong as theirs combined. As he nears their table, they seem for a moment to be in danger and, at the last instant, drop their eyes to ketchup-smeared plates. The worker walks past and then turns in triumph to fix them with an icy look before disappearing into the rest room.

The entire room has felt the contest and someone leans over to the old couple.

"What'd he say?"

"He didn't say nothing," says the old man, laughing over his nerves. "But by God, he better watch out."

If these workers have shown no regard for Prairie City's customary reserve, they've started no fights, and have brought to town a traditionally epic thirst. In a place so small and cleanly patterned, one sees with an instructive clarity the profitable residue that new unordinary business leaves on a town. Successful fields of corn and beans require new silos and the importation of men to build them, men with wages and long thirsts that they quench with local beer. The benefit of "bringing new business into town," that chamber-of-commerce phrase, can be directly traced, and understood as the plainest civic algebra: New towers equal higher profits for the Cardinal. In cities, the municipal planners court industry and continuous refurbishing with the same equation in mind, but it's hard to watch it clearly working and balancing. Diffused through thousands of people and so much space, the terminology loses energy, becomes some "concept" that can't be seen on the street.

A good many Prairie Cities across the land are facing just now—by the grace of their size and isolation—the same dilemmas that took down larger towns years ago. Competitive claims on the space. An economy in need of aid. An effort to find a size that will assure a town its life but keep it a livable place. The amount of government, the purity of its politics. These are no longer the exclusive concerns of cities, and small towns have a chance either to improve upon the cities' earlier failures or to duplicate them. In any case, a plain and open-moving place like Prairie City seems fashioned for study, built to an observable scale and animated by its history, its wisdom and its conflicting ambitions.

My last Chicago apartment was a small place on a one-block street in the Old Town neighborhood. It's a cramped and lovely old street, an unbroken line of vine-covered row houses on one side, my block-long building on the other. I had a large bay window in front that seemed to hang over the sidewalk at eye level. If I sat at the table I'd placed in the swollen space of the bay, people on the sidewalk appeared to be walking directly at me, through my window and into the room. After I got used to the block's tight quarters, I began to think of the bay window as a low-hanging tree house perched over the sidewalk and the street, and I loved to sit with morning coffee, watching the block awaken.

In my Prairie City house, I feel for minutes at a time the weight and power of an unblemished silence, a sound the city could never achieve in its slowest moments. Prairie City's daylight silence is something so full and novel it can't be passively noticed; you must, rather, suspect that it's around and then go after it, all the senses drawing you further down, as in a well, past familiar levels of quiet.

Then, without build-up, a rich, rippling motor breaks in and I jump in my chair as if I'd heard a crack of thunder over the roof. Things come in bursts after a long quiet, and suddenly the streets are filled with motorcycles and on the highway past my house there's a parade of semi trucks shifting for speed, after climbing a small incline, at a spot on the highway even with my living room. I see trucks pulling flat beds piled with all manner of things, from mounds of rough steel to mobile homes.

It's this vast aural distance, chaos coming out of a full stillness, that works on the nerves. A city's noise stays reliably at one volume, allows you to hear it in that frame and learn to block it. But Prairie City alternates silence and noise, irregularly spaced. I cannot predict the motors here, and have drawn my first easy irony: I am lonely in this country town for the peace of an inner-city street. I hear the motorcycles swarming and the charged-up screaming engines of the cars and find myself, at the age of thirty, cursing the innocent noise of Prairie City's youth like a cantankerous old man shaking his walking stick at children playing in front of his house.

I've spent the late mornings walking streets, north end, south end, my eyes lingering on the homes and lawns like a voyeur's, hoping to ride my memories back to an emotional center. I'm anticipating, like someone awaiting the delayed rush of a drug mixing and moving in the blood, some warm, primal flush of "being home" to take me; it hasn't. I'd hoped my walks would release it, but they've given me only subliminal flashes of the past and a great unfocused intimacy.

The fields have turned, yellow and light brown; central Iowa gets most of its autumn from the fields. Trees and brush trim the roadsides and fence rows vividly, but the great reaching planes of quiet colors are the fields. The corn and beans are nearly ready. Storekeepers in town, feeling those first slow days and the streets' perceptible emptiness, know that a few farmers are in their fields taking crops. More and more, the landscape has been opened and cleaned and planted. Iowa now uses ninety-five percent of its land for crops and has become, as I once overheard it described in an airplane circling a floor of spring-black land, "just a big damn cornfield, border to border."

The figures have risen as farmers have learned to cultivate stretches of once unsuitable land—steep rises, swampish bottoms—but the best smooth land has almost always been maximally tilled, a practice with implications I first felt in some small but fundamental way one afternoon when I was in high school. I sat in English class, looking through the room's tall windows at an autumn day, the light-brown color everywhere and the air hot with summer still in it. Our principal came into the room, crisis on his face, and after whispering with our teacher, called the boys out of the room. In the hallway, I saw that he'd summoned all the boys in high school. We gathered around him as he explained that Ralph, a sixth grader, had that morning run away from home and that we were going to search for him. He'd last been seen, after an argument with his father, heading full stride into the camouflage of the nearest cornfield, and he was believed to be there still, or in a neighbor's field, hiding like a fugitive from the hounds. This was clearly high adventure, an event that had released every able-bodied male from school and gotten him out into the magnificent day, and we all smiled and silently thanked Ralph for his disappearance.

We were divided into teams and assigned fields. Each of us was responsible for four rows. On the principal's signal, we walked into the corn, moving through the harvest-high stalks like a young army through a strictly planted jungle. There is a thrilling isolation inside a high cornfield, and I felt it. I could hear classmates four rows away, but they seemed miles from me in the corn. We sent up a huge sibilant rustling as we brushed aside the dry leaves, but there was little talk, everyone feeling that same solitude and each of us concentrating on the certainty that he'd find Ralph, huddled and shaking beneath the next stalk.

We finished a field, found neither Ralph nor his footprints, and a couple of the boys who lived in town and had had no reason until that day to walk a cornfield came out with arms and faces hideously splotched from dormant allergies. Those boys walked sadly back to school, while the rest of us, and some men from town, continued to search. We crossed a narrow path and began another field, moving now on someone else's land in the same straight line. And from there, through a ditch, over a fence and on, the last long row of one field flowing into the next one and becoming one hypnotic tunnel through the countryside. We stopped to rest after the third or fourth field, and I looked up to see that we'd come several miles through an unbroken row of corn and stood on the other side of town. Like Cheever's swimmer, stroking his way across exurbia in private pools, I fantasized that day that one could cross back and forth over the land exclusively in the fields, and I saw them for some time after that in a new way, like a dark and private medium, fields yielding and melding, shaping secret roads. I saw, in other words, what Ralph had understood very well when he plunged into his father's corn and emerged, clocking his surrender perfectly, from a hilltop woods near Colfax around five o'clock.

There's an equal and opposite truth about this land. Prairie City is not only lyrically open, it is also tightly congested; and these two realities—one visual, one emotional—psychically compete. For while it may appear a vast congenial field, people own and work the land in patches.

And there's an accelerating pressure: Farming has made men money in the past few years, and young men want to farm again, to own more and more land. If one looks out at central Iowa with a farmer's eyes, one doesn't see the measureless stretches I saw that day, but a flat, rich real estate, crowded as the cities of India; forty, eighty and one hundred and sixty pieces packed suffocatingly close. The farmer feels every day a claustrophobic scarcity of space, as he looks for room in the land he already has, planting narrower rows, running these rows over ground that was weeds and fence, feeding more and more fertilizer into the soil, working precisely measured rectangles with something infinite in mind.

My father comes out of his cornfield, parting the stalks like a curtain. Standing next to the giant end rows, he appears even smaller than he is. We are the same height, nearly five feet eight, but he's begun to slump from the shoulders and, side by side, I'm taller.

He's youthfully thin. For years he carried extra winter pounds, spending idle months drinking coffee with other farmers in town. Then he would lose them, like an athlete playing himself into shape, when the spring work came. But now he works in a factory in town when there's no farm work and that has made him lean and firm year round. He says he went to work there, as much as anything, because he became so bored with all that coffee and conversation, and the factory, or something else recently added to his life, seems to have energized him. As a young man, he found no discomfort in idleness, but he now seems terrified of it, and spends late afternoons and weekends moving from one chore to the next with an almost comical haste that has become his gait, as if he's hurrying as he ages to finish some enormous private restoration.

His hair has grayed but is full and wavy, and the only unarguable sign of his age is a settling in of flesh and bone around his mouth. Otherwise, his skin is tautly drawn and the sun has built up a permanent red-tan color in his face.

"I knew those August rains would help," he says, showing me three impressive ears of corn. "Everybody said, 'It's too late to do any good now,' that rain we got, but it had to help, no further along than the corn was."

He holds the ears nimbly in his right hand that at first glance seems only unusually slender. Surgery has greatly refined its technique since the time when men of earlier generations were left with the blunt stumps of severed fingers. He lost his index finger in a factory press a few months ago and doctors went into his hand for the rest of the bone, the long deep root of the finger that grew to the wrist, and they took that, too, restyling the hand, so that the thumb now lay aesthetically and in partnership with the middle finger. Dad can already pick coins from a change purse, and in time, the middle finger will inherit the touch and agility of the index.

"Those are just from the end rows," he says, looking out at the field. "I didn't go too far in. But if it's like what I picked farther in, we'll have a corn crop." His crops may be good this year, in spite of seven rainless weeks, because a wet spring kept him out of the fields. He planted late, by all ideal calendars, and his beginning corn was not critically in need of rain that didn't come. In August, after several fields around his had been brutalized by the heat, his got hard, invaluable showers and the crops bloomed, almost like flowers in those Disney films that explode through the magic of time-lapse photography.

He has hired his harvesting for several years, since his corn picker and his combine quit. He hasn't enough land to make buying a new machine worthwhile, for his farming hasn't grown; he hasn't wished it to. He manages exactly the land his father did—these 140 acres that surround the home, and the adjoining 80-acre farm of Byrdie Rush, the old maid with the vicious dogs. Byrdie was taken to the nursing home a few years ago, when her mind was finally overrun by demons that had once come only at night.

My father has watched in recent years the manic

explorations for profit going on all around him, and has marveled at an impulse he cannot identify in some of his farming neighbors that sends them to borrow money unblinkingly in order to accumulate more ground, bigger tractors to cover it, new combines to pick it. "They must just not even *expect* to get out of debt in their life," he has said. "Just decided to pay themselves a wage every year."

Nothing more obviously speaks of a farmer's complexity of feelings for what he does, for his private counterbalance of risk and security, than the size of his farm. It's there, sweeping or humble, never so far from a road that it can hide, and I believe some of the competition for land here, the heated purchases, has to do with an instinctive understanding that a man's ego is visible in his farm.

My father's farm expresses well the essence of him. It's some of the state's best land, on a flat, narrow ridge that the topographer would represent with a southeast line between the parallel meanderings of the Des Moines and the Skunk rivers, safe from floods and perfectly sloped for draining rains. (He loves the story of an old man in town, gullible to the wildest story, who was told that the highway bordering the south end of our farm was flooded after a hard rain. The old man repeated it, eyes wild with catastrophe, to everyone he met on the streets. "If that road was flooded," my father laughs, "all central Iowa would be under water.") He inherited its advantages, but has immaculately maintained them, taking no risks with the way he's used his land. His machinery has been adequate for the work and well cared for, perhaps a size smaller than would have been convenient, and a couple of sizes smaller than the latest models.

I have recognized his need for security only since I've been back and have seen the adventurous drive of other farmers. I'm not ashamed of his unfashionable timidity, his hesitant ambition, his rejection of conventional greed.

He's reached an enormously difficult time. Nearing sixty, he knows that the farm will soon be hard on him; on the longest days, it already is. Since Grandma's death, the farm is his and his sister's, my Aunt B. They equally divided its 140 acres, and in order to own 80, the historical denominator, he must buy land from her. "If I had just an eighty," he's said, almost wistfully, "I could really take care of it, work it right, by myself, and come out about as good as I am now." Yet the idea of taking on debt at his age touches Depression-raised fears.

From the small back porch, my father and I survey the fields and soundlessly share his preoccupation. Finally, he gives words to it. "I could just sell the whole thing, too," he says. "A fella could live pretty well off the interest. I tell ya, you see what they're getting for land, it makes you stop and think." Temptation has come as close as a neighboring farm. From where we sit, looking straight south and across the highway that was flooded in the lie, we can see 70 acres generally considered nearly as rich as my father's; they were sold a few weeks ago for $2340 an acre.

"Man!" Dad says, and exhales loudly, as if to relieve himself of the pressure from all that money across the road. As when anyone else speaks of local land prices, his voice fills with an almost fearful wonder. He recites a litany of purchases that the town apparently regarded as unsurpassable foolishness when they occurred. "Everybody thought T was crazy when he paid five hundred an acre for the Lamson place, and that was only ten years or so ago. And then everybody said S was completely out of his mind when he paid fifteen hundred for the Carter place, and that was just a few years back. I said then, I just didn't see how a man could farm that back out of a place. I still don't. Now it's up to twenty-three forty, and they say it's not a corporation, either, just some guy down around Monroe with a lot of land and wanting more."

We sit for several minutes, thinking of this major decision that has come at a point in his life when he assumed all his hardest choices would have been made long before. He turns and says to me, "What do *you* think I should do?" With that sentence, he has laid himself open and vulnerable to me, has drawn me past all parental guises into the intimacy of one man exposing his humanness to another. Immediately, in some defense, I suppose, I move the moment back an entire generation, to him and his father. By the time I was old enough to share any of the work, my father was clearly making the daily decisions regarding fields that should be tilled, with what instruments, and by whom; and Grandpa easily followed them. In my mind, I've drawn their life lines many times and have imagined that seismic moment when they crossed, when authority passed from father to son; and I've only guessed at the measureless ambivalence of feeling that must have been involved. Now, fully unprepared, I'm sitting with my father and he's asked me into his hardest problem and I begin to understand that the exchange comes gradually, in delicate steps, and that we've taken one.

But it's surprised me. I want to remind him that I'm here to claim my own feelings about the farm, and so I'm carrying some very selfish notions that wish the place left undisturbed. I want to say that I've seen some rootlessness in the past few years, and felt some also, and while there may be a lot of money just waiting for him, if he wants that, he now has something else—a piece of the planet with a consistent and unfinished history.

And when I try all that out on myself, it sounds easy and lofty, the sort of thing a spectator to a problem would say.

"I don't know, Dad . . . it's up to you and Mom. I don't want to tell you what to do." I look at him, expecting to see my failure on his face.

"I know," he says softly, but he makes no effort to free me from our new equality. "I was just wondering what you thought. It's hard. All I know for sure is, this is the last year I'll farm Byrdie's place. It's too much for me, by myself. I said the same thing last year, but a fella gets a little greedy, I guess. All the years. . . . I get a statement from the bank every year that shows what I'm worth. And for years it was in the red. And then you see it go a little bit in the black, and now, in the last few years, it's been *way* in the black, and you just hate to give any of it up."

"Sure," I say, and find something easy: "But if you're too tired from making it to enjoy any of it. . . ." I'm still trying to get back to that safe place beneath his fatherhood, and I conjure us together on the tractor when I was quite young. I was driving, the steering wheel big as a tire in my hands, and he was standing behind me on the hitch, but seemed all around me, body and arms, blocking the sun, and I felt tucked into him. I was fighting the tractor, and losing, as it hopped up out of the furrow again and again, and in a sharp turn jumped completely free, like a derailed train. At last he gave up on me and, without warning, angrily jerked the wheel with my hands still squeezing it, jerked me, also, and I felt in his takeover the strength required to keep the tractor in.

"Did you ever think what would have happened if I'd been interested in farming, and any good at it?" I ask. He looks at me quizzically.

"I mean, it would have changed your life, too. You might have felt like you had to get more land, get bigger."

He understands now, and says, "That's right. And it would have been a problem. I see it happening all over. I was talkin' just the other day with Harley Lammons. He asked me if I wanted to sell some ground. His boy wants to farm, and he's looking for some to get him started. He said, 'I've tried to talk him out of it. I told him, it ain't great, ya know. But it's all he wants to do.'

"No, I never really minded that you weren't interested, 'cause I never really loved farming, myself. My problem with farming is I've never been able to just settle in and accept the conditions. Always wanted things ideal. A wet spring'd drive me crazy. I'd worry I'd never get in the fields. A dry spring would drive me crazy, too. 'Why plant, if it's gonna be a drouth?'

"But farming was the safest thing to do, and it's worked out for the best, financially. Otherwise, I'd just be workin' for a wage somewhere and I couldn't stand that."

I try to see him in that way, a man whose working life was beholden to something smaller than nature, and can't. I've already seen his subservience to his part-time factory job—worrying about some extra minutes that spilled over from a half-hour lunch break—and can imagine that anxiety magnified by forty years.

Mother joins us from the kitchen. I realize that I have less to learn from her than from Dad. She and I have an almost extrasensory kinship, picking up each other on a wordless spiritual register. And yet, we've talked more than Dad and I have, often disagreeing. But such confrontations leave an inimitable closeness.

"You guys ready for dinner?" she asks, and then sits with us, while her marvelous cooking steams inside the house. She specializes in what I call "Iowa soul food": creamed chicken over baking-powder biscuits, ham and soup beans with corn bread, beef stew, and fried chicken served with the Western world's definitive potato salad, rich with eggs and mustard and mayonnaise. I've often told her that if she would move that menu, with her fruit pies, to Chicago, find a North Side storefront and do it over in a kind of early Willa Cather, she'd have the beautiful people lining the sidewalks of Clark Street.

Her presence on the porch completes us, a circle coming closed, and activates a soothing, almost mirthful warmth in me. This is the deep, effortless pull I've not felt from the town, and perhaps I should not have expected to. This is my center, and I find it now, as always, in this big white house. I sit very still, so as not to disturb it, and wonder if the ease with which I've been able to find it throughout my life has in some way ill-served me. I've been content with the center and paid no attention to what feeds it—the farm, the business of it and the way it works, the people in town on whom the farm and my parents depend.

"You never know how many's going to show up over there," Dad says of the factory's transient work force. "There were four guys there today. Makes a fella curious to go to work, just to see who left town during the night."

"If they'd pay decent wages, they'd get some people in there who might work and stay," Mom says.

I agree, and am pleased within the wholesome inanity of a family sharing its day. I feel the adhesion in the act, and a comfort that stays through most of the meal. Then it begins to fade as a small and dreadful hallucination I've fought off a few times works its way in. It is the premonition that something tragic is going to occur while I'm in Prairie City. And, more than that, it's the fear that, after being away for a dozen years and coming back now expressly to put the coming months on paper, my parents will oblige me in the most unfathomable way; that one of them will die while I'm home. From behind my fear, I watch their mouths moving.

In the middle of the park, a dilapidated grouping of furniture—couch, leaning floor lamp, chair and coffee table—sits surrealistically in the bright morning light, the park's dead grass for a rug. Yesterday, the Lions Club held its annual auction of donated goods and these few remnants were prankishly arranged during the night. It's as if an invisible family were sitting in its open-air living room, drinking morning coffee and watching the towns-people move up and down the sidewalks, watching trucks and tractors pass by.

A thick orange dust and corn silks dried to parchment have started to cover the streets, especially on the south side of the square, where most of the field traffic waits to do business. It's a curious parade, equipment old and new pulling grain in single file on the south side of the square. People inside the shops glance out through plate-glass windows and measure the progress of the harvest by the length of the line. It is long and its trucks and tractors are moving like cars on a rush-hour freeway, into the elevator's driveway tunnel, dumping grain, sending dust into the air.

Harold "Hoop" Timmons emerges from a dust cloud, looking as if he'd stepped clean from a shower. For more than thirty years, with some interruptions, he's worked at the elevator, has for some time now been the man in town who sets the dust free, and has fought it every minute with the tidiness of a spinster. In the summer, before the crowds, he sweeps and cleans and straightens his silos as if he were expecting royalty. Atop his two new silos, there are scraps from the labor—concrete chips, piles of welded metal—and he frets with the knowledge of a mess on his roof.

His striped overalls, his gray, wash-faded shirt, his red

cap are filled with dust, and yet he magically gleams. A plastic air filter hangs from his neck like a surgeon's mask, and covers his nose and mouth when he's receiving beans. He can breath corn dust, but after thirty years around beans, he wheezes and coughs in their unfiltered air.

Harold hurries to the front again, surveys the growing line, and removes his cap to run his hand over the long bald avenue atop his head. He slaps the cap against his thigh and a small dust cloud jumps out of it. Something athletic in the gesture puts him back twenty years in my mind, when he played for the Prairie City Lions and I studied his movements for clues to skills one doesn't learn.

When I was young, and sport was what there was in life, the Lions were among the state's best softball teams. Formally, they were the Prairie City Lions Club, named after their sponsor, in the way that other teams were known as Al's D-X of Reasoner, Pella Chevrolet, or the Sully Merchants. But we abbreviated the names, because Lions, alone, sounded authentically zoological, like the Baltimore Orioles or the Detroit Tigers.

Few of the Lions wore their complete uniforms, preferring tight white T-shirts with their blue-trimmed baseball pants. All, except the pitcher, were local men who'd played baseball and softball together for years and reacted unanimously in a game. The pitcher, Elmer Hocksbergen, worked in Newton and lived near one of the many surrounding hamlets that trees and the world have grown around. He was capable of wizardry with a softball, sending it with extraordinary speed into the catcher's glove and coating it with a spin as it left his hand that made it drop at home plate. He suffered a genius' mercurial temper, however, and a corresponding wildness, and if he fell to one of his moods, a thick brooding hung over the bench like a blanket, and the game was finished. But when he touched the core of his gift, something transcendent took place, evident from the first inning, and through the crowd the words were passed: "Hocksy's *on*."

So my passions were rarely wasted on the Lions. They won seriously, and often, and sometimes melo-dramatically with scripted victories. But I was from the beginning loyal to Harold Timmons. For several years, I played catch every summer with our neighbors' visiting grandson. We gave each other high fly balls, making the most prosaic catches appear miraculous. Back and forth, all day long; volleying heroics. We were Lions, and he usually chose to be the first baseman or the center fielder, while I invariably was Harold Timmons.

Timmons is a small man, was bald even then. Before each game, he packed his cheek with Red Man chewing tobacco. Everyone called him Hoop and still does. There is no anecdote that left him his nickname. He was a high school student, stacking shelves and carrying groceries at DeWit's store, and Don DeWit one day, from nowhere, called him Hoop'ndasher. He didn't resist it, heard it contracted over time, and there is no more story than that.

I'm not sure why, in our games, I always pretended to be Hoop Timmons. Perhaps I sensed his kindness. Although he always hit well, and fielded flawlessly, there were more apparent idols. Hocksbergen, the pitcher; Lowell McFadden, the tall, thin center fielder, who covered ground with smooth, deerlike strides; John Shuey, the first baseman, who did everything well and with the quick, mincing steps of a speeded-up movie. Timmons, on the other hand, performed with an econ-omy of movement that became a kind of flamboyance if you watched for it. I have a clear picture of him rounding second base toward a triple, his legs chopping the earth and his arms uniquely stiff at his sides, only his hands flapping loosely behind him, paddling the air.

He has changed little. He could get no balder, so he looks no older. He's added a dark mustache, filled with work dust, and his eyes twinkle with a boyish mischievousness that is true, the front edge of his chronic concern.

Timmons believes firmly in Murphy's Law—that if anything can possibly go wrong, it will. Last summer, as June and July passed without rain, he watched the new grain silos irremediably rising and was convinced that they would hold nothing but air at the end of autumn. Rain came in August, breaking the sun, and since farmers had opened the earth the previous spring as never before, planting fence to fence, there now grew the possibility that the crop would surpass any in history. And Harold Timmons began to wonder how in heaven's name he was going to fit his harvest into so few grain silos.

He replaces his cap, tugs at its bill as if he's cocked for the pitch.

"Oh, me, oh, my," he says, looking at the line waiting to dump grain. "Ain't never seen a year like this. I tell them every year, if they'll organize their line, according to what they got to dump, they'd move a lot faster. But nobody wants to give up 'is spot, see. They get downright hostile at you."

There are loads of beans, usually the first grain harvested, loads of corn, and, in each case, the moisture of the grain varies. Timmons makes certain not to mix, in the same silo, corn with beans, wet with dry. He controls, like a chef keeping his various flours in their specific canisters, the necessary segregation. From a set of dials and switches mounted on a wall, he directs the destination of each load—which of the several silos it will end up in, after it has first been emptied into a grate-covered pit in the middle of the central silo's driveway, then carried in metal buckets mounted on conveyor belts that run in a vast, veinous internal network through all the silos in the cluster.

It has reached that point in the season where all the possibilities of a harvest are overlapping—a truck of wet beans might be followed in line by a wagon of relatively dry corn. A tractor and its load pull to a stop inside the central silo, where Hoop receives the crops. If Hoop has dumped dry beans, and now receives corn, he must wait for all the beans to be carried in their conveyor buckets out of the pit, leaving it absolutely empty, before flicking a switch that changes the course of the flowing grain. Beans in their silos; now corn. If the conveyors are running at full speed, the pit can receive at least four thousand bushels in an hour, my father's entire crop in a very good year.

Hoop walks out into the sunlight to receive his customers, and rides back into the elevator tunnel on a truck's running board, talking with a young farmer through the window.

"This's the last you'll see of my face," the farmer says.

"You plant corn on your place this year?" Hoop asks, knowing the answer.

"Well, yeah."

"Figure you'll pick it, do ya?"

"Yeah."

"Then I guess I'll be seein' your face so'more," says Hoop. "Wish you were right."

He laughs, and the farmer laughs, and Hoop turns to me and winks. "I don't know what I'd do if I didn't have farmers to shit on all day. This job ain't no beda roses, but it beats some."

The truck stops in the tunnel, rear end above the grate,

and I step behind to lift its tail gate and start the beans. I carry an artisan's tools, fashioned from scrap metal and from years of this chore—raising tail gates, pouring grain, scraping floors clean. I slap onto the back of the truck a doubly bent rod that keeps the tail gate up, keeps the beans coming. With the rod in place, I lean toward the back end, feeling absurdly important, point my thumb upward and the farmer starts his hydraulic lift. The truck bed starts up, rises like an elephant on its haunches, and comes back on me, with beans. Gravity gets them going, a slow hiss that builds and builds with the rising truck bed until beans pour through the grate and into the pit, dust coming off them. They are moving through the grate, but gravity isn't enough, and I stick my head and shoulders through the tail gate, my nose and mouth protected by an air filter. With the second handmade tool, a flat metal square soldered to a long rod, I pull the spilling beans into me, hurrying them into the pit. Great haste is ordered here; the tunnel feels like a racer's pit stop—Whoah! Up! Unload! Down! On your way! The whole transaction takes seconds, and the farmer roars away, his truck bed still coming down as he leaves, racing the past week's magnificent weather to clean his fields before a long rain stops him, stops him for a week that might be followed by a deathly frost.

"Beans, beans, beans," says Hoop wearily, staring down through the dust, watching the mound of beans sink in the pit as if it were quickly melting. "I've seen enough beans."

I nod, knowing I cannot speak through the air filter that's holding off my asthma reasonably well. Instead, I smile through it, feeling marvelous in my imposter's role, working with Hoop in the nucleus of the harvest. Last week, I'd asked his boss if I could work in the elevators— to participate in something I'd never gotten near. I have learned an elemental vocabulary in the past few days, listening to Hoop and the farmers. Now, talking with them, I am having my first conversations in my mother tongue, the language I heard my classmates speak.

"What's it testing?" I've asked a farmer, asking casually about the moisture in the corn he's carrying.

"'Bout seventeen percent," he's answered, and I've nodded solemnly.

"You dry this?" I've asked, in the farmers' pared idiom, seeing dust in ferocious clouds coming off the rushing grain. More and more, farmers have driers on their farms, saving the money they'd be charged for drying at the elevator.

"No. It's right outa the field. We're takin' number-two corn outa the field."

"Incredible," I've said, knowing now that it is. Number-two corn, I've learned, is high grade, standardized by commodity exchanges and signifying moisture of fifteen percent, a condition rarely found in corn on the stalk. The rainless summer had advantages, too.

The line continues without pause, trucks and wagons, corn and beans, corn and corn. "Little more. Little more. Whoah, that's good. Whoah!" Raise the tail gate, however it works. Get it up, and quickly. "O-kay. Lift 'er." Hissss. A nearly dangerous sound, the threat of moving tonnage, a landslide of grain. Whooooshh. Slap the tail gate down. Wiggle it down its home-built grooves or turn it shut with brand-new gears. "O-kay." And away.

A truck bed, with corn, begins to raise and Hoop dips a cupped hand into the stream. He takes a handful of corn, sifts the kernels in his palm like salted peanuts, and pops them into his mouth. He chews them clinically, a distant expression on his face. He chews, and a few stray kernels mix with his tobacco juice and appear on the line of his lip as neglected teeth. Hoop walks to the farmer in the truck.

"Eighteen?" he asks.

"Last load was seventeen," says the farmer, who has stopped at the elevator office to have his grain weighed and its moisture measured. Hoop jerks his head, a quick, satisfied nod, and allows the corn to be dumped. Amidst the powerful driers, the twenty-minute moisture tests, the generally sophisticated technology of harvesting, he relies on his mouth, chewing the corn for moisture as he has done for thirty years, and is consistently accurate within one or two percentage points.

For the past week or more, there has been a lot of news concerning grain-inspection fraud at Gulf-port terminals. Grain exporters are mixing bad corn—and far worse—with good corn, so that foreign buyers have opened their purchased cargo to find rotted corn and small stones and rodent feces in their grain. I think about that as I watch Hoop move fastidiously about, tasting corn, keeping his ingredients separated, reading from the master control panel the temperature of stored grain, which is measured by heat sensors placed every six feet in the silos. Grain that's rotting gets hot and Hoop detects it. Every year he worries the crop in, imposing an absolute surveillance on more than a million bushels of central Iowa grain.

And then it is gone from his care. Long semis pull away from the elevator with thousand-bushel loads, drive the grain to a regional terminal, from where it's taken east to the river and floated down the Mississippi to the Gulf. There, unregulated exporters mix rocks and rat shit with it, and sell it overseas as Iowa corn.

Late in the morning, the last man in line drives in and through.

"Call again!" Hoop says. As the wagon leaves, we look back from habit for the next truck or tractor, but see instead an empty square of daylight.

"I can't believe it," says Hoop. "No more countries heard from? Better take a sit-down while we can."

We leave the driveway, walk back to his office—a plywood shack, four feet by eight feet, where he keeps a portable radio, an electric heater, a wooden bench.

He reaches for a pouch of Red Man and withdraws a handful, shaking free the dangling strands, mechanically inserting it like a partial plate. It's a modest portion, not swelling his cheek as I'd remembered.

"Both my grandpas chewed," he says, positioning a coffee can at his feet. "I thought it was the dirtiest, most disgusting habit I'd ever seen."

"You never chew any other brand?" I ask, remembering the pouch of Red Man folded neatly into his Lions' back pocket.

"Noooo!" he exclaims. "In the Army, I's with a bunch from Oklahoma that chewed. We chawed and chawed. So Red Man was hard to get. I took some Key and, *Lord*, I got all white and sick to my stomach. Couldn't stand up. I thought I was gonna die."

"I remember you always had a big wad for games."

"Yeah," he chuckles. "Me and Lowell McFadden."

"I didn't remember Lowell chewing, too."

"Oh, yeah. We both did."

There's a long silence in the shack, and we both stare straight ahead, back to that glimmering place. I feel a sharp, renewed envy of Hoop's place in it, but he feels something more difficult.

"I guess a fella never really gets it out of his system," he says quietly. "I go down now and watch 'em play and I get to thinkin', Gol damn, I'd like to try it. And I know, sure as billy hell, my legs'd break down and I'd be so slow and stiff, and I wouldn't be able to hit. And yet I get to believin' I could still do it. Now, ain't that silly?"

"When did you quit playing?"

"Nineteen sixty-two," he says. "I wasn't really that old when I quit. I coulda played three, four more years. But I got to looking foolish at the plate. Some of the other guys played a year or two after that, and the same thing happened to them." He leans over the can, waters the kernels at the bottom. "We coulda played for fun and horsed around for a few more years, but we never played that way. We always took a loss real hard. We did. Nobody wanted to play, just for fun. . . . What it amounts to is, we didn't want to go out mediocre."

The August rain, and this ripening October warmth, have helped both corn and beans. It's best to pick beans that are dry: The pod pops open with its berries. Corn should be picked slightly damp, so the kernel won't shatter as it's stripped from the cob. After August, it was alternately wet and warm, giving both crops some of what they needed, and now farmers are taking beans and corn in unprecedented quantity. In some small towns, the silos are already filled, and newspaper photos have shown sloping ranges of unprotected grain, dumped outside and relying on weather.

Naturally, that seems to Hoop a fool's act of faith, and a sloppy one. But something more than housekeeping is involved. If elevators all over the country fill up before the end of the season, farmers will not be able to hold their crops while they watch the grain market and wait for a price; they will lose all leverage to the winter. Grain that cannot be stored will be forced onto the market, sold for that day's price, high or low.

Hoop has ridden to the top of the silos for the past several days, removed a manhole-cover lid from the roofs, and dropped a string with a bolt tied to it, as if he were ice fishing. He's dropped the bolt until it hit grain, and has measured the distance. Every foot equals one thousand bushels. For the past few days, Hoop has been fishing in shallow air, touching grain at five feet, six feet. The silos are almost full, and the prospect of bluffs of grain piled up on his driveway causes him a long-suffering sigh. As if that drier out back, overworked with all this crop and running through the night, weren't enough to think about.

"I just lay there at night, waitin' for that phone to ring and tell me the drier's blown up," he says. "That's stupid, but I can't help it. I toss and turn. The most a fella can do is clean it out ever' day, get in there with a brush and get them corn fines, and when it blows up, at least it won't be 'cause it was choked up on fines."

"What are fines?" I ask.

"That's them little ends on corn kernels. They break off when you run 'em through a drier and they build up a terrific dust layer. It's the kinda job a fella can put off, cleanin' 'em out ever' day. But you gotta do it," he says and shrugs.

There are distinctive dusts, then. Corncob dust, red and velvety. Fines. Stalk and vine dust, pale yellow and apt to make you itch. Dark bean dust, like swirling dirt and the most malignant of all. Thinking of dusts, I psychosomatically wheeze and clean my air filter, spit into its sponge to clog it.

"That damn bean dust," Hoop says. "It gets my sinuses, is all. It don't bother me otherwise. Guess that's what you call an occupational hazard, huh?" We chuckle. "Bean dust and rats, my occupational hazards. There's always rats around here, of course, around grain, and the sight of a rat just scares the bejezus outa me. I swear it does— Oops!" he says, peering through his windows.

"We got us a customer." And we leave the shack, walk through the round room's door, and stand on opposing sides of the driveway as wagons of corn come in.

"Damn wet corn," says Hoop, as he eats a handful of this new load. "Tastes just like last year's. 'Bout a third of the corn I ate last year tasted like meal, like a mulch. This's the same, but it's the first I've seen that reminds me of it. That was the sorriest damn crop I ever saw. It was . . . it was just nothin'. It was wet, and then a frost hit it and stopped it and it was just holla inside. You'd bite down on it and there was nothin' to it.

"And heavy! Crimanee! It was like shoveling sand." We each take a corner of the wagon and draw wet corn out. "It was the worst of both worlds, like they say. Wet and hard to shovel, but it didn't really weigh anything in terms of quality."

He steps into the farmer's rearview mirror and points to the ground, then comes around to talk with him as the wagon descends.

"Where'd you get this stuff, anyway?" he asks.

"Oh," the farmer says, "some of that bottom land. Kinda wet was it?"

"Shee-it," says Hoop. "Why don'tcha plant rice?"

"Yeah," says the farmer. "Well, you just keep it off by itself and we'll send it overseas. Let the Russians eat it."

Hoops laughs, then seriously asks the farmer if his neighbors have begun to pick their crops. In Hoop's mind is a map of farms. He knows who's finished, who's still picking and, from reporting neighbors, whose grain is next.

Some of the farmers jump down from their tractors to help Hoop and me, shaking and rocking their wagons while we scrape with the long-handled squares. Others behave like employers, waiting atop their machines. Hoop is not a lazy man, but the implication that he is something less than a partner in this harvesting rightly works on him, and after three or four unassisted unloadings, he watches the next man come to a stop, catches his eye and with a hooked index finger beckons, "C'mere." The farmer hops down and lends his strength to a sticking tail gate.

Now a big, friendly, sunburned farmer drives in. He wears gray sweat shirts against the field wind and, like almost everyone else, a baseball-style cap with a sponsor's message on the front. His says "Enjoy Pork Often" inside a yellow logo. He joins us behind his wagon and watches his corn fall.

"Let's have no more of these stalks in your corn," Hoop says and winks. "You leave the stalks in the field; didn't anybody tell ya how that works?"

The farmer puts his hand into his corn, as if to filter it, and lets the corn run liquidly through his fingers. "Hell," he says, "let ol' Kissinger eat some of it. He's so damn smart. Tryin' to tell the Agriculture Department what to do." The grain embargo, finally lifted, has inspired these feelings all over town. "Let Kissinger eat it," says the farmer. "He's so dumb he can't even talk the language. You ever hear him talk? He knows all those big words, but he can't pronounce 'em." The farmer laughs. "It's like they say, 'He knows about the birds and the bees, but he can't do no stingin'.'" He laughs louder. "You heard that one, ain't ya, Hoop? 'He knows about the birds and bees, but he can't do no stingin'?' Ha!"

Hoop looks into the farmer's grinning face and says, deadpan, "You can go now."

After the farmer drives away, we sweep once more. A lot of foreign policy has passed through his driveway during the week, angry declarations about Americans' right to have open markets, to sell to any buyer holding good money. Yet beneath these opinions, I've sensed a small, confused guilt that much of this crop may have been grown to feed Communists.

I am tidying the floor, during a temporary calm, when I look outside and am surprised to see my father waving. He's standing on the loading docks behind the factory, directly across the street from me. He's wearing a navy-blue zippered sweat shirt, and his silver shock of hair glistens in the early sun. Between the elevator and the loading docks, the ground slopes away almost impercep-tibly, then rises back up, so that we are standing on small hummocks above the terrain and we seem to be occupy-ing neighboring freighters on a low sea, nothing but still, dead-brown water between us. Living the illusion, I wave back across the water with an exaggerated sweep of my arm, the kind of wave that goes with a long echoing call of "Hellloooo!"

There have been moments, as dust-covered farmers have roared past me, when I've thought of my father as a truant from his own harvest. It's a foolish and romantic wish, that he farm exclusively, remain pure to a passing life. I know that he has too little land for that, and I've seen that his factory job has provided him a release from isolated work he has never loved. Still, I have these selfish regrets.

But I'm also feeling, more deeply than I have since coming to Prairie City, an almost aggressive warmth, caused by this elevator work that has allowed me to join the town's synchronous labor. Everyone seems to have a manual role in the season. There's a sense of communal assignment about the jobs men have settled into and, for the moment, I feel I have mine. Now, seeing my father doing his job on the factory docks, I feel that warmth even more. I imagine him moving busily around the factory at the same time I'm shoveling and scraping grain here. The notion of our coordination shapes my work, and I walk and stand and lean against the tunnel walls with a mannered ease, trying to imply a reserve of undemonstrated strength, and laugh at myself for the fraud.

His fields are ready, the cornstalks and bean vines have an inimitable dust-dry brown. For the past few years, Mark Walker has picked Dad's crop. More and more, the specialist has come to farming, the man who has the massive machinery that requires several hundred or a thousand acres to make its purchase worthwhile. He picks many farmers' fields and, finally, his own. Mark has been such a specialist, though he has been paring his client list with retirement in mind and has agreed to pick only my father's crop and one other farmer's this year.

From the road at the northern border of our farm, one can see Mark's red picker above the crop, appearing to sway precariously down the rows. He has opened the fields, made his first rounds. So far, the beans have snapped eagerly from their vines, leaving an immaculate path after the picker has passed. The big pale-yellow berries have filled Mark's truck quickly, and promise a fine yield, perhaps as much as forty bushels per acre.

Mark Walker lives on a farm near Monroe, the next town southeast on highway 163, and was raised just a few miles from my father's fields. He worked at the Maytag washing-machine plant in Newton, one of the county's largest employers. Later he farmed, and eventually bought 300 acres of his own, the land he belatedly picks nowadays, after finishing his contracted work. A few years ago, Mark and his wife built a new house in the town of Monroe, a low white ranch between older houses on a curving street off the square, and they bought furniture to fill it. Soon after they moved in, the Walkers began to miss their farm home and they decided to move back. Now they are living once more on the home place, back in the company of growing things, while the town house stands vacant and completely furnished. He will not sell it. He will not rent it. He will not live in it. For Mark, the house is simply one more acquisition, like a new machine or an additional piece of land. He has more equipment than he did twenty years ago. He has more land. He has more homes. There's nothing temporary, nothing fluid in his responsibilities. He regularly tends the lawn of the new house, maintains its surfaces. He owns it.

He's a magnetically cheerful man; his voice is high and buoyant and always close to laughter. He nearly shouts every word he says, a common habit here, formed from many years of speaking over engines' volume.

The huge machine seems to float over the fields as it mows. Now it suddenly stops in a half-completed round and swings laboriously into a freshly picked path that leads to our house. The red combine whines, as if wounded, and comes to a stop at the edge of the lawn. Mark climbs out and peers down into the smoking innards of his machine. His right hand is swathed in gauze and tape, a white mitten. A few days ago, he reached impatiently into the vine-clogged gears and they seized his hand. He lost none of it, but fainted from the shock of gear teeth drawing him in. Dad found him on the ground, his hand badly swollen. No matter how long men have farmed, and know the danger of moving parts, there often comes some moment of suspended judgment, when they are tired, hurried, racing diminishing light or rain clouds, and that is when they try to clean a running engine. I recall as a child hearing the report of each season's field accidents and hearing also the observation that the men injured were usually older farmers who'd gotten away with their flirtations for years, had become so used to poking and probing among living parts that they had lost an edge of fear of their machinery.

Mark seats himself atop his combine, adjusts comfortably, like a man on his roof awaiting, with every hope of rescue, a rising flood. He sees me driving into the farmyard and waves his white-mitted hand. Help has arrived. I climb up onto his roof and he begins to laugh.

"I got me a little bonfire down there, ain't I?"

I look down into the smoking hole and see exactly that, a small crown of flames flickering over the wheels and rods. He seems absolutely unconcerned, and, taking cues from him, I ignore the fire also.

"How's your hand, Mark?" I ask.

"Oh, it's fine. Just a little sore now is all it is." His few front teeth are symmetrically balanced in his mouth and protrude like small fangs over his lower lip. "No, I was real lucky that I got outa that thing with no real hurt. No, it was purty dumb, all right."

Smoke rises steadily from the hole. As casually as possible, I look down at the healthy little fire and say, "What's causing that?"

"Oh, I'll tell ya, I washed it all out last night, see, and it's still kinda wet in there and it's just all over bean dust. Bean dust just clings when it's damp, see. Damned thing, anyway, I never gave it a thought that we'd have us a fire.

"But that's not why I quit here. I just noticed the fire there when I stopped. I got transmission trouble down there and I can't reach it, see." He moves some smoke aside with a wave of his mitten and demonstrates the futility of reaching down into the combine to repair it. "I'll have to call down to Lynville and have them come up with some parts. Damn, I's goin' so good, too. This'll cost us a whole day."

"The way those elevators are filling up, a day right now really hurts," I say.

"Damn, ain't *that* so. I tol' ol' Hoop, 'What the hail, Hoop. You guys tell us ta hurry up and get everything in, and then we gotta wait in line all day.'

"I grew up with the fella had Hoop's job before Hoop. Ol' Carl Jennings. We called him The Colonel. The Colonel never got excited about nothing, and he's always that way from the time he was a kid. We'd all be playin' ball or something, but that looked like a lot of work to The Colonel. And he's like that at work, too. So things always moved purty slow at the Co-op while The Colonel was runnin' the elevators. Hoop said the other day, 'If you see The Colonel, tell him things ain't changed since he was here. Still got lines.' Ha, that Hoop's a good one, ain't he?

"I remember when Hoop had to go to some kind of class to learn how to run that big drier they got over there. He went for, oh, quite a few weeks, it seems to me. And somebody says to him, 'What the hail, Hoop. You gotta go to school to learn how to do The Colonel's job?' Ha!"

Smoke intermittently separates us, comes like smoke signals from the hole between Mark and me. He reluctantly quiets and looks down. "Well, I guess I let this thing burn long enough. I better go get some water."

"It's smoking less now?" I ask.

Mark measures the smoke for a few moments. "No," he says, "I think it's burning a little more now than it was."

"Jesus, why didn't you say so?" I step back quickly, with new respect for a fire I'd thought was dying.

"Oh, it won't hurt nothing down in there," Mark says, chuckling. He studies the flames for a while. "No, like I say, if I don't get held up no more'n a day with this, I'll have them beans in another two, three days."

"I'll get your water."

"Like I say, if this weather holds. This gol damn weather is one sweet stretcha bliss, ain't it? I never have seen a fall like this one. I said to somebody the other day, 'Them Dutchmen musta put some extra holy in their prayers for this stuff, huh?' Ha!"

"I'll be right back." I scramble down, leaving Mark to speak with his bean fire, and return with a can of water.

"Too bad you didn't bring some wienies, Doug." He laughs. "We coulda had us a wienie roast." Mark stands over the growing smoke and delicately pours, gives the fire small helpings. It hisses angrily and sends up a retaliatory cloud that briefly engulfs him, then flows slowly out into the bright-skied afternoon.

I'm beginning to distinguish the work-marks these men leave on their grain. For a few weeks, I've bent and half-crawled into the wagon holes as grain rushed past me, climbing quickly to my knees, flowing between my legs, receding like quicksand through the grate. I've seen the harvest microscopically, and have noticed that the kernels and berries betray their owners. Corn filled with broken stalks has been brought consistently by a farmer known for neglecting his land, his machinery, his buildings. Kernels of corn chipped and shattered, forced through a combine that was too closely set, has come from someone south of town, whose hired help and machinery seem inadequate to the land he's working. We have seen to it that black and spilled corn has been dumped separately, treated leprously, and given payment penalties for its deterioration. It came from a farmer who dried it at home, then stored it before it had sufficiently cooled. He has the latest appurtenances—driers, tractors, more gadgetry than his farm's size requires—and his corn is rotten. And so one matches men with their offerings. Dusty beans with dusty faces. Broken corn pouring from tail gates held by baling wire. And, conversely, grain that seems scrubbed to a polish arrives in tight-feeling wagons, some of them old but conscientiously kept.

These deeply secretive men surely know what's revealed in their autumn deliveries, sense a slow, revealing leakage of themselves. Perhaps that helps explain their apparent coldness, the assessing rural stare, the miserly dialogues. Their expressions say: You know more about me through unavoidable exposure of my work than I care for you to know.

Hoop and I stop to let the pit take beans, and Hoop checks his dials and gauges, checks the drier to see if it has exploded. The recent loads have been so dry from the fields, naturally dry, that for a few days now, Hoop has been drying very little, has been merely "keeping air" on the stored grain, cooling it in the silos. Fans at the base of a silo send air struggling up through grain-packed space, to reach the top four days later.

Near the doorway, Hoop adjusts a heavy wheel that controls the speed of the pit. Every day, as I watch Hoop move fastidiously about, some new image comes to mind. Today, as he turns the big wheel, checks the dials once more, he seems a ship's captain, worrying his battered vessel home.

The elevator is going through a storm. For a week, its gears and pulleys have run without rest through ten-, eleven-, twelve-hour days. Leaks have sprung in grain ducts, spilling yellow mounds into the bowels of the silos. A conveyor leg broke yesterday, its buckets jamming, and Hoop spent several hours reshaping the crop-carrying buckets. Last week, he climbed to the top of the mast with heat-sensitive tape to patch a hole in the drier's exhaust duct. Hoop works every day encompassed by mechanical fragility. He feels about the elevator the same sealed-in pessimism that farmers have for the skies.

"You ever in the Army?" he asks me.

"No, I wasn't."

"Man, I hated ever' minute of it. It's kinda funny. There's a lotta good guys there that I hung around with, had a lot of fun with. But, ooh, did I hate it. I was so homesick I like ta died. You ever get homesick?"

His question requires an answer longer than the time we have between unloadings, and so I simply say, "Not really."

"I'll tell you something, it's the worst pain there is. God, it hurts, all knotted up in the pit of your stomach. I got it the worst on Sundays. The rest of the week, they'd keep ya busy so you wouldn't have much time to think about it, but Sundays there wouldn't be nothin' much to do except lay around, and I'd lay there on my bunk and think about Sunday dinners back home. It'd make you sillier'n a pet coon if you let it get to ya."

Noise comes up the drive, interrupts him. "Oh, here we go. Here comes double trouble." We see a big Farmall 1066 tractor, pulling two wagons. A young farmer, blond, tall, and very heavy, his broad face red as sunset, jumps down to help us.

He kicks the wagon violently and it rocks free of corn. Then he jumps back onto his tractor, a tremendous breadth of snow-white back showing below his sweat shirt.

"He's about a big one, ain't he?" Hoop says.

He returns to the Army. "I's in Korea nine months, and Japan nine months. With the medics. I never got hurt or nothin'. We used to worry about land mines, though. You'd see a buncha guys go down to the river to wash their Jeeps or somethin' and step on one of those suckers. Mmmmm. It's 'Good night, Josephine.' But I's never hit, and that's kind of a funny deal. They'd already got that 38th Parallel, see, so they's on one side and we was on the other. And our strategy would be to run across the line, shoot up a buncha' people, and then run back. We'd set up, then go ahead and have our battle, see, just shoot the bejezus outa one another, and hitail it back. Crazy ain't it."

"Did you get any good R and R?"

"Oh, I saw some a' Japan, but I's always so blamed *homesick*, you see, I didn't really enjoy it like I should. One thing I would've liked to see over there, I wasn't too far from it, either, was Hiroshima and that other place, too—Nagasaki—but I just didn't get there. That was only five years after it happened, so there'd been a lot they wouldn't have fixed up yet. That woulda been interesting."

"Did you have any trouble readjusting when you got back?" I ask. Hoop had left, seen cultures exotically opposed to his own, and had unhesitatingly returned.

"I was worthless. I was absolutely worthless when I got back. I admit it. That was really a funny deal, but I didn't wanna do anything. I'd saved a lotta money from the Army. Sent it home to Mom and Dad to keep for me, and so I bought a car right away, but I still had some. And I just squandered the rest of it. I'd get up about noon. Eat. Then go uptown or somethin', and then ever' night—I didn't get drunk, but I'd drink beer at the Tower with a buncha guys. I wasn't married, and I didn't spend nothin' on girls. And this went on for months. All my jobs was just real temporary, you know? Work here a few days, work there. Didn't care a lick. I was living at home, so I didn't need much. Finally, the folks began to ask me, 'What ya gonna do?' And I didn't care what I did. Ain't that pitiful?

"And then one day, I woke up and I just decided, 'This has gotta stop.' And I got a job, and haven't been outa work a day since. Now, that's the truth, and I'm not particularly proud of it, but I don't know, when I got home from the Army, I guess I just felt entitled to goof off for a while."

He withdraws his pocket watch from impossibly clean overalls and says, "Bean time. If you hafta leave before I get back from my break, just tell 'em at the office that the door is open and the pit is empty." He smiles brightly. "Hey! Yessir: 'The door is open and the pit is empty'— William Shakespeare."

He walks out into the sun and hears the Rock Island train moving listlessly through, hears its ghostly whistle claiming the tracks. Hoop breaks into a jog to beat it, looks left and right as he crosses the tracks. His arms are stiff at his sides, only his hands flapping behind, paddling the air. And the long clanging wall of train eases past, closing after him.

I straighten my shop for business, an eager merchant, draw broom-wide roads through the dust and, ridiculously, dust myself off with a hand broom. I listen for motors and, therefore, listen to the town and hear one of its sonorous silences. It is moments before noon, before the dismissing whistle, as if the entire town were a schoolroom class awaiting the bell. I move to the doorway of my shop on the square, wearing a velour of harvest dust, and scan northeast, across the empty park, thinking of my fellow storekeepers. Don DeWit, the grocer. His brother, Snub, whose restaurant is filling. Travis Walters, who sells good furniture to the townspeople on the north side of the square and eventually, as the town's undertaker, arranges them in silk-lined sleep in his funeral home on the south side.

Now the whistle sings, and the sidewalks become populated. I watch quick lunch-break routes—grocery to Snub's; pharmacy to car; post office to Van's coffee shop. The people exchange each other's names, toneless conversational equations, as they pass.

"Jim." "Raymond."

"Nettie." "Anna Bernice."

"Chuck." "Al."

I see that I have a customer of my own. After being weighed on the drive-on scale and a sample of grain taken, a truck lumbers toward me. It is the size and shape of all the others—barn red, with a peak of corn above the box line—but this one feels familiar in some way, as if I've driven it. It rocks and wheezes as it crosses the tracks. And now it's near enough for me to see, inside the dark cab, a white mitten waving metronomically across the glass. I can see Mark Walker's smiling fangs as I step up onto the running board to greet him. As he rolls down his window, laughter rushes out through the slit. "You open for business?" he shouts.

I'm tempted to quote some Shakespeare. "Come in, come in. Good to see you." I ride the running board in, and notice for the first time that he has company. His wife has ridden in with him, so that she can drive him to another field and return the truck to our farm.

"Lookee here what I found, Doug," Mark says. "I found ol' Byrdie layin' out in the weeds!" Mrs. Walker tolerantly shakes her head. She's long been immune to her husband's sense of humor.

We all ride through the open door, over the empty pit. Mark brakes and lifts his truck bed while I raise the tail gate and let gravity have the long orange slope. My father's corn behaves ideally, starts with a slow, tremulous shifting at the top that pushes corn evenly through the wagon hole. The tremor moves down, rippling the surface, and I step into the opening, my long-handled square in hand, and lean obstetrically into the flow. Corn flies past me, around and between my legs, becomes a tidal roar in the echoing truck bed as I move it delicately down. My father's labor is swirling liquidly around me, flooding the pit, and it seems the purest corn I've seen, dustless and immaculately made. I see no broken kernels, no rotting teeth, not a stalk. Nothing but the freely spilling evidence of my reunion. I scrape almost maniacally, and the corn responds, cooperates with me in a way that steering wheels and plow bottoms never did. It gives no asthma dust. Breathing hard through an air filter, I inhale smoothly. The corn rises to my thighs and I instinctively let go, suspended in it. I pull the square again and again and shake Mark's wagon box for the last kernels. Now the truck bed starts to drop and the corn sinks slowly down my legs, but I am held firmly by its emblematic strength, having helped my family's crop; received it.

Exactly two weeks ago, Jim Billingsley hung a hand-lettered sign above his bar, posting his party.

RABBIT BAR-B-Q
October 29
FREE. 7 p.m. till it runs out. FREE.

Jim gives a party every June to celebrate the anniversary

of his business. Except for the sign, he advertises not at all. Jim knows that anybody who wants to eat free rabbit will have seen the sign or spoken fairly recently with someone who has. He can also anticipate just how thoroughly publicity from his poster will travel. A poster displayed for a week reaches too few. Three weeks allows news to move too great a distance—through the town, out into the country. Two weeks, he's learned from previous parties, is just right. The poster has enough time to reach his regular customers, and some others not so habitual. He gives the parties to thank the people who've eaten his food and drunk his liquor. He has little patience for those people in Prairie City who find the Cardinal only when the food is free.

Jim and his wife, Betty, have been cooking all day. In the morning, the sweet, heavy smell of spices inspired the appetites of early drinkers. Jim stirred slabs of rabbit meat in a dark sauce the color of iron-rich blood. Betty baked beans in huge tubs, tasting and embellishing. They've prepared for several hundred people, a higher number than might have been expected to come a few weeks earlier, when nearly every farmer had crops remaining in the fields. But most of them have been taken, and Jim believes his crowd tonight will want to celebrate a finished season. He's readied the big square main room and opened both spare rooms that flank it. If he needs more space, he'll let people use his pool and air-hockey tables in the long room off the bar.

By five o'clock, the cement-plant workers, the crew from the factory where my father works, the thirsty grain truckers, begin to watch the time, suggest an earlier dinner hour, and predict the crowd's size.

"Won't be as many as he had in June."

"Why do you say that?"

"Ever'thing ain't free. Beer was free in June."

"Where'd he get the rabbit?"

"Pens. It's tame rabbit. It ain't wild rabbit."

"Tame, is it? Shit. That's a buncha shit. That's like eatin' house cat."

"I'll watch to make sure you don't have to eat any."

"Jus' never you mind. I may get weak later."

"Don't make a shittin' bita difference to me if it's tame or wild. I don't care if it comes when you call it."

"I'm so hungry I could eat the ass out of a skunk."

"I don't believe that'll be necessary. What time is it?"

"Six. . . . Give us four more here."

Jim walks from the kitchen to check the gravel parking lot in front. At this hour in autumn, the interior of his bar is dark amber, the sun still coming strongly through the plate-glass windows. He stands in the doorway between the bar and the kitchen, alternating his supervision. In the kitchen, his wife, his elder daughter and her husband, his son's wife, Jim's two weekend employees—the Birkenholtzes—are all terrifically busy over vats of food. In the main room, there's loose and steadily growing noise. Jim watches both rooms, a fulcrum of calm management.

He's a short stocky man, bald, with a large sad face and narrow eyes that make him look like a morose rodent. He moves and talks slowly and smokes Pall Malls continuously. He drinks great quantities of coffee, strong and black, but rarely drinks what he pours for customers. There was a time when he did, quite a lot of it, he says, but no more. ("There's two things a fella should never do if he's gonna run a bar," he's said. "Don't work both sides of the bar. And don't screw your barmaid.")

"What time we get this show on the road, Jim?" shouts Vern, knowing the answer, but wishing to be part of the mood. He's sitting at a table covered with empty beer bottles and a fine gray powder of cigarette ash. Other factory workers sit with him. They cross the highway to the Cardinal at four o'clock, when their shift is over, and they stay. If anyone merits a generous portion of free rabbit, Vern does.

"Seven," Jim says and points to the hand-lettered sign.

"Well," Vern says, "be sure to let me know. Like I say, you can call me anything but late for dinner." He laughs at his joke, and when he does, deep lines in his forehead and around his mouth move animatedly, flow like rivers. His eyelids, heavy from drinking, lift momentarily when he smiles.

"You're just gonna have to take care of yourself tonight, Vern," Jim says.

"I reckon I can."

In front, by the big windows, there's a small dance floor, and a microphone for the country-western singer Jim has hired especially for this evening. Next to the dance floor, there's a big mahogany-colored organ. Virginia Rowe played the organ on weekends before she remarried and moved away last summer, but now there's no one around who knows how.

The singer is local, one of the Kain girls. She graduated a year ago from high school and has been singing and playing guitar at dances around Jasper County. There are many Kains in Prairie City. "Kains is thick as sparrows," someone said the other day. There are Kains just south of town and Kains southwest, near the river bottom. There are Kains nearly everywhere around here, all of them somehow related, cousins and second cousins, third and fourth cousins, some of them spelling their name Kane, a family tree dense and snarled and deeply planted in Prairie City soil. Marla Jo is a river-bottom Kain and, like her father, a woman of untroubled spirit, easy cheer. She's small and blonde and stands before the microphone, tuning her guitar and sending fuzzy chords through the room.

"Hey, hey, we're gonna have some music. Ol' Jim spared no expense tonight."

"You ever heard her? I hear she's real good. That's what somebody said."

"She usually has a couple others with her."

"Can she play *Willie Nelson*? I fuckin' *love Willie Nelson*."

"I don't care what she plays, just so she keeps bringin' it."

The room has nearly filled and cars and pickups are arriving in a rush, as if a meeting were about to start. Men and women, old and young, crowd into the Cardinal, taking the remaining tables and standing against the walls. Some of the men, a few with women trailing them, know the Cardinal well and roam freely with a bottle of beer in hand, waving and shouting. Others act with an adolescent skittishness, clinging to corners and forming tight clusters. The men, and many women, emanate the polished cleanliness of people who work outdoors, the unduplicable clean of often-washed denim and starched khaki. I remember seeing my father achieve it every night, coming onto the back porch with his long day all over him, his eyes peering out through the dirt, then emerging an hour later from a bath with brilliant skin, having roughly scrubbed his labor away before putting on freshly laundered old clothes. He had gotten "cleaned up for supper," and whenever I've heard that phrase since, his pink, raw skin has come to mind. These people tonight have gotten cleaned up for the barbecue. Their skins show violent contrasts of color—forearms and faces a brown that began years ago, foreheads and biceps as milk-white as infants'.

Jim joins his son, Jimmy Joe, and they mix drinks and draw glasses of beer, moving up and down the bar and crossing nimbly in the tight space. People shouting orders are all around them, a solid wall at the bar and tiers of customers standing behind, jumping up to be seen and ducking between cracks in the wall.

"Give us a round here."

"Two Blues."

"Can a Bud, you can keep the glass."

"Let's see, I need two Buds and two sloe-gin fizz."

"Give us a couple here. VO on the rocks."

Jimmy Joe thrusts a short cocktail glass into the hill of ice below the bar, packing the glass, and colors the ice like a snow cone with a generous shot of whiskey. Jim holds draft glasses at an angle beneath his Schlitz spout, gradually righting the glass as it fills and achieving a nearly headless draft, only a thin white scum on the cold, gold beer. ("What'm I supposed to do with this?" a customer once asked, rejecting a thick white draft. "Shave?")

Jim's hard drinks measure slightly more than a shot, sometimes slightly more than that, satisfying something in his customers other than a thirst: an assurance they're getting their money's worth. Jim believes himself that quantity, and the suggestion of it, is a noble concept. He recently passed up an opportunity to buy, on sale, a smooth, expensive whiskey and paid more for an inferior liquor with a raw, sedimentary force. When mixed with 7-Up, Pepsi, sour mix (as liquor here usually is), the better whiskey vanishes on the tongue and the drink seems diluted. The rough-edged liquor holds up in solution, tastes like a shot's worth at the bottom of the stomach.

"I'll have a glass a beer. It's cold, isn't it? Give Wesley another one, too."

"You finished out at your place, are you?"

"Well, we got a few acres of corn on the north place, is all."

"How'd it do? Say, give us two more here."

"Here, and here, bartender."

"A whiskey sour and a PBR."

"A round."

"Two more."

"A can of Blue."

Betty carries the first big tub of baked beans from the kitchen and places it on a table near the bar, a look of proud mission on her face. Almost immediately, a practiced line forms single file along the walls leading up to the tables of food. Aromatic steam rises from the tubs and blends with the cigarette haze, spices it. The line moves forward, taking helpings of rabbit, beans, potato chips, French bread.

"Help yourself, folks," says Jim, smiling. "There's another tub of rabbit."

Soon all the tables are filled, the other rooms are crowded, the pool and air-hockey tables have been set with paper dishes and plastic forks. Some of the younger people sit on the floor by the dance area. Smoke and laughter rise in the Cardinal. Behind the bar, Jimmy Joe keeps a hand on the draft beer handle, snapping it forward and back as if he held a gearshift. He skims away the useless foam and it slowly drips through a hose to a large coffee can, finally spilling over and sending up a smell like rotting fruit, the smell of soaked wooden floors in old bars, an incongruous smell in this clean new room. Jimmy Joe covers the spill with towels, too busy for anything more, and shifts gears.

Vern gets slowly to his feet, liquor stiffening him, and moves to the bar. He's alone among these local people, not really a citizen of Prairie City, though he shares an apartment in town with a few other men. He has no crops to talk about, no field work. Vern came to Prairie City with the construction crew that built last year's grain silos and when the work was finished and the crew moved on, he stayed. He has been a migrant nearly all his life. He was born in Kansas and when he was a child, his family followed the wheat harvests around the state. He has worked in Oklahoma, Missouri, the Texas panhandle, always with his hands and always in the flat small towns. He's stayed in Prairie City nearly a year, longer than most of the places he's paused to wait in. He looks out from under an eyelid and seems to lead with it, as if it's the only spot on his body still sensory.

"Tarbender," he says, and winks. "Tarbender, another beer. Ya know, I'm not as thunk as deeple pink I am." Vern repeats this line at least nightly, and no matter how elusive the rest of the language becomes for him, he can swiftly and without stumbling say it, just that way.

"How do ya like the rabbit, Vern?" asks Jim.

"Say," he says, suddenly quite serious, "this is good rabbit. I'm enjoyin' this rabbit, I really am."

Vern wears a faded denim Western-style shirt with a stitched yoke and long rows of shiny snaps along the cuffs. He normally wears Western clothes, cowboy hats and boots, jeans, a thin white Western jacket. Many times on weekends, especially on Sundays, when the town is locked, one sees Vern, hard and bone-thin, dressed in old Western clothes, walking the streets or the through-town highways. His wrinkled face appears shrunken under the wide white hat, and he walks with a tight, restricted step, his body squeezed in against itself, so that even in this hot autumn, he seems to be feeling a chill. He walks up and down the highway, an apparently aimless stroll, as if his horse has thrown him and left him stranded here.

Vern turns toward the first music from Marla Jo Kain, cocks his eye to receive it. Marla Jo fills the room with country music, sings a mournful layer of sound over the shouting and the laughter and the beer-loosened whoops. She sings and plays strongly, her voice coming from that place in the back of her throat where women make their country songs, a lilting hitch of sound.

Her audience puts down slabs of barbecued rabbit and applauds.

"Sing *This Ol' House*," says a fat woman.

"Sing *I Like Beer*," shouts a heavy young man on the floor, his face field-red, his legs drawn awkwardly up under him.

"I don't care what you sing," says Vern quietly, to no one. "Just so long as you keep *bringin'* it." He squints toward Marla Jo and the crowded room, and tilts his head radically. "I sure would love to play like that," he says. "And I wouldn't mind playin' *with* that, either. She's about as purty as a freckled pig on a pink blanket."

Vern's similaic speech separates him from the people of Prairie City, many of whom suspect all but the most essential spoken language. Vern seems to know that they find him foolish and faintly embarrassing, but at least his language gives him some identity: that fool with the monologue of bad jokes, stories of wives in heat and stupid niggers. Still, he talks on, probably knowing that he's talking to himself, talking at strangers, and he has perfected over the years the verbal hooks—words and phrases and dangling voices precisely timed—to keep another drinking body near him and silent. He will allow a sudden silence to fall, and let it last exactly long enough for you to think the words, "Well, I got to be going," then end it before the words can actually be spoken.

Marla Jo continues to bring it, a medley of recognizable hits. The crowd claps and pounds and young couples, then older ones, begin to take the floor.

"Whooooeeee!" Spinning and catching and low, re-membered dips. "Come on, Mother. Aw, come on." Trochaic stomping on the parquet floor, fumbling for Marla Jo's time. Stomp and bounce and bully the beat, kick it up out of the floor, loose from the wood, up into your legs. "Yaaahaaa. Let's look for it, Moma." Men and women, women and women, a man and a man—"Lookit Lyle and Mike! I think they're in love! You shure purty, Lyle. It don't *look* right." A clean-drunk crowd, fed for free, doing what it needs excuse to do: let go.

"Sing it, Marla, honey. Allamande left, you sons of bitches!" Finished with a day, a harvest under roofs. Let it rain. Blow. Snow and watch me give a shit. "Whoaah! I need a beer."

Vern turns back to the bar, sobered slightly by the noise and the swirling motion. "Lookit that over there," he says, pointing to a young wife holding hands with her husband. "She's got an ass on her like a Montana mule. I gotta find me a new dolly. I had me one over in Newton. She's a good ol' gal, too, but we fought all the time. All the time. I couldn't understand it, like I say, she's a good ol' gal. She'd chew ass, then I'd chew ass, and we'd go back and forth. I couldn't figure it out till I sat down and thought on it. Like the man say, 'I thunk about it,' and I finally decided the problem was simple. I just hated her."

He smiles and the wrinkles move sleepily around his mouth. He lights a cigarette and sips his beer. "But I'll get me another one. If one gets away, it don't take me too long to train another one. Like the fella says, it don't take nothin' to find a good wife. It's watching out for their husbands that's the problem. Ain't that right? Ha!" He becomes immediately serious. "I gotta get my ass outa this town. There's nothin' in this town for me. I could stay here till Christ kicked a football and nothin' good would come of it. I been thinkin', I got a brother wants to go down to British Honduras and work in the oil fields and he wants me to come. Good money down there and I feel like I need to get outa the country for a while. Fella can make seven bucks an hour down there, my brother says, and that's a shit load better than I'm doin' here, I'll tell ya. I got me a camper that's parked down at Sully and I want to get that fixed up and get the hell outa here. I'm gonna leave this town like a ruptured duck in a hailstorm. I could drive to Kansas, where my brother is, and we could go down to British Honduras from there."

Vern cannot legally drive his camper or anything else. His license was taken from him after too many drunken-driving arrests. To get it back, he must go to school, complete a course given by the state highway patrol. He refuses. "I'll show those bastards," he frequently says. "They're not gettin' my money. They're not gonna make me go to no drunk-driving school." He walks from his basement apartment a few blocks north to the factory, and from the factory to the Cardinal across the highway. He walks home; some nights he's driven. On weekends, he walks along the highways, around town, to the P.C. Drive In and to Casey's 7-Eleven for beer and cans of beans and soup. Sometimes, on Saturday afternoons, he gets a ride to Dick's Tavern in Colfax.

Two young men hurry into the Cardinal and walk to the microphone. Marla Jo has taken a short break. One of the young men, heavy, tall, with long brown hair down the sides of his face, is a stranger. The other, Mike, is a Prairie City boy, the son of a feed salesman who has been one of Jim Billingsley's best customers. Mike is twenty and seems to have inherited his father's capacity. He speaks to the crowd.

"Listen up, everybody. Listen. Gary, here, was passin' through town on his way into Ankeny and ran outa gas. He gave a holler on the C.B. and we picked him up. I told him we were havin' a good time here and it turns out he's a professional entertainer and he's gonna sing some songs and do a few impersonations he knows. So let's give him a hand. Gary, come on."

The heavy young man walks reluctantly forward and

the people, digesting rabbit, beer and inspired dance, seem confused. Gary looks uneasily about.

"Hello, folks," he says quietly.

At the bar, the hunchbacked drinkers look irritably over their shoulders.

"What the hell is this?"

"Where'd Mike drag up this guy?"

"Says he's some 'professional entertainer.'"

"I'll tell you what. No 'professional entertainer' runs outa gas in Prairie City, Iowa, by God."

Gary picks about on Marla Jo's guitar, explores the strange instrument for its music. Softly finished chords come from the guitar and gain the room's attention. He strums again, a seemingly casual pass over the strings, and richer sounds come out, and others build from those.

"Ooohh," says a woman at a table near the microphone.

"That's purty."

"Real nice."

Gary says, "I'll play a few for you. Anything you'd like to hear?"

"How about *Folsom Prison Blues*?"

"Okay," says Gary, and he plays the introductory chords, turning his back momentarily to the people. He swings around again and begins to sing. The voice from the microphone is low and breaks up into rumbling shards of sound as it meets notes. *Folsom Prison Blues* is Johnny Cash's song, and so, almost exactly, is this voice.

"My God. Would ya listen to that?"

"I'll be go ta hell," whispers a man at the bar. His eyes are disks of awe. "If I had my back to him, I'd think that was Johnny Cash for sure. That sona bitch is good."

At the end of the bar, Vern's head comes slowly up from a posture of prayer. His eyes open and blink bewilderedly, and he turns cautiously in the direction of the music, as if not to frighten away this hallucination. He blinks again, seems trying to determine if a liquor dream has taken life. For a long time, he stands raptly, until he seems to understand that the moment is real, and less than it had promised in its warm suspension. Finally, he slowly exhales and shakes his head. As the song ends, he says, "That son of a bitch is onto Johnny Cash like stink on a skunk."

"Whoooeeee!"

"More!"

"Hey, ain't he *good!*"

Gary bows, relaxed now in a friendly place, and speaks with more force and a Southern accent.

"Thank you, folks," he says. He sings *Sunday Morning Comin' Down, Behind Closed Doors,* sings Waylon Jennings and Tom T. Hall songs, and between them does impressions. John Wayne. Jimmy Cagney. Johnny Cash, again, singing *I Got Stripes.* The crowd enjoys his songs, his guitar, but what it clearly loves are the voices, celebrated voices coming through the microphone in the Cardinal Inn.

"Hey, buddy! Do Gomer Pyle!" yells someone from the bar.

Gary says, immediately, "Gol-lee, Sarge!", has the high moronic whine of that television character precisely. People bend over with laughter, shake their heads, send sonic whistles back to Gary.

"Listen to that guy. If that ain't Gomer Pyle talkin,' I'll be damned."

"That son of a bitch is *good!*"

Gary performs for half an hour and hypnotizes nearly everyone. People move closer to him, up to the edge of the dance floor where he stands, and some of them squint into his face, as if looking for the place where he hides the voices. They urge him to bring them back. Do John

Wayne again. Do Glen Campbell. Do Johnny Cash once more. Especially do Gomer Pyle.

"Gol-ol-lee, folks," Gary says finally. "I gotta go now, but it sure has been enjoyable meetin' y' all."

They roar, and a number of men rush to him and shake his hand. Jim walks quickly up to Gary and offers him free drinks and many thanks. He asks Gary back, to return when he can, and to bring his voices.

"Thank ya, folks. Bye, now. Take care!" Gary shouts. He stops at the door and semaphorically waves, the exit of a professional entertainer.

The room is silent, seems half as full now that Gary and the famous people have left. The bar drinkers snap back first, begin to look around and whisper.

"I swear," says a man at the bar, "that was just about the best damn thing I've ever seen. I woulda swore ever' one of those guys he done was right here in the room."

"Sure as hell."

"I'd like to see that guy come back. I mean, I'd really like to see that guy back here anytime."

"What'd he say to you, Jim? You were talkin' to him. What'd he say?"

Jim speaks with the authority of one who's been told secrets.

"Just passing through. He's selling restaurant supplies. He's got apartments all over. Got one in Kansas City. One in New Orleans. The guy's strictly a floater. Here today, gone tomorrow. . . . He *was* good, though, wasn't he?"

"Good? I'll say the sona bitch was good."

"I know I'd sure like to see that guy come back."

"Me, too. I'd love to see him in here again."

Jim says, "The kid's strictly a floater."

"Well," Vern says, *"floatin'* is a damn sight better than sinkin'."￼ He lights a Camel and says, "Better have one more here," and when the beer is placed before him, he moves the glass around on the bar like a chess piece he can't decide to commit.

"Like I was sayin', I can't come up with a whole lot of reasons why I should stay in this town. Once I get my camper fixed up, you know what I mean, once I get it runnin', like I say, I'm gonna clear out of this town so fast they'll think a posse of husbands has sniffed me out. I got me an idea, anyway, I been tossin' around in my head, most people would think it's crazy, but that don't make no never mind to me, 'cause people think I'm crazy anyway. But, like I say, I's watchin' TV the other night on this show, oh, whatchacall, *Wild Kingdom?* And they was doing something out in Utah, or Montana or one of those big fuckin' states. And they was talking about all the minerals they got in the mountains out there, ya know what I mean? Minerals. Like your copper, and your nickel, but especially your copper. And I was thinkin' I might just drive out there and do me a little prospectin'. I know a fella made a million prospectin'. He was telling me once, I was talkin' to him, and he said that ya gotta know what you're looking for, 'cause when you look at it, whatever, copper, tin, whatever, in the mountain, it don't look like nothin' at all. Looks like, oh, like maybe gray sand, I'd say. But those mountains are just loaded with minerals, and if ya know what you're lookin' for, you can make a million. I been thinkin' I just might do that. Fix up my camper and head out there and do a little prospectin'."

People have begun to leave, thanking Jim formally as if they were his guests, not customers, explaining that early chores await them. Marla Jo, smiling bravely, packs her guitar. Vern backs away from the bar and walks toward the door, shaken awake by the room's percussive emptiness.

"Good night," he says, waving over his shoulder at the

chairs, the tables, the big empty tubs, sauce-scabbed.

Hours later, Jim and Betty finish cleaning up. They step outside and Jim locks the door, locking the exuberant night inside. Neither he nor Betty will speak of this evening's specific flourishes; Jim believes that events that take place in his bar must remain there. Not that there's anything about this night to conceal. But Jim knows the possible dangers of a small town interested in itself. Some of the attraction of the Cardinal is the chance it gives to escape that intimacy for another, more manageable kind. If his customers wish to discuss late-night conversations they've made or heard outside the Cardinal they will, but Jim understands that if anyone suspected that he were carrying overheard opinions past his door, he'd soon be presiding over empty barstools, vacant tables.

At this hour, the highway is empty and there is a quiet that is nearly as absolute as the night. There are two sources of distant sound, steady motor-humming sounds that continue imperceptibly like a furnace or a refrigerator motor. From the silos, one block north, wind from the grain drier blows through moist corn. West, on the highway, diesel engines idle. Long-distance truckers have pulled their semis to the side of 163, onto the parking surfaces in front of the P.C. Drive In and Casey's 7-Eleven. Here the truckers slide down in their seats and sleep for a few hours, until the sun comes east down 163 and into their cabs, or until they get their wake-up call. Arriving in town, the truckers frequently page Prairie City's policeman, Terry Massick, on their C.B. radios. Massick's tour of duty lasts until three or four o'clock in the morning, and he happily accepts their calls and drives up to the side of the trucks to pound on them at the hour they've requested.

"Time to get rollin', good buddy," Massick says into his C.B. microphone. "You take 'em easy, take 'em careful."

"Hey, thank ya, good buddy," says the trucker, and moments later, his semi moves out onto the highway again.

Jim and Betty live exactly two blocks north of the Cardinal, with only the grain silos standing between their business and their home, but they always drive a long, ritualistic path between the two. Leaving the parking lot, they head west down the highway, driving slowly past the Tower Cafe, dark and locked and boarded. They continue west to the P.C. Deep Rock gas station and, across the street, the P.C. Drive In. Billingsley owns the Tower, he owns the gas station and the drive-in. Now he turns north, following the street over the Rock Island tracks, toward the small house where his mother lives. She has been in Prairie City for a few years now, as his sister and her husband have. Jim's father died last year. The car slows to a crawl past her house, as he and Betty closely inspect the dark house and the yard around it. Satisfied, Jim turns east again, toward the street of shops and offices off the business square. First, they pass their own home, a huge old frame structure with ornate trim and asymmetrical additions, random gables and sagging porches all around. Opposite their house is the simple concrete building that was Billingsley's first real estate in Prairie City. Across the street from that building is a vacant lot, also his property, on which he parked used cars, the first item he sold here.

"I came to Prairie City because it was a little town, where it looked to me like a man could make some money," he once said. "Simple as that." At one time, before he moved here, he worked two jobs—in a Knoxville garage during the morning and early afternoon and, from three to eleven at night, at the Maytag washing-machine plant in Newton. He drove to the plant with his father, who worked the same shift, and after work they ate at a late-closing diner and, between them, drank a pint of Paul Jones whiskey on the drive back to Knoxville.

"I couldn't hold a conversation in those days," Jim said. "I couldn't stay awake. I'd sit down and in two minutes my head would drop, bam, and I'd be asleep." But he made more from his Maytag shift than from any part-time job he could find locally, even figuring that he had to earn two dollars more an hour from Maytag to make the drive to Newton profitable.

The Billingsleys arrived in Prairie City in an old station wagon and parked it in the concrete garage. They slept in the back of the wagon, cooked meals on a hot plate, made a living space in the building, which Jim tried to warm with a small gas heater.

Now they drive down the street of shops and offices, and Jim checks the buildings he owns, nearly all of them on the south side of the street. He does not own the Zaayer Insurance Agency, and wishes he did. He'd like to own an unbroken line.

At the northwest corner of the square, Jim turns again, drives south past the old, empty State Bank Building, which is his. Steps lead up to its door, and Jim believes those steps have much to do with the fact that the building has no tenant. "Nobody likes to climb steps. It's the only building in town where there's a lot of steps in front, and it's hard as hell to rent like that." He must continue down the west side of the square to the end before reaching another of his buildings, a small and relatively new one, Beek's Barber Shop. Jim owns the bookends of this street—the barber shop and Van's combination grocery, coffee shop and bakery. It's been clear in town for some time that Van has not been able to draw business from DeWit's grocery, on the northeast side.

"Van'll be out of business by spring," Jim predicts.

"He's got all kinds of problems. I'll tell you what he needs to do. He needs to get some elderly lady up front on the cash register, some local lady who everybody knows, and who will give you a smile when you come in, say 'Hi.' Van's got all his kids running around in there now and kids ruin a business. People don't want kids running around. You gotta watch kids every minute."

Jim and his wife shop exclusively at Van's; Jim eats his afternoon meal at Van's lunch counter, buys bakery buns there for Cardinal sandwiches. Jim says that he has nothing at all against Donnie DeWit but believes Prairie City needs competition wherever possible. He also feels loyal to someone fairly new here who is trying to draw a living from a town that has shown a historic fidelity to its old families.

"I'd of starved if I'd had to depend on Prairie City people. When I first came here, I worked on some old cars for a bunch of Missourians down at the cement plant. And they bought some cars from me. Otherwise, I never coulda got started in this town." He has sold cars, houses and beer in Prairie City, and all these goods have in common the same element of potential controversy—a house with severe and undetected faults; a car that abruptly breaks down; the simple merchandising of liquor in a community so divided on the subject. There's defiance in the pattern of his retailing, just as there was a certain defiance in the evening just closed. For such a party could not have taken place ten years ago, perhaps even five.

There have always been social gatherings sponsored here, by someone showing gratitude to the community. Probably there have been such gatherings since the plains were settled, farming neighbors coming together over food, to lose some accumulated solitude. From my own childhood, I remember huge Co-op dinners in the spring;

Pancake Days sponsored by various clubs; church suppers; and every local business' open house when a new room was added, a remodeling completed. But these were always abstinent affairs, the air mercilessly chaste in the basements and gymnasiums that held them. Every gathering looked the same. Set out on a long row of folding tables, covered with white cloths, were gelatin squares, red, orange and lime, and big wedges of pie baked by the wives of the sponsors. Between the salads and pies, the women stood behind the tables with tubs of potatoes, meat, deep lakes of brown gravy. They scooped and ladled and sliced the meat, their work-formed arms sleeveless in summer dresses. I can see the long meandering lines, the same kind of line that took Jim's rabbit and beer tonight, moving forward with a shuffling meekness, a social shyness fighting with a fundamental belief that it was a waste bordering on sin to ignore a free meal. People ate the beef or ham, praised it, compared it favorably with last year's pork, the men working clumsily with plastic dinnerware, their faces frowning with a child's concentration. They talked of little else but the food, and tillerman's business, and paused for long appraising looks at the crowd around them, interested not so much in how many had come but in whom. After the pie, over strong cups of coffee, the hosts made speeches—reports of profit and loss, praise for the customers' loyalty that had made the new addition possible, summaries of fund-raising progress toward the new pews. And then everyone went home and more candidly assessed the evening. Had the beef truly been equal to last year's pork? D said his was plainly tough. L found the rolls cold and stale. R disagreed, had eaten a fine meal, the best in years. For the next few days, in the coffee shops and gas stations, a collective verdict took shape.

These open houses continue in Prairie City, but they

are no longer the exclusive entertainment. People have new choices, and Jim Billingsley has been their merchant, openly hoping for profit. Even those who've welcomed the change in the town find Jim's success surprising. Tonight, at the height of the evening, amidst the swelling noise and stomping rhythms, people said: "Can you believe this?" and "Who'd ever thought this could happen in Prairie City?" and "Did you ever think you'd see this here?" watching themselves in a way peculiar to plains people and essential to the restraint we place on public emotion.

There's good reason for people to be surprised. As recently as the early 1970s, a special election was held in Prairie City to decide if its high school students should be allowed to dance at a spring banquet. Dancing won, but I remember being startled to hear that a vote had been taken, for I'd assumed that the issue had been settled long ago. A decade before, we had danced, had changed the law with a revolutionary spring prom when I was thirteen or fourteen years old. But apparently a new school board, with rejuvenated narrowness, had tried to draw out of the town a measure of its old intolerance.

And roughly five years later, Jim Billingsley has not failed, has made money from the Cardinal Inn, money he's used to buy more of Prairie City. He gives a lot of credit to the young people, and to new couples in town. He feels that the town still resists him—"My best weekend business doesn't come from Prairie City," he says— and he won't accept the explanation that people seek relaxation in strange towns, away from the crowd that knows them. He prefers to believe that Prairie City people will drive to another town in order to spend their money with someone else. His gratitude to the customers he has is all the more fierce, and with his parties he has done more than any other resident to change Prairie City.

At the end of the street, Jim slows his car again for railroad tracks. He has not checked all the property he owns, some houses in town that he rents out ("Rent 'em cheap, keep 'em full"). He has buildings, too, in the surrounding small towns, in Colfax, Pleasantville, Baxter. He would like to have a building on the square in Monroe.

"Why?" asked a man from Monroe, with whom Jim spoke one evening in the Cardinal.

"Just to have one," said Jim.

He sees the flow and the pattern of this town's commerce with dispassionate clarity, anticipating, acquiring, spreading. It's as if he views Prairie City as a Monopoly board, knowing that if he owns enough of it, people eventually must land on some square that is his. If they don't buy his beer or eat his food, perhaps they'll need his gas or some of his space. "I never did take much interest in the stock market," he's said. "I like to invest in things I can see." Had he been born in a city, raised among black-topped lots and high tenements, he'd no doubt have become someone like Arthur Rubloff, the landlord of Chicago, or William Levitt, or another of the city monarchs who have the identical need to own things they can see. But Billingsley came from a farm in Pleasantville, Iowa, has lived fifty years in Marion and Jasper counties, has not slept one night in a motel bed, but has had hard ground under him, and the floor of a station wagon. He has come recently to Prairie City, has no ancestry here he might not wish sold: "It seemed like a town a man could make some money in."

There must also be in him some drive for revenge. When Jim had been in town just a few days, he spoke with one of its prominent people, a doctor from one of the very old Prairie City families that watched the town's growth with almost feudal concern, worrying about the expansion and the new people coming in. Jim had opened for business, was living in the concrete building and sleeping in the station wagon. He and Betty were looking for a house, and finding it hard. Houses large enough for their family were scarce or expensive. Jim knew the doctor's place in Prairie City, and one day he asked his help.

"I'd like to find something soon," Jim said. "I'd like to get the kids up here and started in school."

"I don't think you want to find a home here," the doctor said. "I don't think you're going to be in Prairie City very long."

He has never gotten over that. In the tight spaces of Prairie City, he has operated with an occasional rudeness, tearing down or covering up in days what had merely faded or shifted slightly in a hundred years. When he first arrived, he shrewdly bought and sold Prairie City houses to make what he calls his "fast money," the capital he used to start his real-estate purchases. Some of the farmers and the small-risk merchants see his rental profits, his real-estate sales, his late-shift hours at the Cardinal as easy, sweatless work. Jim's successful bar is only his most recent provocation and to those who've resented him all along, it simply validates their feelings.

And he has met the historic discrimination, especially against those from southern Iowa, where Pleasantville and Knoxville latitudinally lie, barely below that arbitrary mind-drawn line that central Iowans trace across the state, separating their cooperative soil from the bleak border towns near the Missouri line. Indeed, in some minds, south-central Iowa and Missouri are one place, and both are mostly populated with hillbillies, people quite relaxed with their timeless poverty and sure to bring it into any new settlement. The first cars Jim repaired were owned by Missourians working at the cement plant, and that confirmed a kinship. It may not have occurred to some people that he'd have welcomed work on any car that came into his garage.

Jim had tried his own business before, run a small grocery and gas station in Marion county, his home county. His receipts grew slowly but were holding reasonably well, well enough, at least, for Jim to feel he could take his family on a three-day vacation during a Memorial Day weekend. He kept the grocery open, leaving it to a visiting brother-in-law, a stranger to the area.

When Jim returned, he found the shelves of the grocery absolutely clean, all the stock sold, and in the cash-register drawer a thick pile of charge slips bearing names, signatures, that Jim had never seen. They were false names, given by the people of his home county, some of whom had patronized his store, and hundreds more who'd made their first trip while Jim was away. His brother-in-law had naïvely written the names next to grocery totals and had locked the slips safely in the register.

Jim and Betty reach the stop sign at the highway, turn back onto the quiet strip and pass the Cardinal again, finishing the long rectangular circuit of their property. It's nearly one-thirty as they pull up beside the marvelous old house, all of geometry represented in its architecture, that dominates its street, as it would any street in town.

"After I quit my job at the garage in Knoxville," Jim has said, "I didn't do anything for a long time. I just went down to the river and laid on the bank for about six months. I thought about how I'd worked all my life. I'd even worked two jobs for a while, and where was I? I was no farther ahead than I'd ever been. I thought it all out, about what I wanted to do, and I decided that whatever it was, I wasn't ever gonna get ahead if I kept on working for somebody else, or working with my hands. I was gonna have to get into something that would work *for* me, and would go up in value fast. So after I'd come here, and made a little money from the garage, I sold some cars, and then I sold houses, and that's the quickest money I've ever made in my life. I made more money by inflation than I ever did working for a living. The Cardinal is a different matter. It's slow money, and I never had any intention of running it. I leased it once, but the fella got in trouble and I had to take it over. But the building is bought and paid for and if I locked the doors tomorrow, I'd have enough to put three meals on the table for the rest of my life."

They walk slowly into the house, and after a moment, kitchen light fills the big windows. Jim sits at the table, removes his shoes, and wiggles some of the standing pain from his feet. He looks out to the concrete garage, diagonally opposite his house."I'll never sell that building," he has said. "It's worthless, but it was my first, and I'll never sell it." Directly across the street, he can see his big vacant lot, high with weeds at the moment and a few humpbacked, old used cars. There is no sign, no feeling, not even the inhabiting currents that sometimes remain, of the huge old landmark house that he tore down when he bought the lot, the house that belonged, until the day he died, to the doctor who'd welcomed Jim to Prairie City.

Through October and the first days of November, the weather has held to summer, and the farmers cannot ignore it. Around town, at Snub's lunch counter, in all other gathering places, they quickly gulp coffee, then drive back out to their farms to make some use of the weather.

"I hadn't planned to plow, really, but a fella can't sit around in weather like this."

"Well, guess I oughta do something as long as I can. You can always drink coffee."

So the conversations go, and doughnuts are left half-eaten on the counters as the men spin their stools away from long easy mornings. Some of the stores, Vroom's men's clothing, Walters' furniture, Beek's Barber Shop, are nearly as empty as they were at the height of harvesting, and the town has the atmosphere of a resort whose season has been hurt by foul weather.

For farmers, then, even good weather can be harmful. It has stirred their guilt and put them back in their fields, breaking the crust of harvest work that many of them had intended to leave. They are "fall plowing," opening the earth once again with the plow's huge shining scythe blades, so that it can breathe more easily, receive air and the winter's moisture, and so that, after thawing, it will be more finely crumbled for planting. In central Iowa, the rich loam is ideally porous, and autumn plowing is not as essential as it is in northern Iowa. There the soil, generally a type agronomists call gumbo, breaks behind the plow into heavy black chunks and autumn plowing works it to a texture that can hold seeds. Still, some farmers have always plowed their Prairie City farms after harvesting, to make the land open to melting snow and to save time in spring. And also, perhaps, so that they can look out over white winter fields and imagine the turned soil beneath, alive and still at work.

But fall-plowed fields lose the firm holding surfaces of stalks and vines that crop taking gives them and they can be susceptible to erosion during a dry winter. The land around Prairie City, dry in early summer and dry again in this remarkable autumn, will need immoderate snow. But that concern belongs to the next season. Right now, there is this damn compelling bliss to deal with. The countryside is busy and from the gravel roads near our farm I've seen small spots moving up and down the fields. Tractors pulling plows, surrounded by a thick dust, like an obedient cloud, that becomes high above the tractor the same pale blue as the air.

My father has never plowed in the fall. He is dubious about the advantages, and, in any case, he has never had so much land that he could not prepare it in the spring. Certainly, he has planted later than his neighbors many seasons, and has been teased about that, but he's never missed a crop and sometimes, as with the one just finished, he's shown that the community's calendar and nature's do not always agree.

When I was growing up, the school bus I rode followed the same route year after year, stopping at the same farmhouses for the same students. There were small shifts of order, so that one year I'd be picked up after the Laurens girls and before the VandeLune boys, rather than the reverse, but the people on my bus remained mostly unchanged. New kindergarten children began to ride, and seniors graduated, and there was a firm unwritten rule that the youngest started at the front and moved toward the back as they passed from grade to grade, eventually graduating to the status of the last two double seats. Here one could look out the rear-door windows and shout or wave or gesture obscenely to traffic behind the bus. The driver and discipline were far away, in the front.

During the years that I enjoyed the prestigious seats, my friends and I played a card game called pitch, the playing surface a briefcase set in the aisle between the two double seats. Always, we fought time. We hurried to complete as many hands as possible before the bus arrived at school, and we became so practiced at saving time that the hands would be dealt and waiting for whoever was the last to board. One of the younger children, recruited as a kind of silent apprentice, kept a second deck shuffled and waiting. He gave us freshly dealt hands for distribution and scooped up the one just played. Gather the cards. Stack and shuffle them. Deal four hands down. Wait. Here.

But as keenly as I can feel that sense of fraternity, I can also hear the conversations we had in the fall, and can see the bright-red arms and faces of the other players, the particularly intense complexion that one can get only in the fields.

"Shit. Who dealt this mess? That you, Bass? I'll kill ya. . . . Oh, I bid three. We worked till dark last night. Didn't eat supper till nine o'clock."

"Plowing? Us, too. Eighty acres a stalk ground. I pass."

"What're you pullin'? A four-bottom? John Deere? John Deere's for shit. Massey's the only plow to have."

"Massey? Massey my ass. I'll match our Deere against it anytime."

"I bid four. You don't have any ground to plow, that's your problem. You don't know what plowing is. How deep you plowing?"

"Don't make a shit what ground. Hills or flatland. Don't make a shit how deep."

"What gear?"

"Don't matter what gear, either. You name it. What model you got? 1016. Fourth gear. Overdrive. Hard stock ground on a little hill. Some gullies. Deere. Massey. Over/ under. Six bottom. 1280. Conversion. That new A.C."

"I'll pass, " I would say. "What a shitty hand."

I couldn't see then that the best care my father could give his fields was his neglect. For me, studying my cards and listening mutely, there was only a sense of separation from classmates whose fathers practiced fall plowing. Not only did I feel hypocritical about being a farmer's son but sometimes I even blamed my father for not giving me work that was simply not part of his farming. Not only was I no farmer's son but he seemed, compared with his neighbors, less of a farmer.

Now I've seen how naïve it was to think of him as some kind of part-time farmer. Although he has not physically participated in a season since planting and early summer weeding, he's been a farmer every moment—tracking grain prices, stopping daily at the Co-op office to check market reports and to speak with other farmers, standing each evening on our back porch to find the weather in the skies ("there's no rain in that sunset"), *thinking* about it. The hardest form of field work.

No one's running for mayor. Not the incumbent, Dick Charls, whose term expires at the end of the year. Not Hank Ostlin, who was defeated by Charls in 1974 after sixteen years, by a margin of fourteen votes. Not anyone else.

For several weeks, the *Prairie City News*, published Thursdays, carried a small paragraph notifying everyone of the filing deadline, urging civic interest. Every Thursday, a small paragraph, the same words: "as of press time, no one has filed" . . . "Nomination papers are available" . . . a paragraph of motherly nagging. Don't forget. Four more weeks. Three. Two. The notice moved around in the paper, back to front, ever more prominent, finishing in the October second issue on the front page, middle column, among obituaries, with the news: "No one filed for mayor and this position will have to be filled by a write-in vote."

The men at the Cardinal looked into foamless beers and shook their heads. "Typical," one said.

"Just like this town."

At Snub's, over hot noon specials, a man giggled and said again, "I shoulda run. I thought ol' Hank was gonna run again."

His friend smiled. "You couldn't run. The rules say you gotta be white and half-bright. You only meet one of the requirements . . . and I ain't so sure which one."

"Shit."

In the check-out line at DeWit's grocery, a woman said, "We barely got anybody to run last time. There again, seems people would just rather sit back and criticize."

"Let the other fella do it," said her friend.

"It's always been so," said the woman.

All over town, one heard that assessment that Prairie City's people have been reluctant to serve, and such conversations put a clear distance between the problem and the people lamenting it, as if those shaking their heads were exceptions to the rule.

The theme is an old one here. Whenever some notion that's dependent on public participation or money or both has come to Prairie City, people have skeptically sighed and said, "That'll never go here." Often, they've been right. Few people were willing to work for, or against, a new high school, and several proposals were rejected before one finally achieved a majority. The town seemed to have no clear opinion, or at least to have opinions it did not wish attributable. Only voting day forced them out, and even then, in one remarkably inscrutable gesture, it endorsed at the polls the construction of a new school, then vetoed any bonds to build it.

Still, to some extent, Prairie City may have maligned itself through the years, for when faced with issues that truly have seemed to threaten its self-sufficiency, its integral balance, the town has responded. Funds were raised for a medical center, without which they could not have drawn a doctor after Dr. Ella Rheinertsen retired. The center was built and the doctor came. Also, plans for new churches have always found stores of idle funds. Indeed, churches have been built in the recent past with an almost competitive urgency—the Methodists' blond-brick structure in the south end, its roof line running low and subdued above corn rows; the Christian Reformed congregation's sweeping barn-roofed sanctuary, huge as their love of God Almighty, on the northeast side. They rose nearly simultaneously and in an air of serious aesthetic comparison.

"Fancy," said some of the Methodists of their competition.

"Puny," said the Reformed members of theirs.

As might be expected, matters of the soul inspire Prairie City's generosity, and when anything needs money or willing bodies, someone usually says there'll be enough of both if the citizens can be assured that God's for it. God loves new sewer systems; He endorses the Old Settlers Day cleanup committee; God wants paved streets.

But when service alone is sought, the difficulty goes deeper than plain miserliness. A man who serves on committees, runs for election, sits on city councils, must inevitably release his feelings, with his name on them. Finally, he subjects himself to the risk of discovering what his opinions are worth in Prairie City—what he is worth.

There are no issues debated in local elections, no ideologies clearly marked. No Democrats and Republicans, no centrists, moderates, no neo-Mugwumps, so that, when beaten, one could ease the defeat by saying, "They like me, but they don't like my politics." There are no politics in Prairie City campaigns, though there should be, because there are, in fact, issues, strong ones, as elemental as in any city. Federal intervention, fiscal health, philosophy of spending, government regulation, patronage, clout: All of them are here, and beginning to matter. But no one discusses issues, perhaps because that would seem a pompous sophistication of the process, giving these elections a city sheen. We're just a little town, not fancy. What do we need with issues?

Those who finally do run begin and end their candidacies with a quiet advertisement in the *News*. No one campaigns, for that might raise the suspicion that he actually wants to win, and what man of clear mind and sensible modesty would honestly want the job? The town understands a man who sacrificially agrees. But for some candidate to state to his neighbors that he's best for mayor, to list supporting reasons, amounts to the sort of preening that insults the plains sensibility. There are no speeches, no debates, no house calls. (In the last campaign, Mayor Ostlin mailed a letter of his accomplishments in office. "Now, that kinda irked me," said one who voted Ostlin from office. "It made it sound like he's done all those things for the town when it was really the council as much as him.")

And so one deferentially submits an ad, small and square and framed in heavy black border, and waits for the verdict on his personality, which has been exposed to the voters long before Election Day.

That has been custom. But this year, no one's running for mayor.

Must Register to Vote in City Election

City election will be held November 4, 1975. Voters who are not already registered may register with the city clerk. Final date to register, according to City Clerk Hugh Williams, is October 25, 1975.

The *News* has begun to speak imperatively, as if annoyed by the town's inattention. Throughout Prairie City, there's a feeling of frivolous expectancy that might justify the concern of the *News*. It's as if, freed from the demands of authentic candidates, people feel no obligation to behave like voters. For the past several days, folks have been suggesting that small children, dead men, coalitions of pasture cattle, be mayor of Prairie City. Alterations of government have been proposed. A man in the Please-'U' declared himself king and before he'd finished lunch, he'd been overthrown by a triumvirate of queens from shops around the square. A waitress at Van's suggested that the town be minimally governed, City Hall closed, no mayor chosen.

"That'd be okay," a customer said, "but we gotta keep the men's can in the basement by the jail open for all the tourists that come through."

"And for the little kids to have a place to pee on Old Settlers Day," said his friend. Then he smiled, pleased with the oratorical meter of what he'd just said, and took it as his campaign theme: "If elected, I promise to close down City Hall, except for the men's can in the basement, so all the little kids can have a place to pee."

"I'd vote for ya."

In the dark-brick Co-op office, men sat in folding chairs by the east window, looked out to the season-bleached grass in the park and nearby lawns, while tractors drove by, delivering the end of autumn. They spoke above the ticker-tape machine against the wall as it statically typed grain and livestock prices and news that might move them. Tape lay, untorn, all about the men, white ribbon with Monday's prices flowing into Tuesday's, Wednesday's, on and on, days of continuous fate running a river's course over the floor.

A tall, thin man stood, walked to the machine, read the river.

"Hey," he said. "Says here Rockefeller just quit. Announced he'll not be a candidate for Vice-President next year."

A farmer who regularly watches the morning from the Co-op windows nodded. He wore cowboy boots, shit-freckled, a cap that said "Eat Beef Often" on the front. "Well, god damn," he said. "Poor ol' Rocky sure as hell's gonna need a job. There again, why don't we get him out here and run *him* for mayor?"

Men leaned forward with laughter.

After a few moments, the man holding the tape said, "Either that or we get that fella who's mayor of New York City that's having so much trouble out here. He's got more than he can handle, looks like. We'll let him be mayor out here, see if he can run a little bitty town any better."

"Who's that?"

"Oh, you know. The mayor of New York City, got the town where it's near broke."

"*Is* broke."

"Is broke. Right."

"Boom."

"Beame."

"Beame?"

Dick Charls TV is one of the shops in the long, full row on the north side of the square, D and L Clothing on its right, the Uptown Beauty Salon on its left. It's long and narrow, like the others, with a big front window displaying Zenith cabinetry. Above, a brick second story holds parts, boxes, attic smells.

Clyde Jarnagin is in the front at his counter, where he receives messages, bent stereo arms, burned tubes. In a big, square room at the back of his shop, the mayor of

Prairie City circles a blackened screen. Screws, wires, tubes topped with dust spill out of its back. He holds a screwdriver, has a carpenter's pouch of tools at his waist. Television sets sit everywhere in the room. On the floor, on tables, on top of one another, three tiers of carnage; one senses leaking wattage.

Mayor Charls has a roomful of company. Lucille Ball, Merv Griffin, three bright-blue women Searching for Tomorrow. Lucille and Merv are merely bright pink. Charls puts down his screwdriver, turns down the sounds. He's perhaps five feet ten, solidly built, and has kept the crewcut, now nearly gray, he's worn for years.

His father settled south of town, bought land that runs steeply to the river, and bits of land in the flat draws, small patches of bottom soil wedged among the rock hills, small woods, the ungovernable terrain where "all a fella gets done is turning around." But Mr. Charls acquired enough of it to make some money, and he left, at his death, a number of bottom pieces scattered through the hills; and on the pieces there are a number of Charlses.

But Dick has never been a farmer, and he opened his television business when black-and-white screens maximally measured twenty-one inches and few local people could afford anything beyond seventeen. He delivered our family's first set in 1954, seventeen inches, in a rose-hued cabinet with a grid of thick gold thread crisscrossing the speaker cloth below the screen. Saturday nights in front of the set, friends and relatives of my parents used to say, "Are you sure that's only a seventeen-inch screen? It sure does look bigger than that to me."

Discussing the election in the big square room at the back of his store, Dick Charls says, "You're really torn between two loves." His voice has a permanently hoarse quality. "You hate to see things in town go to pot, and I'm afraid for that now. But you've also got your business to think about. Being mayor takes at least an hour or two a day, and you spend many, many sleepless nights."

He's asked if that is why he's chosen to retire.

"There were a lot of things. My business, of course. But I've also got two kids coming up into high school, and I think they'd stand a pretty good chance of taking a lot of abuse if I was still mayor. It hasn't gotten too bad so far, but there's bound to be some of that. . . . You get flogged once in a while." He smiles, laughs hoarsely.

"I got shanghaied into running in the first place. I didn't want to, I didn't have the time, but people wanted a contest. Hank Ostlin had been mayor so long, some people thought it would be good to shake things up. But I didn't think I had a chance of beating him."

His margin, fourteen votes, was two more than the majority of all votes cast. Inevitably, names are written in, some seriously, some in the spirit that has prevailed this year, and constitutionally a candidate must receive a majority.

"Hank put out that letter. I didn't. I said I wouldn't. I said, if they were gonna elect me, it would be because it was me. And I never did one iota."

A bell rings faintly. Clyde, at the front desk, sends the customer back. Roy Buitenwerf, tall, thin, dressed in D-X blue, the father of the dentist, Dr. Mark Buitenwerf, walks back to check on a piece of his stereo.

"Should be in next week," says Charls.

"No hurry. Just walking past, thought I'd stop in."

"Where was I?" says Charls. "Anyway, so far as I'm concerned, in small-town government, the mayor has no real power, per se. He's strictly an administrator. That's where Ostlin and I have the greatest disagreement. I was on the council while he was mayor. We'd vote one way and then find out that our vote was, uh, let's say, overturned afterwards by the mayor. Then we'd have to go around and try to block him.

"The new fire station's a good example. We got fifteen

thousand dollars in grant money and he had plans drawn, an architect appointed, everything. We saw the plans, and they called for only two stalls. We needed three. They called for prestressed concrete, huge metal doors. Lord, we're not that fancy in Prairie City. We finally got the building we wanted and overrode him and it came in at fourteen nine. But that kind of thing went on all the time."

Bling. A young couple stands near the window, moving through the cabinetry and reading tags. The mayor, a salesman now, saunters toward the front of his store. Easy conversation drifts back. "Thinking about one. . . ." "Good as any. . . ." "This one?" "Good, too." Mayor Charls leans against the wall and seems more an observer, like the Stage Manager in *Our Town* watching newlyweds.

"Whenever you're ready . . ."

"Thanks, Dick."

He returns to the back room. "The town gets its operating money from property taxes, the state road-use tax, liquor-profits tax, some revenue sharing. We get income from water, sewer and rental properties. Altogether, it's about a two-hundred-thousand-dollar annual budget. And I'll tell you something." He smiles. "We're limited by law how much we can go in debt. We've had to keep our pants up all these years." He nods, satisfied. "If New York City had had that imposed on them, they'd be in a lot better fix right now, wouldn't they?" He smiles again, an italicizing smile. "But that's the way it is everywhere you turn around. The federal government tells us if we want any revenue sharing, we have to build a new sewer-filtration plant. Now, we needed a new system, I got no squabble there. But they set the standards when you use their money, and they're always way high. Cost us three hundred and eighty thousand dollars, and we have to run test after test after test to show that we're not polluting. And then, here's my point, they turn around and give Des Moines permission to dump raw sewage into the river."

He slowly scratches his temple by turning his screwdriver, as if he were adjusting a tube. "Same way on the city payroll. We hired Howard Van Wyngarden to answer all the ambulance calls, but the government stepped in. They said we had to pay him more, because he was technically on call twenty-four hours a day, whether he was actually *answering* any calls or not, just because it was his number people were supposed to call. Good crimany, paying for all that extra time added up to about four hundred dollars a month. What we finally worked out was a deal with the nursing home. We put in an extension phone there, so Howard could leave and he wouldn't be 'on call.' But it's just something like that all the time."

He laughs fully, a lame duck's laugh, free of responsibility.

Asked for an assessment of his term, Charls rolls the screwdriver in his palms and it clicks against his ring. He thinks for a few moments, glances at Lucy and Merv as if they were eavesdropping consciences.

"I guess I'm proudest of the library. I wanted to get it out where people could see it and use it. We had revenue-sharing money for it, and people in town didn't even know it existed. It's not much, but we're building it up all the time, and at least it's fixed up. We got that little space in City Hall, and folks are aware of it. . . . What else? Well, the water tower, was in the works already when I took over, but we got that completed and for a lot less than it could of run. So I'm proud of that, I guess."

The bell rings. A man walks back to the room looking for his appliance or some assurance that it's still there.

"Been a few weeks now, Dick," says the man, tall,

young, fat, dressed in jeans that have a week's work on the knees, more than a week's on the seat. Together, Charls and the man rummage archaeologically among the sets, opening and closing cabinets, stepping over some. Charls separates networks of wire from two or three sets that seem to have grown together organically.

"Here it is," Charls says softly. He reads the tag. "It'll be a few days, the end of the week. Okay?"

"Sure, Dick." The man has seen his set, is pleased with the one Charls has given him to get his family through. "Thanks."

Charls becomes a politician again, a reflecting statesman. "The thing I worry about is that the town will just turn into a bedroom town for Des Moines. People living out here, working there, taking no interest in the place. Gosh, I'd hate to see that, but I don't know how to prevent it. We talked about it on the council. You can't keep people out, that's for sure. But it's getting harder and harder to keep people from doing their business out of town. We can't compete pricewise. The wholesalers penalize us because we order small quantities and we make them ship to a remote post office. Just no way we can match Des Moines on price. Which leaves service. The only thing we can offer is better service, and honesty. Our businesses are more honest out here. You take up in Des Moines, they advertise low prices and get you up there, but once you're in the store, you can't take the low-priced stuff they advertised out of the store. Hell, they'll nail things to the floor. Things like that go on in Des Moines all the time. But I'm afraid honesty isn't enough anymore." He's managed to articulate a gloom, and the back room darkens with it.

"So, you've got the new people coming in who see the town as a suburb, really, though it isn't, and won't be, at least until somebody breaks up the land west of town.

Then watch things go. Once they start building west of town, geemanee, Des Moines'll be right out here on the edge of town, breathing on us. Ten years, I'd say.

"And, on top of that problem, you've got the natural tendency of people here not to do their part. I don't know why that is, but it's getting worse. The fire chief was in here just this morning, upset because he can't get people to work on the fire department. I was on the fire department for sixteen years and there used to be guys who really wanted on. No more."

The mayor moves up front, saying as he walks, "I don't know what's going to happen next Tuesday, but I don't see how anybody can win with a write-in. You need a majority, and what'll probably happen is that a couple will finish high and they'll have runoffs. What a mess." He smiles and hesitates, with something on his mind. "I hear," he says, finally, "that Hank's getting a lot of pressure to run, or at least to take it." He smiles again. "And I also hear that Erlene's gonna run as a write-in. And wouldn't that shake up the town? Hm?" Mayor Charls turns at the front counter to his customer. "What can I do you for, Mel?"

Vote in Council Election Tuesday

Regular General Election will be held Tuesday, Nov. 4, for the election of city officials.

The polling place will be the Town Hall in Prairie City and polls will be open from 12 noon to 9 p.m.

Absentee ballots may be obtained by calling Hugh Williams, city clerk. The last day for voting absentee is Nov. 3.

No one returned nomination papers for mayor. However, Mrs. Joe Veverka has indicated she is a write-in candidate for mayor.

• • •

The word had been out several days before the *News* printed it. In Prairie City, the newspaper's strongest competition is conversation, and the paper is always scooped. The function of the *News* is not to report the news but to preserve and legitimize it, lending it the credibility of printed columns. Otherwise, the paper serves as the town's bulletin board, posting meetings, coming events, times and dates, devoting its front pages to detailed obituaries, its insides to the colors, fabrics and music of teenage weddings. No editor could possibly compete with the speed of spoken gossip. Certainly not with something as good as the news of a woman's candidacy.

"I hear she's got a campaign manager and everything."

"I wouldn't be surprised. She's always about two squares aheada ya."

"I bet she wins."

"She's quite a gal."

"She's sure as hell gonna win if nobody runs against her."

"How *can* anybody? It's too late. No one returned nomination papers."

"Run a write-in just like she is. We got to get a serious candidate instead of dickin' around with putting ads in the paper for some kid or Elsie the Borden Cow."

"I bet she wins."

"Phil Frank. I bet Phil'd take it. He's on the council. Maybe a fella ought to go see Phil."

"Or Truck Randall. I hear he was a good councilman."

"I bet she wins."

"You know, really now, seriously, the mayor ought to be, at least this is what I think, the mayor ought to be a retired fella. You know, some guy that has a good head on him, knows about the business deals that a mayor has to know about, but he's retired, so he's got plenty of time to concentrate on being mayor. Now, this is what I think; like I say, this is just my opinion."

"A woman's got no place bein' mayor."

"I know I'd never work for one."

"Well, she'll sure be spending money if she wins. That's one thing she knows how to do. We'll be votin' on new swimming pools and Lord knows what else if she gets in."

"I bet she wins."

Most of the new homes in Prairie City fill the far north end of town, a thick residential finger off the flat square palm. In the north end, low ranch houses run end to end over several blocks, a tract with all the proud banality of a genuine suburb; it could as easily adjoin any city. Here many young married couples live, among them some of the new people who've moved to Prairie City for its space and emanative comfort. Scattered among them are couples who have been raised in Prairie City. The Veverka home, at the top of the palm, is frame and brick, planes of white and red squares, with sun decks and patios and glass-doored additions. Inside, there's a swimming pool, a feature whose construction was reported urgently around town.

Dr. and Mrs. Veverka came here in the early '60s, after the town had built the medical center and interviewed physicians seeking the captive practice of a very small town. The job was attractive. Des Moines and its affiliated hospital were near, the medical center was impressively equipped, Prairie City eager to offer up its broken limbs, its viruses, its reliable scleroses.

A small town and its only doctor cannot avoid a fragile dependency, the doctor aware of the prominence of his comings and goings, the town feeling a kind of grateful resentment, contradictorily pleased to have a doctor and uneasy with the hold he has on them. Are we getting our money's worth from him? Why's he take so many vacations? Is he thinking of leaving? But Prairie City has been generally well satisfied with the care Dr. Veverka gives it. A few people complain that he doesn't take enough time with each patient, and there are those who believe, as a given principle of life in small towns, that one should take his illness—and his bankbook and his tax returns—out of town. But, Dr. Veverka was professionally welcome, and the couple moves socially with apparent ease.

I heard about the first party from my parents, who were invited, and afterward described its largesse, the cuts and casseroles, the tangy dips, the trays of meat—turkey and ham and beef sliced and stacked in undulating rows. The party has grown each year and the quantity of good food has grown with it, as abundant for hundreds of guests as that first night's offering seemed to dozens. Now, eleven years after the inaugural dinner, cars line the streets around the Veverka home on that Saturday night in January, the kind of line-up one used to see only around the high school for basketball games or class plays.

Prairie City had seen nothing like the Veverkas' party. Men and women, dressed in best clothes, crowded this big new house for no other reason than to eat and talk and *be* with one another. Dozens growing to hundreds, people who might weakly smile and trade names on the street on a midweek afternoon.

People talked for days about the first party. One could sit down almost anyplace in town and find a conversation about it. The size of the crowd, the food, the noise, the cars, the late hour.

And the liquor; mostly, the liquor. There had been liquor served, in amounts that grew in estimation with each day of analysis. Hundreds of dollars' worth. Thousands. Enough to fill the Skunk in spring. There were bottles in the street. A lawn of broken glass. Drunken voices into the dawn.

But the Veverkas continued to hold their party, and other smaller social events. They invited couples for food and bridge, and the gathering at the end of January became a kind of annual taking of the town's moral fever, which slowly fell. There was still a great deal of disapproval, of course. The superintendent of schools ordered his teachers not to attend, and a few others boycotted, but gradually the strongest protest quieted, the evening became accepted. A year after he retired, the superintendent of schools and his wife came, and seemed at ease among people he'd directed his teachers to stay away from.

New and old feeling in Prairie City meet here, then, with the Veverkas, with Erlene, and she has often confronted her critics by inviting them in. So there was probably a certain inevitability about her mayoral campaign, for she persistently tests the town's presumptions and women's acquiescent place within them. She's served on boards, sat with county Republicans, solicited research funds for all the diseases, urged the construction of the new school. She spends days at a time at out-of-town meetings and, in Prairie City, drives about in a flashy red Mercury Cougar convertible. To those who find fault with her energy, she appears to be patrolling the town at an assessing, proprietary speed.

There was, of course, a quick response to her candidacy. Men gathered in small groups to determine alternatives. Their urgency varied, and so did their motives. Some spoke of her inexperience, a woman's unfortunate ignorance of a town's moving parts—ducts, pumps, engines. They claimed nothing personally against her, worrying simply that with a woman for mayor, the village might break down critically, might find air in its water pipes, cracks in its streets.

Other men spoke with the certainty of those who take the Bible literally. "It was not right, a woman running for mayor." A few cited the verses of *John* and *Timothy*. It was not right.

A small committee once more visited the offices of Prairie City Concrete, to ask Hank Ostlin if recent events could not persuade him to accept the job after all. Weeks before, he'd been delivered nomination papers, filled out and ready for his signature, and he'd refused them. But he'd assumed then, as had everyone, that Prairie City would have no declared candidate, that a name would somehow surface out of all the apathy.

Another group, smaller and younger, sat at a table in the Cardinal Inn and asked Jim Billingsley, who'd decided to seek a place on the city council, if he'd instead allow his name to be written on the ballot's open line. His fiscal sense was needed, the young men said. Prairie City had been spending extravagantly, its new projects lavish for so small a town. The town needed a mayor who'd spend its money as if it were his own. They gave Jim Billingsley twenty dollars to pay for an advertisement in the *News*.

In its October 30th edition, the paper carried these advertisements:

CITY ELECTION
Prairie City, Iowa
November 4, 1975
For Mayor
MOVE
J. E. Billingsley
up for Mayor and

run the city as a business
instead of a yes bank.
Ad paid for by Concerned Citizens.

Erlene Veverka sips coffee and reads a typed list of
registered voters. She scans more than six hundred
names, but many of them are farmers, voiceless in city
elections, and so she edits as she reads. Her campaign
manager, Phyllis MacRae, has the same list. They sit in
the MacRaes' long living room, filled with sun and
Colonial furniture. A big bay window gives onto the
narrow north-end street. From the window, one sees
small brown lawns, rectangles laid down one after another like ceramic tile in an autumn-brown design.

"I've got about forty, forty-five names on my 'for sure'
list," Erlene says. She has large round eyes that dominate
her face, and they appear to widen and dilate according to
the speed and volume of her voice. She has light hair,
held in a high constructed wave, then falling long and
loose below.

"I count forty-five," she says to Phyllis MacRae. "And I
figure Hank's got a hard core of maybe fifty. I'll need sixty
or better for sure, and I don't know if I can get that
many."

Phyllis studies her list. She's a tiny woman with short
brown hair. She runs her finger down the names.

"I think there's more than that," Phyllis says. "Gee, I count, oh, seventy-five anyway."

"Really?" says Erlene. She looks across the room at Phyllis and her list, as if the secret of compiling votes were in the way you read the names. "Well," she says, "let's see. Here's what I was thinking. I figure I should get the teachers, since I worked so hard for the new school. I have the staff at Joe's office. And I hope I'll get a lot of votes around this neighborhood."

"I've heard lots of support all around me," Phyllis says. "I know you've got my neighbors. And I was talking to Joann across the street. She says you've got support in the bank."

Erlene snaps her head at those words, looking across the street, as if she were trying to catch voters in the open.

"There goes Lila from up the street!" Phyllis says. Erlene snaps her head around again. A blue sedan passes slowly across the window. Votes in slowly moving currents. "She's for you. She told me she thought it was great."

Phyllis lived in Des Moines before moving here, was married there to a local court judge, and she helped him in his campaigns. After their divorce, she remarried and has come with her new family to Prairie City. Crime, drugs, street meanness, all have reached Des Moines' best neighborhoods, she says, and she wanted to move her children to a small town.

She's bewildered only by Prairie City's politics. "We used to worry in Des Moines about not getting our campaign started soon enough," she's said. "Here, you have to worry about timing everything. If you do too much too soon, people think you're showing off or something." She and Erlene have decided to divide the names of those they consider doubtful but at least receptive to a phone call. They'll wait until the last two days, Monday and Tuesday, then make their calls and hope they'll not offend anyone with their eagerness.

Erlene, given to lists, composes one of items that might keep voters away, or away from her. "First, I come right out and say I'm a Republican."

"*Every*one's a Republican here," Phyllis says.

"But they don't like you to state your politics," says Erlene. "They think politics ought to be kept out of a campaign. . . . Anndd, oh, they think I'm a big spender. I've got that reputation, but I didn't spend much at the Nursing Home Guild and there're lots of people who know that, so I hope that gets around. . . . And, the woman bit. I *like* men. I think women can do some things as well as a man, but they're limited. People think I'm a libber, but I'm not."

Here, a woman who has organized, served on boards, chaired some, and, most of all, has had opinions, is clearly a feminist. Women in this culture have always been trusted with hard work, with livestock and steering wheels. These past weeks, women in hooded sweat shirts have driven into the Co-op tunnel with high loads of grain and have handled the machinery with a fine and sensitive touch. They've casually waved down to Hoop, and he's waved up to them. No surprise, no mockery.

Women have also been accepted as athletes, basketball players, and, more recently, members of track and soft-ball teams. Indeed, men have always packed the gym-nasiums to watch high school girls play basketball and have sat over Saturday-morning coffee, comparing the moves and speed and touch of various women players.

But these are admissions of a woman's physical ca-pabilities. Erlene Veverka, on the other hand, has repeat-edly expressed her mind on all manner of things, and in places other than classrooms and Sunday school.

"Joe's telling everyone at the office to vote for me," Erlene says, checking names and drawing pencil lines through those she concedes. "I hear some people are saying that Joe doesn't want me to run. That he can't hold me down. But he *does*. It was his idea, actually. I'd thought about it, but I didn't think I had a chance to beat Hank. Joe said, 'Go ahead and run.' Then I heard nobody had filed and I said, 'Prairie City's too good for that to happen.' So I did it, and now I hear a rumor that Hank's going to resign immediately after the election if he wins." She stops and her eyes constrict, then widen again. "I've already asked the council to consider me if that happens, and I've been assured they will. Anyway, if I lose this year, I've done some groundwork and built support for the next election."

Phyllis pours coffee into thin cups. Blue and yellow flowers grow serpentinely up their sides.

Erlene returns to a previous list. "I'm not sure about the bank. Dwight can't say, because he works for John and John's an old friend of Hank's. But I think I have a lot of support in the post office. Bob Bowen said he'd vote for me if I'd do something about zoning in this town. He lives right next to the Osgoods, with their junk yard flat up against his back door." She continues down her pages, as Phyllis does, running her fingers over the names and reading their dispositions, a kind of intuitive Braille. "Dick Zaayer. I love him. He's a friend. But I don't think he'd vote for me. I saw him in the grocery store and we were talking about the football game tomorrow night. He said, 'If they lose that one, I'll move out of town and then you can be mayor.'"

"I was at the back of the store," Phyllis says. "I heard you talking."

"There were quite a few around," says Erlene. "I don't know about Tom Stoner, either. He's always been so friendly, and the last few times I've been in the store, he hasn't had much to say. I wonder if he's avoiding me because he's not going to vote for me."

"He just had a new baby. Maybe he isn't getting enough sleep."

"The businessmen have to be noncommittal, anyway," says Erlene. "Now, I wonder about the Van de Lendens? They're good friends with the DeGraags, and Wilbur DeGraag's cousin married a friend of Hank's wife."

"But they don't get along."

"Oh," says Erlene and makes an asterisk, coding years of feud. "I think the Jennings might be for me. We bought some apples from their orchard a few weeks ago and they seemed nice."

"How are their apples? How were the prices?"

"Good. They were lower than everything else around. Good apples. I might have the Aldens. I spoke with her at a rest stop on the way to the Iowa game last weekend."

"Good. Friendly?" asks Phyllis.

"Yes, she was. I think she was."

"The Roberts clan?"

"Hard to say. I know I don't have the Strucks. She's mad at Joe."

"How about the Vanderheisens?"

"I think you can cross off that whole bunch," says Erlene. "Them, and the cousins, all the in-laws. The DeZaks, the Van Astenbergs. In fact, I don't think anybody in that church will vote for a woman. Very few of them."

"The Van Astenbergs?"

"Hank Van Astenberg married a DeZak. They're all related."

"I didn't know that," Phyllis says.

Erlene laughs suddenly after reading a name. "I have to tell you. Edna Van Halden called me last night. She wants to be city clerk. She said she wouldn't vote for Hank, because Hank thought city clerk was a man's job. But she's worried she didn't have a chance, because she doesn't doctor with Joe. I told her, 'Heavens, that doesn't matter.' And she said, well, she wanted to call, she didn't know. She was just worried that since she didn't doctor with Joe, she might not have a chance. She sure wouldn't vote for Hank."

"Great."

"And I had to laugh, the other night. I was out in the yard and our local cop, Terry, he drove by and I thought he was going to fall out, trying to roll down his window to wave at me. He's never waved at me in his life."

"What about the Pomeroys?"

"Well, they're neighbors to the Wilsons, and he's a friend of Hank's."

"Rankins? I heard she was for you."

"Hmm. That's surprising. They're friends of the Brouwers. He is, and she and Jana are best friends."

"What about the south end?"

"The only ones I know for sure are the Kurlisses. As friendly as we are with Al and Nancy, and their daughter, too, I should get Lila's vote . . . if she's registered. She's not on this list. But then, she just turned eighteen, so, gosh, I hope she's registered." Erlene looks up, closes her eyes, tallying. "Maybe fifty or sixty. Gee, I don't know. I think about three hundred will vote, but not for mayor, just the council. Oh," she says, "here's one. Wilma, at the *News* office. She'll vote for me."

Phyllis grimaces. "I, gee, I don't know . . . I heard she wasn't going to vote for you."

Erlene's eyes widen. "Really? Hm. That's . . . hm . . . mm. Well, maybe she doesn't want to vote for me because she'll have to cover council meetings for the *News* if I get in. Ha!"

Phyllis sips coffee, bites a butter cookie. "Are you going to ask the *News* to write about the council meetings?"

"Well," Erlene says, a candidate's rhythm suddenly in her voice, "I do think things should be opened up. It might be good enough the way they do it now, with the clerk publishing the minutes, but all the meetings should be publicly announced, and open. Somebody said, 'If they opened up all the meetings, they wouldn't get any work done,' but the way it is, everything gets decided at special meetings and we read about it afterwards."

Phyllis says, "I don't think they should say in the minutes who was there."

"I know," says Erlene. "It keeps people from coming. You read in the paper somebody's been at a council meeting and you say, 'What do you suppose he was doing there?'" She flips through the pages once more, tapping the sheets with her long yellow pencil. "The people my age aren't going to vote," she says. "They haven't been able to change anything in town, so why try now? Most of the young people will vote for me, I hope. They should. They're the group that comes to the party."

"Oh," Phyllis says, "by the way, I know a couple who'd really like to be invited this year. Tom and Carol up the street."

"Oh, well, fine. There probably are a lot of people who'd like to come that I'd like to have, but I just don't know about them. I hate to be too pushy about it. People told us when we first got here that if a doctor entertained, he'd lose all his business, and we said, 'If we can't live the way we want to, we'll just move.'

"Now it's the social event of the season. I send invitations two years in a row, and if they don't come, or respond, I assume they don't want to come and I drop them off the list. But, like I said," and she nods to Phyllis, "I'm always glad to hear of somebody who wants to come to our party. I'll just add them to the list."

She makes some notes. "So, I guess, when we call, we should say that our issues are zoning—this town really does need some zoning, especially if Des Moines gets busing and people start moving out here—zoning, and . . . and getting petty personalities out of politics."

"Do you think we should mention the competition?" Phyllis asks.

"Not unless they do," Erlene says. "And then, the only thing is that he's out of town so much. He leaves for Arizona in December and doesn't come back until it's warm. Someone was complaining about that at bridge the other day and somebody—who was it?—Alma? She said, 'Yes, but he gets everything cleared up before he leaves.' Three or four months' worth? Jeez."

"More coffee?"

"No," Erlene says, "I've got to run." She leans over the coffee table to assemble all her notes. Phyllis simultaneously stacks plates and cups. Erlene walks through the room, curtain-dark now. "So. We'll start calling, and I'll stop in to visit some people on Election Day—John Carlson at the Co-op and a few others."

"Monday," Phyllis says, "and we're going to *win!*" Erlene smiles, and the corner of her mouth catches briefly.

"Thanks," she says. She walks out into the sun, her arms burdened, like a student's, with her pages of lists and notes, and starts down the sidewalk. Her round eyes dart about, and she has the kind of beaming smile one puts on when being introduced.

There's a full row of analysts at the Cardinal bar. With

only three days until the election, events seem to have settled. When Thursday morning passed without revisions, it was clear that there'd be no new candidacies, no time for any more. The *News* will not publish again until after the election, so there's no place to formally announce, no chance to make news or take a small box of declaration. Furthermore, with just a weekend in which to work, the news would languish, especially after church on Sunday morning, when the town moves indoors.

Although the talk runs the length of Jim Billingsley's bar, everyone feels free to discuss the candidates as if Jim were not one of them. Few beyond the group that convinced him to place his advertisement have felt he'll receive many votes. First, he's a beer merchant, and that fact alone alienates three congregations. Furthermore, Jim freely admits that he's not widely liked, and he's asked anyone who does consider him a friend to vote him a councilman, not mayor. He knows, too, that he should not consider his customers in any way loyal to his candidacy. To regularly drink beer in the only bar in town is one matter, to carry that patronage into the voting booth another altogether. So his constituency might not extend too far beyond family, in any event, and small as it naturally is, he's urged it to vote for Ostlin.

"People are going to get all confused with that ad. Think I don't want on the council," he says. "I just agreed to go along because I heard Veverka was running. A woman's got no place bein' mayor."

His wife, Betty, laughs. She's sitting at her customary place, an end stool near the kitchen door. "You just don't like women is all."

Jim slowly shakes his head. All his features appear sad-angled—eyes, cheek-lines, the corners of his mouth, sagging at the same emotional pitch. "No," he says. "They just got their place.

"The editor said nobody else had come to him with an ad. Then I see Hank'll take it, and that's fine with me."

Midway down the bar, a young man leans forward, away from his neighbors' talk, and listens to Billingsley. He is thin, has short hair, glasses, and a long face that he lengthens even more by lowering his jaw as he listens, as if he's laboriously chewing. He says, "I'd just as soon see a woman as Ostlin." His mouth moves imperceptibly, like a ventriloquist's. "What's Ostlin do for this town? Hell, he's gone half the time. Spends six months in Arizona. He's the Sam Yorty of Prairie City's what he is."

Jim says, "I'd rather Hank part time than Veverka all year."

The young man owns D and L men's clothing store on the square, between Dick Charls TV and Travis Walters' Furniture. He is D, Dick Vroom, and his wife, Lana, is L. Vroom leans forward again, his arms crossed on the bar, and he absently rubs his right biceps with his left palm, and picks at the arm as if he had a peeling sunburn. "He's been in my shop exactly one time in five and a half years," he says. "One time. Big supporter of the town, you bet. Came up to drop off some dry cleaning. I saw him coming in and I thought, Well, I'll just have some fun. I said, 'What's the name on that?'" Vroom twists his pursed lips as if he were holding in laughter. "I knew damn well who it was. I thought ol' Hank was going to faint. He says, 'Ostlin.' And I said, 'What's the spelling on that?' He spells it. 'Go a little slower,' I said. 'O, s, t? You say t?'" Vroom lets out an indignant exhalation, "Humph," that causes him to jerk on the stool. "Yessir, that's some mayor we got. Really civic minded, oh, sure. I've seen him uptown maybe three, four times since I've had the store. Sam Yorty, as far as I'm concerned. Least Erlene would be here and run the meetings."

Jim says, "That's exactly what I'm afraid of. All she

knows how to do is spend money. I don't care about gettin' on the council. I'm just tired of everybody saying yes to everything. If I do get on, I'm gonna be sayin' no."

A huge man in khaki clothes sitting between Vroom and Billingsley has been watching their conversation and suddenly intercepts it. "By God, I'm gonna vote for you for mayor, J.B. Your ad says you gonna run the town like a bank. I figure that means we get eight percent on our tax money, right? Huh? Ha. Ain't that right?"

Jim seems to sag even more. "No. The ad said I'd run the town like a business, not a yes bank." He sounds embarrassed to be quoting his own prose. "It just meant I'm tired of the way the town's spending money. That new maintenance shed shouldn't've ever been built. Their payroll's ridiculous. They got one man getting a thousand a month and now they hired another guy at three fifty an hour to help him." His voice remains low and weary, but a regular energy comes subtly into it as he speaks, as he hears what sounds vestigially like a speech. Others seem to hear it, too, and stop their own arguments to listen.

Jim says, "They let Emery Sheerer go and he used to do the whole thing—graded the streets, plowed snow, maintained everything—and now they got one full-time guy and another one on top of that.

"Plus, they got two full-time policemen now. They got a guy on from seven to three in the morning, and another guy from midnight to eight o'clock. So from midnight till three o'clock, we got two cops on duty. That's just about the most ridiculous thing I ever heard of for a little town like this. Does it make you sleep better knowin' you got two cops on duty? Doesn't make me sleep a damn bit better. In fact, it keeps me awake, thinking how ridiculous it is." He speaks as if he's personally offended, as if this carelessness has been specifically intended to anger him.

He tends bar reflexively, pouring, mixing, wiping, washing, casually sweeping the change into his palm. "If I don't like something, I'll tell you about it, face to face. I'm tired of certain people in this town getting special treatment. If I get on, that's gonna stop. Now the council's passed a resolution that you can't put a house trailer on a lot anymore. Well, Brubaker and McKlveen are on the council. Brubaker owns the trailer park and McKlveen has the lumber company that builds the houses. There you are.

"They had a Model A fire truck up for sale, worth, oh, three or four thousand dollars, which Brubaker got for five hundred. Nobody else even knew about it. I'm tired of that kind of stuff."

"And you think it'd be any better with Ostlin again?" asks Dick Vroom.

"He ain't had a thing to do with any of this," Jim says. "This's all happened in the last two years. All this spending."

"You weren't talking about spending, just now," says the huge man between them. "You were talking about secret business. That's what you were just talking about. And Ostlin ran the council like a dictator. Those guys couldn't do nothing without Hank's say-so, the way I heard. They couldn't say shit if they had a mouthful of it." The huge man leans back again, extremely pleased with himself.

"That's right," says Dick Vroom, rubbing his arm furiously now. "If you're worried about an open council, you'd be a hell of a lot better off with Veverka than Ostlin."

Jim looks at Vroom and at the huge man, and at all the other faces in the row. He shakes his head very slightly, but there's exasperation in the gesture, more eloquent than anything he's said. They wait smugly for him to respond, believing they've caught Jim in confluent prejudices that he's going to have to reconcile for them, and maybe for himself, right now. Finally, Jim says, "Well, if you want an idea what it'd be like, just watch the way she spends money on that house."

Albert Kurliss moves from his stool at the far end of the bar and walks down toward the politics. He makes a place for himself at the very end, moves Betty's coffee cup and cigarettes, fastidiously dusts with the edge of his hand a small spot on which to place his forearm. Settled in, he says, "Jim's right. We just can't hack her. I'm not talking about liking her or not. I mean, we just can't *hack* her."

Jim says, "Well, what are we gonna do about it? If that's the way you feel, get out and work for Ostlin."

Albert Kurliss sadly shakes his head, sipping a gin and tonic through a straw, rocking his head and the glass together as if they were attached. "I can't do that, Jim. I *can't.* Erlene and my wife are best friends. Lila's always over there. Erlene's like her second mother. And Joe and I are buddies. My God. I can't do anything. But, oh, my God, we can't *hack* her." Kurliss is quite drunk, sufficiently drunk to believe that what he's just said will stay right where he's spoken it, in the immaculate little space on the bar.

Dick Vroom has had enough. He steps off the bar stool and collects his change. "Whoopee," he says through his frozen lips. "Sam Yorty for mayor." As he walks out, he says, "Who you suppose is gonna pay for all the phone calls he'll be making to Prairie City from Phoenix if he's mayor?"

Everyone is quiet for a moment after Dick Vroom leaves, and then Betty, seeming to feel a hostess's responsibility to break the silence, says, "Well, it's gonna be real interesting, anyway, that's for sure. Jim'll probably lose a lot of friends over it."

Jim looks at her as though he were wondering if she'd been living these past dozen years in the same town he had. "That's the farthest thing from my mind," he says. "I'm not worried about losing business, either. My best business, my weekend steak business, doesn't come from Prairie City, anyway."

The huge man in the khaki work suit leans toward them. "Well," he says, "I'm gonna vote for ya, J.B. I figure since you're gonna run the town like a bank, you'll pay me dividends ever' quarter, ain't that right, hum? Ha!"

Jim gives the man a fierce, steely look and adds a futile shrug. Finally, he says, "As far as I'm concerned, everything's black and white. Everybody should get the same treatment. If I get on, everybody gets the same chance."

"By God, I believe ya, Jim," says Albert Kurliss. "I'm gonna vote for ya for council. And, and . . ." his voice rises now to a childlike wail, "oh, we just can't hack *her*."

Hank Ostlin's principal business, Prairie City Concrete Products Company, sits at the west edge of town, next to the Kent feed mill, part of the small and tight light-industrial cluster. For years, Prairie City clearly stopped on the west at this spot, before a few blocks of new houses spilled out past it, and there's still a sense of the town ending there, because the last street that runs north and south the entire length of Prairie City runs past the front door of Prairie City Concrete.

There's a small white office building and, behind it, several hundred feet of open work yards and warehouses. Huge earth-moving machines painted construction yellow move laboriously about, machines that dwarf the largest tractor and smoothly lift tons of dirt or concrete. Tight, even rows of concrete tile run back from the street. The powerful machines and the precisely spaced tiles, lined up and ready, lend a kind of armamental atmosphere to the yard, as if the purpose of the work here ultimately aided a war somewhere.

Ostlin bought the business in 1944, from a Prairie City man who had not operated it at all for a few years. He bought, he says, "a few pipe forms and a mixer and a lot of weeds as tall as the office, and not very much more." With luck, he believed, he might in time do fifty thousand dollars', perhaps as much as a hundred thousand dollars', worth of business in a year, and his first few years were in line with that goal. But Hank had all along been applying to the work a gift for anticipating the manner and places of growth, and for finding ways in which his concrete could participate. To that he added a perception—part vision, part accountancy—that sees with certainty from plans and blueprints the texture of a finished product, and the hard costs of labor, materials, logistics, breakdowns, idle and expensive days. Consequently, he began to win contracts and make money from the work, and by 1950, 1951, his original hope of a small gross of a hundred thousand dollars a year seemed perhaps the only outrageously inaccurate estimate he might ever make.

Now, a quarter century later, his company has government contracts throughout the state, has begun to lay sewer lines all over Des Moines, and has men and construction-yellow ton-lifting machines working where new highways will run. Hank owns farms as well, and herds of cattle in the Dakotas. There's a completion in that, for farming was the work he first knew, when he came to Prairie City in 1942, by all accounts—including his own—too poor to hide it and not particularly trying to.

A traveling salesman sits in Hank Ostlin's dark paneled

office, his swatch books and samples spread all around his feet. He's the type of salesman whose job is to persuade businessmen to buy calendars, fly swatters, pens and pencils with their company's name printed on them. He's making his regularly scheduled call at Prairie City Concrete and it must certainly be one of the least pleasant points on his route.

Hank Ostlin leans forward in his big swivel chair to listen, a position not so much of interest as of challenge. He watches the salesman flip his charts and spread like a hand of playing cards his profit-enhancing products. Hank's eyes follow every small movement that the salesman makes, like a man at a carnival booth watching the pitchman for the first sign of swindle. All the while, he says nothing, or at most makes an inaudible growl. The salesman talks on and on—"How about this calendar, Hank? These are *real* nice. . . . These double-ink pens are great, Hank, don't you think?"—talking and sweating furiously.

Hank watches. His oval face is a surface of lumps and crevices, looks like lines carved into a potato. He's a small, thin man, and wears an old gray suit, and underneath his suit coat, a blue cardigan sweater buttoned to the top. The look on his face says, "I have built this business for twenty-five years by being smart and mean and damned persuasive when I had to be, and its success has had very little to do with having on hand a supply of letter openers with my name printed on them."

"How about these ter——"

"No."

"Well, then, Hank, we've got some——"

"No."

At last the man has nothing at all left to say or show and he leans over in his chair to gather up all his samples while the expended effort of his ordeal hangs in the office air like weather. But when he stands to leave, he's smiling again and thanks Hank for his time and says, "We'll be seeing ya again next time, Hank."

After he closes the outer door, Hank waits a moment more and then says, "Damned peddlers."

There's more than a map of a life in this face; there's recent sickness in it, too, skin cancer, and although his latest checkups have found no more of it, the fact of his cancer has caused many in town to wonder how much longer he'll actively run the business. It has also given several people in Prairie City some reason to question his fitness for public office.

Hank knows this, the way people who've lived in small towns can sense at times a vulturous focusing of interest in their movements. He says, "So far as mayor's concerned, I had no intention of runnin'. I didn't take their nomination papers. I thought maybe somebody who'd be well qualified for it would come along, but they didn't. So, well, I finally told a few of 'em, if they wanna write me in, for the good of the community, why I would serve again."

It was the news of the other candidates, then, the thought of Prairie City run by either of them, that worked through Hank's resistance. "I don't think they got any business bein' mayor. They just don't understand the mechanics of the sewage and the water, all the utilities, and they don't have any experience that way." There is in his raspy voice an old realism.

He ran eighteen years ago against Wiley Roberts, the incumbent. "I beat him by one vote," he says and chuckles for a moment. "And I ran against him twice after that. Each time, I beat him that much worse.

"The first thing I did as mayor was start the garbage pickup. Before me, it was hired out to some outfit from Altoona or Colfax that charged two hundred and twenty-five dollars a month. We bought that first garbage truck for six hundred dollars and it ran about twelve years. Then shortly after, we got the ambulance, Then we got the fire station and new fire trucks." As Hank lists the ways he's helped, he uses the political "we," and one hears clearly the differences between his politics and those of Mayor Charls, the opposing emphases. Charls was proudest of his library, and spoke of services and the town's selfish temper, worried about the effect of that attitude on the future. There's nothing abstract about Ostlin's recollections. They're filled with acquisitions. He sees the town practically, as a machine that needs maintenance, occasional repair, equipment to keep it moving. "We also got the streets, a hard surface on the streets. There was nothing but dust when I took over. And we got highway 117 paved through town. I remember we had some people from the Highway Commission down to a council meeting and they said, 'It'll be six to eight years before you get paving through this town.' Well, I knew several of those people quite well, from the business we do with the state, and after that, we had a meeting in Chicago of some kind or another, and we were all out to dinner, these same fellas and me, and we talked about it. And you know it wasn't a year after that we got it paved. Didn't cost us much, either. Eight, ten thousand dollars, maybe." Hank stops and nods, one of the deep crevices of his face turns up into a faint smile.

"Other than that, well, the police department got started under me. We hired the first guy that was more than just a night cop checkin' on the stores."

He believes now, as he reluctantly consents to accept a last term during which he'll do little more than watch the town for two years, that its future is out of his hands. "We don't have enough young people in town, and we need some kind of new industry to attract them. But there again, if they could find some ground in town, or buy some ground—but nobody'll sell any. That's the whole sad part of it."

One visualizes as he speaks the town of Prairie City bordered by the country's best soil, and the new young farmers watching for any sign that some of it might be for sale. And that, against the town's hope for new houses, Ostlin's thought that industry could keep people here. An intensifying pressure to spread outward meeting an opposing pressure—the land's coalescent acceleration. And at the edge of town, an abrupt collision—the grid pressing out, the land sweeping in, leaving precious alluvium. Hank's office and grounds sit exactly on one of the edges and as he describes the town's problems, one begins to feel it as a fragile fault line, and recognizes, again, the illusion of space in this landscape.

"Some developers have come in from Altoona and Marshalltown and all they wanted to put up was some eggshell houses, so I discouraged 'em. I told 'em I didn't think they'd find any land anybody'd be willing to let go of, and that their sort of thing wouldn't go over in Prairie City."

All the owners of the land surrounding town—Harold Jennings and Dwight Hanel on the east, Max Williams and Harold Verheul on the north, Don McFadden on the west, Buck Johnson on the south—have said that they've been asked their price and have resisted, asked by farmers wanting to press in, by builders wanting to spread out. In almost every case, their land has been family land and they don't wish anyone else working it; they don't wish its purposes changed, either. So these owners, more than Ostlin or anyone else, have a deter- mining power over the future—collectively to keep Prairie City as it is, or individually to free it in one direction or another. For now, their individual attitudes are the same—to farm the enveloping fields, or have them farmed.

"The thing a lot of 'em are afraid of," Hank Ostlin says, "is, we can't all farm, and we got all the jobs filled we're gonna have with what business there is here now. So unless we get something else, Prairie City's gonna turn into a 'dinner-bucket' town. People live here and go to work in Des Moines or someplace. I know lots of people around here are scared of that and scared that nobody's gonna care about what goes on in Prairie City if it does. I'm not as afraid of that, I guess. I think so long as a fella lives in a place, he's not gonna let it go to hell. Even if he works in Des Moines, or he don't really pay much attention to the town except to his own house and that. I mean, he still lives in the place and he'll make sure it's a good place as long as he lives in it."

Ostlin may not be frightened by that possibility because, in a way, he's had such a relationship with Prairie City, himself: He's lived in it, paid little daily attention to it, but has tried to help it. He's been, as its mayor and one of its wealthiest inhabitants, a dinner-bucket citizen, moving from his home to an office that may as well be in Des Moines.

"So I'll try to see it gets its basic needs that a town has to have. Water. I want to get another well. Just your basic things." He adds, "Of course, nobody's gonna stop me from takin' my time off in Phoenix. I ignore my own business to go down there. . . . Well, I don't really *ignore* it. I call up every day to see what's goin' on." He straightens up in his chair, posed for a day of work. He seems obliged to show that he's eager to get to his business, that all this talk of Phoenix does not mean for one minute that there's significant idleness in his days.

There's a warm and slowly falling rain on Election Day, giving all the people around the square a second conversation—the election; the weather. They do not see one as important to the other, as the political meteorologists in cities always do on Election Days.

Of course, there's only one polling place—the fire station, no more than five or six blocks from any corner of town—but for those who've lived in so small a place for some time, a distance of five or six blocks will keep them home if it's been raining all morning and seems likely to last all day. The fire station will be open for voting at noon, and remain available until nine o'clock.

"Nice rain," says a short, fat farmer in stiff new violet overalls. He's standing at the Co-op's east windows, watching the day. He has his hands tucked inside the bib of his overalls, as if he were protecting them from a cold wind.

"Nice," says another farmer.

"Nice rain," says a third.

Entering the Co-op, each new observer steps to the center of the room and stops to take its measure, the lacquered plywood surfaces of the counter and the dirty linoleum floor, looking about with that flat Midwestern look that lacks all subtlety. All the while, he nods slightly and after a minute, says to no one in particular, "Nice rain."

He eases toward the floor-to-ceiling windows and nods again to the others who must move their chairs or themselves to make a small space. When that's done and everyone has settled in again, the new farmer says, "Nice rain," but this time clearly as a greeting, and one is reminded by the words that what might sound like a redundancy is not. Farmers do not hope indiscriminately for rain. Nothing ravages a season like rain that whips and tears and beats down a crop. Rain can be the worst thing skies put on a field. But for this kind of rain, a free, rinsing shower, he saves a rare hyperbole.

"Nice," agrees the short, fat farmer in the stiff overalls.

"Yeah."

"Yeah, it is."

"Nice rain."

Only Hoop, running the elevator, resents the warm rain. He has been worried for several days about the rising heat from the grain inside his silos, a heat that threatens to rot the harvest. The ideal condition of the delivered crop, dry and abundant from the fields, has come back on Hoop like revenge. Hoop has been checking the temperature gauges, sensors every six feet along the silo walls, to read the heat, and has consistently seen his needles dip immediately to the right, into the nineties. This is not yet cause for alarm, but is cause enough for Hoop to imagine a spreading fermentation in his bins. Wet November heat lay on the barely porous concrete, keeping the walls hot and damp, and, so, the grain.

To make matters worse, the market prices have reacted as expected to the huge crop and have been dropping since October, so the farmers have held on, have kept most or all of their grain in Hoop's hot and crowded silos. There's little he can do but make certain the fans are running, monitor his climate and wait for imminent ruin.

Hoop enters the Co-op office from the back door that leads out to his elevator. He looks grim.

"How's it goin'?" asks the manager of the Co-op, but he's smiling and offers the question more out of respect for Hoop's mood than his own concern.

"We're holding it about the same," Hoop says. Then he looks up and smiles around the room. "Howdy, New Britches," he says to the short, fat farmer.

The farmer says, "Ya voted yet, Hoop?"

"Polls ain't open yet," Hoop says. "I thought I might on my way back from lunch. I don't know. I don't know yet who to vote for. Who'd you vote for if you lived in town?"

The farmer smiles, tucking his hands back inside his bib. "I'm just glad I don't. Two miles out's too close. But looks to me you ain't got a whole lot to choose from. You got a saloonkeeper, a doctor's wife, and a mean ol' bastard spends half the year in Arizona."

Plain as poetry. And as the room fills with laughter, Hoop says, laughing, too, "That's what I mean! That's why I'm stuck." He thinks for a moment and says, "You suppose if we pick the wrong candidate we'll get in trouble and have to do like New York and *dee*fault?"

"I'm gonna write somebody in," says a thin young man, a new employee at the Co-op. "I sure ain't votin' for Veverka."

"How come? 'Cause she's a woman?" Hoop asks.

"Yep," says the young man tersely. The sour certainty of scriptured belief.

"Well," says Hoop, "I don't feel that way. Necessarily."

"Neither do I," says another employee, and then, considering the possibilities of an enlightened view, adds, "but I just don't know if I'm ready for a woman."

Hoop takes the line without hesitation. "You *always* gotta be ready for a woman, 'cause a woman ain't always ready for you. Ain't that right, New Britches?"

"Yeah, I suppose," says the short, fat farmer, and he tucks his hands further down inside his overalls until his elbows stick out like a midget's arms.

At the counter in Van's on the west side of the square, any discussion of the election is silenced by the presence of Jim and Betty Billingsley, candidate and wife. Were these same people sitting in Jim's bar, where he has a proprietor's implicit right to direct the flow of conversation, they'd wait for him to show them the limits of what they could openly say.

Jim and Betty finish in silence and light cigarettes while talk and noon movement go on around them, counter stools filling.

Jim looks out Van's plate-glass window as he smokes and his long scowling face registers nothing at all. He moves his head for a better view of the square, has seen something on the sidewalk that interests him and is heading toward Van's window. Erlene Veverka is moving down the street, her step bouncing with the purpose of a woman collecting for a worthy charity, and having just a brief time left before she has to turn in all her money. She's been stopping at shops along both sides of the square, coming out again a few moments later and moving on to the next one. And now, as Van's window frames her, she turns her head to face directly the people inside, walking briskly left to right across the glass, and gives the restaurant a blazing smile. One cannot easily see the interior of Van's from the street, but it doesn't matter. Erlene is not smiling specifically to people inside, but to the certainty that there will be people inside, watching. She passes out of the frame of the glass and on down the street and a couple of men at the counter say, "Hey, there goes Mrs. Mayor," and "A vote for her is——" but then they catch themselves and become intensely interested in the morning's *Des Moines Register*.

At the bank, there's talk of little else but the election.

"What do you think's gonna happen?" asks a thin, small woman clutching a fistful of assorted bank business.

"I think she's gonna pull it off," says a teller who has just returned from voting. "Looks to me like the votes'll be split up between the men and Erlene'll get it."

"This is what I want to find out," says the woman. "Now, does she have to have a *majority*, or does she just have to have more than anybody else? What I mean, does——"

"Know what you mean," says the teller, "but I really don't know the answer to that. I guess I just thought she had to have more than the rest, but I'm not sure, now that I think about it . . . I don't know."

"Dick Charls was in this morning," adds a secretary sitting in front of a big vault door in the middle of the room that leads back to safe-deposit boxes, "and somebody asked him that same question. But I can't remember now just what he said."

As in past elections, the winner needs a majority of votes cast, but Erlene believes that she needs only one more vote than anyone else. When her campaign manager asked if they should be working with a majority in mind, Erlene said, "No, that's *old* law. I asked Scotty, the town clerk, and he said that was an old law." But Scotty was wrong, and Erlene had been soliciting for a cause requiring much larger pledges than she'd been led to believe.

Conversations continue all over town, as ubiquitous as the rain. In Nichols' Pharmacy, next to Snub's Please 'U' Cafe: "Hank's a tyrant is all. I heard—did you ever hear?—Bob tellin' about when he was on the council and he went against Hank on something or other, I don't remember now what he said it was, doesn't matter, anyway, and Hank got mad as hell and he hasn't set foot inside Bob's shop since that night? *Nosir.* Not a once. Now, that's a grudge, by God, and that's having a tyrant for mayor."

"Ah, bullshit. What Bob didn't tell yas was that Hank never set foot inside his shop *before* he went against him."

In Brubaker's garage, around the corner from DeWit's

grocery store: "Billingsley's votes'll get split up, some for mayor, some for council, since he can't seem to make up his mind what he's runnin' for."

"I'll make up his mind what to run him for. I'd like to run the shyster outa town."

"So what's that leave you? The Veverkas are tryin' to take over the whole town, buyin' up houses, runnin' for everything. You vote for her and watch what happens to your taxes, the way she'll spend money on things we can't afford. She'll want to put up all kinds of new things in this town."

"Well, I'm gonna vote for her. And I's one of the ones that took, whatchacall, Hank, his nominating papers to sign. When he refused 'em, I thought right then, The hell with you, buddy. You're not gonna be paying attention to what's going on in town. I'd rather have a mayor what wants the work, even if she's a woman."

Prairie City feels crowded—the talk, the people, the hermetic rain, all moving simultaneously. At the counter in Snub's, one sees a man who works two jobs—full time for Ostlin, part time for Billingsley. But beyond that, his wife works for Jim at the Cardinal, and his son, freshly graduated from law school and beginning a practice here, would welcome either candidate's business. His son's wife and her parents have regularly eaten dinner at the Cardinal over the past few years—a remote connection that in a city would alone be enough to assume the man's vote for him. But the man's daughter has married someone whose father works for Ostlin, has for years, and will vote for him and hope the others do the same. And so it goes, with almost any person in Prairie City one might isolate and trace, as if the town had more roles to fill than people to fill them. Today, all those competing claims separate and surface and inhabit the town. Prairie City recognizes them all and seems, swollen far beyond its usual population, to be bumping into itself.

The fire station receives slow, steady business throughout the day. As they do for nearly everything, people arrive to vote in pairs, neighboring women, workers from the same shop, husbands and wives, walking slowly up the wide cement drive.

The voting place is dark and damp, moisture lying on the gray cinder blocks like a sealing sweat. The volunteer firemen's long wax-slick coats and high helmets hang on a row of hooks behind three local women, seated at folding tables, serving for the day as election judges.

On the other side of the room, facing the coats and the smiling and efficient list-checking women, sit large garbage cans with ballot slits in their lids, and next to the cans, two voting booths, properly curtained, but stripped inside as if vandalized; no gears and tabs and levers, no gadgetry. Just a hard plain board and a number-two pencil. Nothing fancy. Voters draw back the curtains and in a private moment cast two votes—one for a candidate, one for some part of themselves. Does the man eating lunch at Snub's wish to think of himself principally as a friend, in-law, or fence-sharing enemy? What of himself has he voted for?

A few hours after the polls have closed, the election judges have counted and recounted—the only possibility of vote fraud is an honest mistake in arithmetic—and determined the day has balanced.

Henry Ostlin, 165 votes

Erlene Veverka, 101 votes

Jim Billingsley, 14 votes

Adding to these totals the ballots cast for councilmen, three hundred twenty-seven people have voted, a few dozen fewer than in September's school-board election, and Ostlin has received, by one and a half votes, the required majority of ballots cast.

"Billingsley's got one more in his family than he got votes," says a man in Nichols Pharmacy the next morning, a man who had not heard Jim say he preferred being on the council to being mayor. "He's got a black sheep in there somewhere." Jim has not won election to the city council, either, placing third in a race for two seats.

In the November 13th edition of the *News*, Erlene Veverka takes a brief advertisement that reads: "I wish to thank all my supporters and to announce my intention to run for mayor in the next general election in two years. Thank you." Her ad ends a column of other personal notices that thank friends and relatives for their cards and their faith in a time of illness or loss, and it shares with them the tone of recuperation.

At last, late in November, the weather has broken, turned chilly. A few days ago, there was a winter shower, sharp points of rain blowing against the face. But it has settled now into a steady chill. The town feels full again, and relaxed, and the pickups have been staying in front of Van's and Snub's late into the morning.

Snub has finally begun to make more doughnuts. In the summer and early fall, he mixes batter for roughly six dozen doughnuts; he doubles his recipe during the winter months. Snub DeWit has owned the Please 'U' Cafe, in the middle of the block on the north side of the square, for thirty-one years. He opened the business shortly after graduating from high school, and he's found that ratio— twice as many doughnuts when the weather turns— reliable year after year.

Snub opens at seven o'clock, as most of the businesses do. He unlocks his door and snaps on the lights, and within moments his first customers walk sleepily through the door and settle onto stools around the long horseshoe-shaped counter. Jake Williams, the city's engineer; Tom Stoner, from Snub's brother's grocery next door; Tim Plate, who opens the Co-op gas station on the east-west highway. The insurance man. The Kent Feed salesman. They nod and grunt familiarly. The same faces, with sleep still in them, accustomed by now to one another's morning temper, waking like a family around its kitchen table.

"Morning, John. How ya doin'?"

"Fair and warmer."

"You getting your Des Moines paper in the morning these days?"

"Yeah, Saturday's on Monday, Monday's on Thursday. That god damn paper boy."

"Who is it, anyway?"

"Oh, Jenkins' kid is the new one. Hell, they had a good one and he quit. I wish they'd just let one kid have the whole town. The other one's okay."

"He's all right."

"Huh?"

"I say he's all right."

"He's okay. But this Jenkins kid in the south end. . . ."

"Mornin', Tim."

"You look real good this morning, Tim. Ever hear of stayin' home some night?"

"Tim's out testing his Johnson rod again last night, weren't ya, Tim?"

"Get any nibbles, Tim?"

"Sheeit."

They watch Snub's new four-pot coffee maker drip and fill and finally Snub's daughter, Pam, pours from a finished pot into heavy, diner-thick mugs. Pam quit her out-of-town job last year so she could spend more time with her husband when he returned from long-distance trucking runs. Now she's a waitress at the Please 'U.' But she serves no one doughnuts at seven a.m.; they aren't ready yet.

Snub has been leasing his doughnut machine for twenty years. He pays a fee, the manufacturer supplies dry mix, maintenance, parts. While his first customers drink coffee, Snub, in the kitchen, adds water, whips, forces the batter through a mold, drops the sculptures into bubbling fat. Seventy-five of them in summer, twice as many in winter, except for the first half of January, when everybody's briefly thrifty after Christmas and his business drops a third. ("It's hard on my pocketbook," Snub says, "but it's easier on me.") Raw doughnuts bob in the boiling fat and, when they're nut-brown, Snub lifts them out, lets them drip, and names them, applies glazes that run and harden like sweet wax: "chocolate," "chocolate chip," "white," "coconut," "crunch." A few, left pure, called "plain." Chocolate chip—bits of chocolate sprinkled over chocolate glaze, have always been his most popular, but I prefer "white," the opaque frosting something very close to straight sugar, cooled and set.

An experienced palate can approximate the hour of morning after one bite. At eight forty-five or nine, Snub brings the trays from the kitchen while the merchants on the square are taking their first coffee break. The doughnuts now are warm, the glazes viscous and sweet with a power they'll lose. Bite through a doughnut and discover three strata of taste and texture: the sticky coat; the crust—heavy skin that's crunchy and almost nutlike; the inside—light, hot cake, sweet steam coming out of its pores and hitting your nostrils. At nine forty-five or ten, the doughnuts have begun to cool, the coatings unusually thick and rich, a crust and cake still slightly discernible. At ten thirty, the crunch is gone, the marvelous grease has settled into the cake and put weight in it. Now the doughnuts are merely very good, the glazes saving them. Pity the stranger stopping for a late-morning cup of coffee who thinks his doughnut as good as it's ever been. At eleven o'clock, you can definitely call the time. At eleven, Snub's doughnuts are all gone.

Snub watches tides of business through the day: the first small group he wakes and sends to work; then come his coffee-break people; then the lunch crowd that begins to build as early as eleven thirty. He's usually in the kitchen, where his head and shoulders are framed in the open, arched window and he can be seen, over the grill, a cigarette dangling precariously from his lips. He cooks and shouts inside the frame, arranging food on plates and plopping them on a sill that is the base of the frame. The busier he gets, the less attention he pays to the ash-growing cigarette. He leans down, out of sight, the ash a fragile parenthesis from his mouth. He rises up again into the frame, a short, clean cigarette between his lips. Where did the ashes go? Some people say all that seasoning in the gravy is not pepper.

His afternoons do not so cleanly peak and fall and he has little evening business now. With the Cardinal and Freda's Drive In on the highway, Snub has been closing earlier and earlier, seven thirty at present, moving the time up imperceptibly, a few minutes every six months since the days when he kept the restaurant open until ten thirty or later. It's business he does not mind losing, for Snub has said that when his daughter, Pam, decides to leave, Snub will, too. He'll sell the Please 'U.'

For the past several weeks, I've been walking three blocks, through back yards and an alley, to the post office and from there one block south and half a block east to Snub's. I seem, without really planning it, to be moving against the tides of Snub's business. Just a few stools are still occupied when I get there, my "white" tasting around ten. Usually, there are a couple of farmers, the grocery delivery boy, perhaps a few others, at the counter.

At the back of the restaurant, beyond the left arm of the U, there's an open dining room. This area used to be closed and very dark and narrow, and with an arched doorway and swinging doors. Above the arch, duplicating its curve, a sign read "Dining Room," and at noon, some people even ate in there, but food was not its attraction. From the arched doorway, out of the dark, came constant plumes of cigarette smoke. Everyone referred to that malodorous closet as "The Cloud Room," named after the restaurant at the Des Moines Municipal Airport, and during lunch hours, and after school, and after daily practice for whatever sport was in season, the clouds came billowing out through the door in cumulus proportion. Those were innocent times, and The Cloud Room provided a formal cover for the students of Prairie City who smoked, an offense that carried stiff penalties. If the high school principal had really wished to prosecute, of course, he could have simply raided The Cloud Room any noon, but no one ever did as far as I remember, and that was not the idea. The Cloud Room kept students from smoking on the school grounds, and kept them all conveniently clustered. For the students, it was a perfect decor—a short row of booths; a dim light that cast the room in a kind of jaundiced glow; the swinging doors, requiring a certain outlaw swagger and nonchalant timing. It was the sort of room that spoke of behavior that needed a place to hide, which was the lure of smoking, anyway.

There was another dimension to The Cloud Room, however, for it was a segregated room, making distinctions with that same silent power of the school-bus seats.

But simple seniority was not the only consideration; the fierce, linear morality of Prairie City also came into play. Good young men didn't smoke and stayed in Snub's front room. In the booths and around the horseshoe. Sin was in the back, in the smoky dark.

Those who kept long hours in The Cloud Room were generally older students, juniors and seniors, but freshmen and sophomores were back there, too, and even a few precocious seventh- and eighth-grade boys with a habit they could prove. Naturally, there was the implicit notion of earned adulthood in The Cloud Room, a kind of ceremonial passing out of innocence, and for a big, ornery twelve-year-old, there could be no finer moment than the first time he sat in the dark with high school seniors, breathing smoke and tenderloin batter, and casually lighting up.

I did not smoke. My Sunday-school lessons had been casual, and I knew no Scripture from memory, yet I had an adolescent vision of right and wrong that was absolutely rigid. There was a kind of missionary zeal in me for a while and I often felt a believer's burden as I sat on a stool in Snub's and lost one classmate after another to The Cloud Room. John Macauley, Wilbur Telfer, Marvin Winegar. All around me, dropping like flies.

"Where are you going?" I'd ask, as Mike Danley or Johnny Stravers or one of the Van Zees rose slowly from the stool next to me. The friend would sheepishly withdraw from a front pocket a pack of cigarettes and a shiny new lighter, palming them carefully under the counter as he might a rubber from his father's drawer. He'd nod toward the arched doorway and, squirming with a small betrayal but, more with eagerness, would say, "I'll see you later, okay?" I'd shake my head, let out the heavy breath of tested faith, and watch him go: around the U, through the swinging doors, gone.

The Cloud Room didn't steal everybody, of course, and by the time I was an upperclassman, the edge came off the whole issue. One day I entered The Cloud Room myself, to deliver some message or other—"Karen says she and Connie need a ride after school and wait for her in front of the gym." I've forgotten my exact errand, but the look of the place remains vivid. Faces in all the booths, coming forward out of the smoke, back-lighted and waxy-looking. Opened ketchup bottles dripping lavishly, and playing cards tossed carelessly onto the tables. There was a compressed and sleazy expectancy, and the curious experience of seeing those I'd known in well-lit rooms behaving with new gestures and rhythms, but not quite instinctively, as if they were giving a well-rehearsed performance.

Most of all, I remember their postures of exaggerated indolence, slouched nearly prone in the booths and leaning at what seemed almost forty-five-degree angles against the wall. Everyone moved slowly, if at all, and with tremendous effort. They squinted through the smoke or, simply and sensibly, closed their eyes. The only energy was in their laughter, a kind of humming chuckle running constantly beneath the talk.

"You goin' to Sully Friday night?"

"My ol' man'll probably make me drive him someplace. Like to drive him fuckin' nuts, is where I'd like to drive him."

"Whoo! Mean talk there. Uh, pass me, uh, yeah, thank you."

"God damn, son, ain't ya heard of no other brand except O.P.s?"

"Ha!" from another booth. "We got four, five, six points. Guess I shoulda bid 'em all. Hey, shit, want a little hamburger on that ketchup, 'Reen?"

"Whoa! Whooee!"

"Oh, I am going to flunk that history this afternoon so bad. I am going to flunk it something awful."

They were moments of opiate laziness, and perhaps it was this laziness among strong young farm boys, an indolence stretched to caricature, that was, more than smoking, the great sin that had to be committed undercover. Here, away from herds of livestock and hard fathers, they found relaxation. Perhaps I was never seriously tempted by The Cloud Room not because of some narrow morality but because I had always had the freedom to be lazy in front of my father.

Students don't come to the Please 'U' much at all anymore since the new school on the south edge of town was finished. The walk to the square at lunchtime is too long. Many local people predicted a great drop in profits for Snub when the new school, nearly in the country, opened. But Snub did not agree. He's been feeding this town for thirty-one years and there's no clearer way to know a place than to watch and listen to it over plates of hot food. He's always known who are his customers, who have never been, and he has known their reasons. So Snub was not surprised, after students and their high-pitched noise disappeared, that the Please 'U' soon began to fill with the older people in town, ordering the daily special, not just Cokes and fries. His past year has been the Please 'U''s most profitable.

Fortunately, the Please 'U''s basic pieces—the horseshoe, the arched kitchen window with Snub inside it, the alley-wide dimensions of the main room—restrict its changes mostly to surfaces. There may be new linoleum, a new counter, but beneath them, the proportion, the scale, has remained.

Pam asks, "Coffee?"

"Please."

"Doughnut?"

"Let's see, there," I say, looking for the trays atop Snub's ice-cream freezer. "Got any whites left?"

"One."

I bite through, chewing for the time of morning, and think suddenly of Hoop standing in a storm of corn and measuring moisture with his teeth. I've been missing him and that work, missing the assignment it gave me. But inside the Please 'U,' all duties are equal. Everyone sits on a stool with his appetite. The horseshoe counter makes no distinctions, recognizes no rank, and serves as a kind of central social depot in Prairie City. Shoulder to shoulder around the curves, face to face across the space in the middle where Pam moves and the malt machines, coffeepots—all the furniture of fast service—sit. Everyone perched in identical discomfort.

At Snub's, then, we are all the same, have come for food and democratic leisure, and the restaurant removes that sense of isolation I've felt since the end of the harvest. Pam keeps my cup full without being asked and Snub shouts from the window of the kitchen, "Hello, Douger." He's stirring ham and beans, 85¢, today's special.

"Hey, Snubber," I answer. His name is Bob, and I have never asked him how Snub came to him. It may have something to do with the leg—the nearness of snub and stub—and I don't want to risk that, though he's remarkably free-spoken about the accident, makes jokes about his limp. He even continued to ride motorcycles, drove a small, quick scooter every day when I was in high school. I remember watching him mount it in front of the Please 'U,' swinging his leg up and over the seat, then racing away from the curb with one of those graceful dips to the street, his artificial leg hanging stiffly from the scooter like cargo. If he felt bitterness, it wasn't toward the machine.

Snub leaves the kitchen, comes out to the coffeepots

and pours a cup for himself and another for me. He swings onto the stool next to me and slurps loudly from the mug.

"I don't know how much writin' pays, Douger," he says, "but if you're looking to make an easy hundred thousand a year, I'll sell you this place right today." He smiles into his mug, and I laugh and raise his lie.

"Sorry, Snub. If that's all you gross in a year, I'm not interested. I make that in six months."

"You know," he says, "the damn shame of it is some people think I'm gettin' rich here. If I made that kinda money, I wouldn't be here thirty-one years." He laughs and draws deeply on a cigarette, holding a long feathery ash. Snub seems to have aged very little. He looks much like his father, John the Butcher, who cut meat in the grocery almost until he died. Snub has the same square jaw and wide mouth, usually smiling. He's a bigger man than John DeWit, broader through the chest and shoulders, but has his father's voice, a low growl. John the Butcher used that voice for a false gruffness that scared hell out of me when, as a child, I waited as he worked behind his meat counter, sawed and hacked a slab of beef into lovely leaves, wrapped them in white paper and snarled, "Next!" Snub somehow gives the same resonance a mellow cordiality.

He watches me savoring my doughnut and smiles. "You know, you can use those to bottom fish," he says. "The bass'll lick the frosting and they're so damn heavy they keep your line weighed down 'bout like iron"—this last word drawn out and pronounced "arrn."

"Bullshit, Snubber. These are the best doughnuts in the world and you know it." I realize that I've never seen him eating one. "What's your favorite kind?" I ask.

"My favorite doughnut," he says, "is another piece of meat."

"Are you serious?"

"Don't like any of them. I don't eat desserts at all. If there's any left at the end of the day, or any pie, I send it home with Pam or one of the other gals. Nah, I'd just as leave have another piece of meat."

I have wakened from deep sleep with thoughts of a still-warm Please 'U' white, felt cravings that have swooped down and just *stayed*, unrequited. They've reached me through layers of hard thought and while dreaming. Geography unimportant, state of hunger incidental. So I find what I've just heard hard to believe, and it occurs to me that Snub has much in common with a man I've read about, a fellow in Scotland named Captain Smith Grant. At his historic Speyside distillery, Grant makes The Glenlivet, the world's best Scotch whisky, and John McPhee wrote of a visit with Grant: "He pours a glass of The Glenlivet, drops just enough water into it for a perfece nose, and hands it to me. Then he mixes for himself a gin and tonic."

"Another piece of meat," I mumble. Meat reminds me of Snub's tenderloins, colloquially, "tenderlines," a cut of pork sandwiched in a bun. Tenderloins are a common Midwest sandwich, but what places Snub's above all others is his skillful breading, his touch with the egg-and-crumb batter in which he rolls the slice of pork before dropping it into deep fat. Again, deep fat. Most everything memorable about the Please 'U' has something to do with deep fat. Snub's breaded tenderloins are like a fine French-fried potato, crisp nearly to the center, then firm. It's like eating a huge disk of fried crust, Iowa won ton, mustard and pickle. The pork is irrelevant. It holds the batter, of course, but contributes nothing to the taste.

"You haven't changed your tenderloins, I hope."

"Well," Snub says, "they used to be better." He waits

and inhales, his timing perfect. "We used to use pork. But it got so high we had to go to goat." He turns suddenly serious and his voice assumes the even tone of business, the voice of a man concerned with books and inventory. "I'll tell you, we *did* have to raise our prices a nickel. Pork's got so damn high I had to. My own price on it's up eleven cents, but you can't raise 'em like that in a small town. Folks notice it. The whole damn town'd have a heart attack."

Folks do notice. I heard yesterday in the grocery store that tenderloins had been raised a nickel "on the square," at the Please 'U' and at Van's, making them more expensive than tenderloins "on the highway," at Freda's Drive In, and at the Cardinal. Snub has already been accused of thievery and worse this morning and his response has been easy laughter, the response that's required here. Small-town businessmen seem bound to pretend that profit is merely an afterthought to their work. It's more important to provide a service and wish all the businesses well and if one finds himself competing with someone down the street, well, surely there's enough to share. Nobody gets rich, but all the stores are open, and the town better served. Cities, of course, simply assume that a man ideally hopes for *all* the business, but in cities one's competitor is a stranger. Here, the man selling tenderloins against yours might also live down the street, might share your Sunday pew, stand beside you to recite the Lions Club oath on the second and fourth Thursdays of the month. Familiarity in little towns once again creates a crowding of many roles into insufficient space. With that comes the additional pressure to treat one another kindly, however much a merchant might wish for the release to conduct hard, impersonal business with all the freedom enjoyed by a man with a shop on a packed city street.

On a small square blackboard on the wall facing us, Pam has written:

SPECIAL
Ham and beans, 85¢

"You sure aren't getting rich on that price," I say to Snub.

He has his humor back. "Well, we'd charge more if we kept the ham in 'em, but we got this one cube we keep on a string, see . . ." and he leaves it to me to fill in the image of Snub standing over a caldron of bubbling limas, holding a cube of ham on a string like an ice fisherman.

We sit through several cups of coffee as people trickle in, others leave, the population holding at six or seven. From his stool, Snub announces each new customer, a way of saying hello, as if he were introducing to his restaurant some arriving eminence.

"There's ol' Bill!" he shouts, drawing out the words the way Ed McMahon announces Johnny Carson. "There's Buck." All the time, he smokes and drinks coffee and continues our conversation.

"Did you like it there 'n Chicago, Douger? What was it like there?"

"Yeah, I did. A lot. Of course, I had some very——"

"There he is, ol' Doc."

"Good friends there."

"Yeah?" Snub growls suspiciously. "I'll tell ya, it always seemed like a damn rat-race to me. Those people—there's young John!—those people don't have no idea whether they're coming or going. They's so damn busy they don't know what they're doin'."

Snub doesn't really want to know what I like about cities; he wants to tell me what he believes about them.

Having spent no time in a city of any size, he holds the firm opinion that they offer nothing to a man with any sense.

"Here comes Marinus!"

That attitude prevails here. I've asked people what comes to mind when I say "city" and have been repeatedly told that "things" come to mind—buildings, streets, cars; many cars. "I don't think people there have friendships the way we do here," a young woman with whom I went to high school said. I've not met anyone who wants to know if he might be wrong about cities or who has any real curiosity about them. Some people cling to the one brief city horror they remember. One man told me that he knew Chicago well enough. He was there, drove the Kennedy and Dan Ryan expressways from a point near Fort Sheridan at the northern rim of the metropolitan area to the South Side, on a Friday afternoon about five o'clock. He was nearly killed by a '55 two-tone Chevy, raked and mean, blowing blue oil smoke from its pipes like a god damn cat with its ass set fire. That single journey, slicing through the bleak borders of the city on the world's busiest road during weekend rush hour, was all he needed to know about the way I'd lived in Chicago.

"I was talkin' to this guy who used to live in Los Angeles," Snub says. "He worked for Ostlin here at the cement plant for a while and he ate his supper here. And he was tellin' me those people out there reminded him of a bunch of worms in a barrel, just crawlin' all over each other to get to the rim. All they do—hey, there's Anna Bernie!—all they do is buy things, buy, buy, buy. They never even stop to think about what they're buyin'."

Spaces around the counter are starting to fill, and in the back room, chairs scrape the new linoleum floor. Snub, having watched the cadence of Prairie City's appetite for thirty-one years, says softly, "'Course, it's gettin' about that bad right here. I remember I used to go down to my uncle's cabin in Arkansas and I used to think those gol damn Arkies was about the slowest damn buncha people I ever met. Now I go down there and I think they're the only smart ones left. They don't care—there's Joseph Joe!—they just have fun."

Snub cocks his head toward the front door, which flips steadily back and forth now. From the back of the restaurant, his brother Don, the grocer, enters the main room from the alley between their businesses. He passes quietly behind us and as he does, Snub growls, "Hello, Boone." He calls Don Boone. Snub is also called Doc, layers of nicknames.

I turn, seeing Don for the first time, and know that Snub has not moved his head, could not have seen him, yet said hello just as Don was passing behind us. I look up at the time on the wall, wondering if Prairie City could move with such precision. Snub sees this thought in my expression and corrects me.

"I *smelled* ol' Boone coming."

I laugh uncomfortably, believing I've been admitted to some old and private insulting humor. "No, I mean it," Snub says. "I can always smell Boone. He smells like meat." Snub's brother has for years worn the family's white butcher's apron, presided over his father's gleaming meat case. Snub continues, "I know I smell like that damn kitchen. Standing over the grill all day, I got grease and smoke all through me. Now, you take somebody like Leo Brubaker, let's say, he comes in here. I can smell him coming before he gets into the room." Leo works on agricultural machinery and smells of lubricating grease, Snub says. He gives more examples to authenticate his nose.

Snub as something deep-fried. Don as a side of beef.

Leo Brubaker as a gelatinous piston. The smell of a man's work seeps into his pores until soap can't reach it, and his labor finally becomes his own cologne.

The front door squeaks quite slowly and Snub watches it open, then calls out the newest arrival. But there's another tone in his voice, nothing in it that means hello. And he's not speaking so much to the room as to his waitresses, Pam and the woman who helps at noon. He shouts, "Eddie's here!"

He's visible through the long windowpane in Snub's front door. His face is nearly on the glass, and distorted, like a child's splayed nose against a window. There's no sign of effort on his face; he simply leans serenely against the door until it finally opens wide enough. Inside, he stands in front of the door, blinking in new light. Several seconds pass while he makes the decision—left or right?—that the waitresses already know. They've placed his red Jell-O, his stack of white bread, his knife and fork and napkin at his place on the left side of the counter. At last, Eddie shuffles forward, to the left, and his soles against the floor make the sound of lightly buffing sandpaper. As he moves toward the stool, other customers move around him at what suddenly seems a rude, city speed.

Eddie leaves his house at the north edge of town at eleven o'clock to reach Snub's in half an hour. He shuffles rhythmically along the clean and treacherous sidewalks as if he were moving to a private protracted waltz, completes a trio of steps, then freezes in his tracks.

"Hewwo," he says to those at the end of the counter, but no one turns around. Three steps, four, and he's near his Jell-O. "Hewwo," he says. Cement-plant workers in high rubber boots pass him on his left and he prepares to speak to them, but they're gone and taking seats in the back before he can gather everything he needs for words. Four steps, five, and he's at his place. He removes his ear-flapped cap; his silver hair bristles.

"Hewwo, Shorty," he giggles to the heavy man on his right.

"Hello, Eddie," the man says. Eddie snorts and laughs and now he turns to his left, to me, and says, "Dat's da way I git even wit em." A waitress brings his ham and beans, slides the heavy plate between his Jell-O dish and his bread. Eddie begins painstakingly to break the bread into halves and uses each one as a scoop that vibrates wildly in his hands.

"Hewwo, Shorty," he says again, but this time receives no response, does not get even, so he eats.

Since I grew up outside of the town, I was only slightly aware of Eddie Schultze living in his rundown house on the north edge of Prairie City. I don't recall seeing him on the streets, or in any stores, and during the middle of the day, when I'd have had the best chance of seeing him, I was in school. His name was a byword among the town students, the measure for all ignorance: "My God, you're about as bright as Eddie Schultze." Or, "You get your brains at the place where Eddie bought his?"

Eddie Schultze is one consistent thread in the chronology of Prairie City. He has been here as long as almost anyone can remember, and he fills his days now as he always has; more slowly, of course, and with some accommodation to his fading strength (his mail is now delivered to a box in front of his house). And the remarkable consistency of his route, his habits, the timbre of his hare-lipped speech, even the words he forces through it—has finally made Eddie invisible in a community that prizes, above all else, behavior that can be predicted, relied on.

After a bite of food, Eddie begins to cough, a violent

phlegm-rattling cough, and he chokes and sputters. Mashed potatoes and partially digested bread form a rabid foam around his mouth. Unimaginable sounds fill the restaurant. His face reddens and he shakes on the stool as he rides it out. A minute later, fully restored, he resumes his meal, as if he'd genteelly cleared his throat into linen. A waitress, seeing whatever expression Eddie's seizure caused me to make, whispers reassuringly in my ear, "He's okay. He does that every day."

Eddie says, "If I eat any moe, I donna bwow up." Pam stacks his plates, puts them on a tray and takes them to the kitchen. "I dotta doe home now," says Eddie. "I dotta doe home now."

Of course, it's naïve of me to watch Eddie Schultze speak his simple sentences to no one and to resent the town's deafness. In the larger scope of charity, Prairie City does care for him. A church paid for the meal he's just eaten. The social and service clubs send food at holidays. I realize, too, that he holds on to any conversation he can draw from someone, the few monologues he has, rushing out and holding their victim in a grip.

"I donna doe home now."

But it's safe for me to be kind. I have no shop on the square he'd begin to visit every day if I once allowed him in. He has no idea who I am or where he might regularly find me. I can behave toward Eddie as a curious visitor.

"What are you going to do at home, Eddie?" I ask.

He looks at me, a spot floating dreamily on his eye like a congealing egg white. The lenses in his wire-rimmed glasses are coated with greasy fingerprints and rest on the bridge of a long, hooked nose. Eddie scratches his head and opens his mouth to form a tiny O.

"Oh, I doan know . . . I s'pose I take a nap. I way down and take a nap."

"Sounds good. Do you take a nap every day after lunch?"

"Sometimes I bake bwed. I donna bing Snub a woaf of some bwed, but he doan wan it, though, he says he use my bwed in his pockets so the wind woan bwoe him away. . . . He says he doan wanna bweak his teeth when he eat my bwed. I bake bwed o' I take a nap, but I got a bad eye, see?" He points a weaving finger toward the milky spot. "I say he better watch it and not cheat me"— and he waves his hand limply toward Snub in the kitchen window—"tuz he got two eyes and I got one." He laughs at his joke. "But I hurt it when a piece a straw stuck in it and I use to have two good eyes. I dot one now and one bad eye and you know what? I have a good woman once, but she runned away."

"She did?" I say, and hear a condescension, a moronic encouragement, in my voice. "What happened? Did you bake some of your bread for her?"

He blinks. "She runned away."

"Where'd she go?"

He shrugs his shoulders elaborately, holding them up tightly around his ears for a few seconds. "Runned away. She di'n't like Pehwie City s'pose? I think so, she went to a new pwace, but I like Pehwie City the best and I been in Jasper Cownie seventy-two years since I come from Suwee."

"Sully? Is that your home?"

"Suwee, yeah. My fatha was a bwacksmith and he come fwom Germany and live in Suwee and then we come to Pehwie City and dis is da best."

"How long have you lived where you live now, Eddie, in that big house?"

"'Bout, oh, thirty years. I use to take care a Momma and was in dat house aul dat time and Momma and me."

"Well, that's fine," I say, and hear the tone again, as if I were asking an infant to explain to me his crayon smears.

"Yeah, and do you know my name?" he suddenly asks.

"Your name? Well, yes, uh, your name is Eddie Schultze." I assume he wishes to know mine, and begin to introduce myself, realizing belatedly that I owe him that also.

"My name is Adowf. Adowf Schultze."

"Adolph?"

He nods enthusiastically.

"Why do they call you Eddie, if your name's Adolph?"

He shrugs his shoulders and again holds them up around his neck and while we're quiet, the restaurant noise comes up. "Special!" yells Snub as he slaps down plates of ham and beans on his crowded windowsill.

"I doan know why," Eddie says, dropping his shoulders as he speaks. "My name Adowf. I doan wan Eddie. I like to be Adowf. Adowf Schultze."

His insistence is firm, and leaves me fumbling. As long as his words had flowed foolishly, I'd been comfortable with our conversation, with his defect and with his sensitivity that I'd stupidly assumed as murky as the vision in his clouded eye. But now he's quietly told me that he'd like the town to return his name, and I can think of nothing good enough to say.

"Cheeseburger! Everything!" yells Snub. Clanging pans and the rubber-lined thump of a freezer lid dropping shut. "Cheeseburger, rare, on one!"

"I don't blame you," I mutter finally and stand to leave. "I better let you go take that nap."

"I dess I doe home and take a nap."

"You take care, now."

"Yeah, I take care."

"Bye, Adolph."

He smiles broadly and says, "Yeah, Adowf. I doan know how it got Eddie, but I like Adowf."

I leave Snub's and walk slowly home, crossing streets and taking the long open alley that runs behind my neighbor's houses and leads almost to my back door. I feel guilty, but feel something else, too, that I can't at first identify. Inside my house, seated at my desk, I think how self-absolving a gesture it was to use Adolph's name at the end of our conversation, a piece of melodrama. After a while, I turn to the window that looks north, across Sixth Street, to Mr. and Mrs. Noon's bright yellow house, and see Schultze moving into view. He has a small sack of groceries clutched to his wool coat and his ear flaps are down and moving in the wind like dogs' ears. He takes four steps and stops, and cocks his good eye, scanning the row of houses in front of him on this block of Sixth Street.

Adolph moves through the vast space between my window frames and, watching him, I remember an article I've recently read by a New York City woman who'd decided to leave Manhattan and settle in a quiet upstate New York village. She described the routine horror on her upper West Side block—parked cars being casually stripped to carcasses, doorstep sex, grandmothers squatting like dogs to pee on the sidewalks. She wrote that while she recognized enduring city pleasures, they were for her no longer worth it, so she'd moved with her children to Rhinebeck, a white and gleaming little village on the Hudson. For many weeks, she had loved things there absolutely, all the expected things. But then she began to fidget psychically, and to miss New York, for all its running viciousness. As a writer, she missed talking with writers, felt culturally lonely, and her warm contentment began to feel at times like flannel pressing against her face. She admitted missing, more than she'd anticipated, New York's adrenal variety, and she even missed, I believe it's fair to say, the need to keep her cunning tooled and sharpened. Where's the stimulation here? she'd asked at the end of her piece. Where's the energy? Where, in my sane country life, are those people on the edge, in costume?

Her question comes back to me now as I continue to stare through my window, even though Adolph has at last crept past. By this time, she's no doubt found her answer. Where are the people on the edge? she asks. Who are the ones in costume?

She is the one on the edge, a writer with odd habits and arhythmic routes. She is. And I am. Adolph Schultze and I. What I'd felt, with the guilt, were some things we had in common.

I'm up early this morning, nearly as early as the town. I leave the alley behind my house, meet Fifth Street past Francis Randall's welding shop, and walk one block west, where, at the corner, Dr. Mark Buitenwerf's dental office sits, surrounded by a big dead lawn. His office is a small pink-brick cottage with white shutters and it was built not for him but for Dr. Ella Rheinertsen. During the final years of her medical practice in Prairie City, Dr. Ella was the town's only physician. Her husband, Dr. Keach Johnson, was its veterinarian. (My father says that Dr. Johnson was the only veterinarian he's ever known who truly feared animals and talks of the time that Dr. Johnson reflexively pulled back, hypodermic in hand, from an ass-shifting bull and inoculated himself in the leg.)

The pink cottage was built after I'd left Prairie City, and I remember well the old office, a low white-frame house, its lines settled shallowly. Inside, off the vestibule, there was a door that led back to a private area where Dr.

Rheinertsen kept a sitting room and kitchen and where she had cabinets of medicine and equipment. If you had just come to pick up medicine, you knocked on this door. Her friend and aide, Lottie Wooddell, opened the door and, seeing you, retreated into the cabinets to find the pills.

"Let's see, now," Lottie would shout, her head deep in a drawer, "do you get the blue pills or the pink?" So simple. All the town could be healed with one color or the other. I got the pink, for acne.

But if you needed Dr. Ella, you walked on through the vestibule and into the waiting room. It was filled with old, uncomfortable furniture; a heating stove stood centrally in the room. Dark and faded fabrics. Dr. Ella's examining room adjoined it, closed off only by a full-length velvet drape that hung in an open archway. The murmurous conversation, the zipping and taping sounds of Dr. Ella's ministrations, the creaking of leather from her examining table, all came easily and unmuffled through the velvet drapes and out into the waiting room. People sat out there, heads down, pretending to be reading old *Look* magazines, breathing that strong yellow astringent smell that always hangs in the air of doctors' rooms, and listening hard for the other voice. Who was that behind the curtain with Dr. Ella; what were they saying? You could hear the faint voice of the patient reciting symptoms, hear clothes being loosened or rolled up, or *removed*. There was a powerful sexuality in the eavesdropping. Then, abruptly, Dr. Ella parted the drape, she and her patient stepped out like actors in a two-character play—So that's who! Erma! or Lyle! or Mrs. Main! What's wrong with her?—and she sweetly said, "Who's next?" One of us then moved into the room, into the play.

One day, waiting patients suddenly heard the floor begin to groan. It groaned again, and moved, a clear tremor, and then the floor gave, simply let go, and the heating stove, the furniture, all the people, the copies of *Look*, the years of bored tension that had forced dead weight into that floor, all dropped through the sudden hole, down and to the ground. Among the things those people thanked the Lord for that evening was their good fortune that Dr. Ella's office had no basement.

After that, the cottage was built, but Dr. Ella was quite old by then and used it only a short time before she retired and, not long after, died.

I reach the post office, across the street from the cottage. It's also brick, but older than the dentist's office and a testament to the Federal Efficient architecture of the early 1960s—low, plain, square. It's eight thirty and Joe Sparks, the postmaster, has just unlocked his front door. He and his assistant, Bob Bowen, and the rural-route carriers, have been unsacking and sorting mail for more than two hours and the rural carriers have left for the country. There's a small group of men at the door and as Joe opens the glass door, they rush to their mailboxes like customers at a department-store sale. The boxes fill two walls in the outer lobby. An old man peers into his empty box, opens it, and speaks through the square pipe to Bob Bowen on the other side.

"First class all sorted, Bob?"

"Just a few pieces left," says Bowen.

"Got anything for me back there, Bob?"

"Not today." Bowen leans down and looks through the back of another mailbox as a man, on the other side of the wall, opens it. The man peers in, sees eyes and nose inside, as if he'd selected Face of Bowen from an automat slot.

"Hello, Bobbie," says the man.

"Hello, Dickie," says Bowen.

They laugh and proceed to have a morning chat.

Bowen will retire at the end of the year. To reduce costs, the Postal Service will not replace him with a full-time local person but by part-time employees from the surrounding area who'll work at many small-town offices as they're needed. "It's gonna be a hell of a mess," Bowen has said. "How's somebody from out of town going to know how to sort this mail? How's somebody like that going to know that if, say, Ralph Vander Waal's mail comes addressed rural route and no box number on it, that he's moved to town and picks his mail up here, even if he still farms out there on the place? They're not going to know things like that and people are gonna bitch to high heaven about their mail."

The lobby gains and loses people, but the small cluster of old men who'd been waiting for it to open stay inside. A sign of winter. In warmer months, the old men don't linger so long, but the post-office lobby has become one of the places where they gather to loaf. That is the accepted phrase, defining a respectable form of leisure practiced exclusively by retired men. ("Dad's kinda restless now. He's no fisherman, and he's never been much for loafin.'") There are not as many rooms in town where one can loaf as there were. Rosie's Cafe, the back of Bert's clothing store on the bench by the stove, Shorty Vanderzyl's feed store, where they sat on sacks and played cards, as well as some of the garages and gas stations have all been torn down, or made inconveniently modern. Certainly, the post-office lobby is not ideally designed. No chairs. Too much light. Too clean, probably, with a gleaming linoleum floor that inhibits the free release of spit and juice. But with little to choose from now, they gather in the post office through four seasons of winter.

Joe Sparks stands inside, behind the service counter, the big open room with metal shelves, the meter machine, wooden sorting cabinets at his back. He's tall and thin, with black hair just graying at the temples. I'm not certain how old he is, old enough to have served in Japan during the Korean War, and to have a twenty-year-old daughter, but when he smiles, years go out of his face.

Joe has the slow pace of northern Missouri in his speech. He was raised on a reluctant piece of flat earth near the border, and came here, after high school and the Army, because his uncle Don had a gas station in town. If he met any Missouri bigotry, he successfully countered it, perhaps because his uncle provided him a kind of prior admission, perhaps because in all Joe seems and does, he's the antithesis—smart and quick and glisteningly neat—of the bigot's archetypal Missourian. He worked for his uncle, worked in the bank, and was appointed postmaster; but in his heart, he would like to farm. On weekends, he often visits a friend's farm south of town, where he "sort of plays around in the dirt."

Behind his long, blond-wood counter, Joe looks out a big plate-glass window on one of the busier corners of town. It's as if he stood before a tremendous picture window or, even better, a one-way mirror, for the sun and shadows play on the glass in a way that conceals Joe. From that vantage, he could watch the flow unobserved. But he doesn't watch, seems to have minimal curiosity about the movements outside and, when not working at the counter, attends to clerical business at his desk away from the window.

"Hi, Joe." It's Wednesday, the day my Sunday *New York Times*, wrapped in cellophane, sits on a metal shelf behind Joe's counter.

"Hey, Doug." He looks up from his ledgers. "I'll get your papers."

"It's comin'," I say. Joe nods and clicks his tongue on his teeth. It sure is, the clicking says. We mean winter, which is building like a mood. The wind has begun to hurt as it passes back and forth with nothing to slow it through the flat streets, the alleys, the treeless yards, giving the air a certain frozen sterility you can smell, so that you can say simply, "It's comin'," in almost any context and the pronoun will be understood.

Joe nods toward the outer lobby, smiles. "Warming up between stops," he says of the old men. "You know, Doug. I watch those guys come in here every morning for their mail and it's kind of a sad thing. You look at their faces, and a fella can see misery on them. Here they worked on their farms all their life, thinking about the day they could sell out, get some money and move to town. So that's what they do, and what have they got now? Nothing to fill their days. They're used to being on a farm, where a fella can always find something to keep him busy, something, anything to poke around in. Take that away from guys like them and they're lost. Walkin' uptown to get the mail is the highlight of their day."

I look out, through the glass double doors, at the old men and feel pleased that I cannot imagine my grandfather among them. After he and Grandma moved to town, he still drove daily to the farm, as habitually as if a time clock awaited him. The big green Chrysler turned slowly into the drive and went on toward the barnyard. Many days, most, in fact, he didn't come up to the house at all, but somehow found ways to pass hours among the machinery and farm buildings. I'd find him out there, resting against the rear bumper of the Chrysler, his bad leg stiffly placed on the ground, as if he were leaning against a fence rail. The trunk lid behind him was always open, for his trunk was a portable tool shed, and seemed to me to run back like a mine shaft, an infinite black hole filled with rakes and jacks and long-handled instruments. He'd often be sharpening some tool from the trunk as I approached. I'd hear the soft metronomic scraping, see him drawing the whet stone across a blade. Scrape. Scrape. Then he'd pause to pluck the glistening blade with his thumb, as if he were tuning the tool to some unreachable edge of sharpness. He could lose himself in this process and it seemed, coming from his huge hands, not idle work at all. It was as if he used all his field years to meet the complexity he saw on the edge of a hoe.

I'd join him on the fence rail, and we'd apply his labor—peel an apple, remove the green mulchy covering from a walnut with his fresh knife blade. He'd stroke the apple and long red tongues of skin would fall effortlessly away. Then he'd pick up the hoe, drop it a few times to see how it cut the ground, and resume his slow sharpening stroke. And later in the day, he'd use that work, too. I'd see him in the garden west of the house, standing with his bad hip hitched up high, so that his foot lightly grazed the ground as he walked. He'd reasoned, or simply known, that after he moved to town, he'd still have as much farming in him as before, that he'd need ways to let it out.

"Look there," Joe says to me, and I turn around. Across the street, a pickup has pulled up to Dr. Buitenwerf's cottage, not in his driveway but through his front yard, leaving deep tire troughs of mud. The truck has stopped directly at the cottage door, its front bumper appearing to touch the bricks.

"Jesus!" I say, believing the driver has lost control and nearly demolished the front of the office.

"That's a pitiful thing, you know?" Joe says softly.

Pitiful? Someone tearing up a yard?

"He's got bad the last couple years," Joe says. "I guess he just won't let you help him at all. Gets almost mad if you try." As he's saying this, I see the pickup's door open and a man's head, then arms, come out. The head looks forward, behind, and seems to be playing the scene I'd assumed: What happened? says his nodding pantomime. Where am I?

All the while, as he looks, some kind of incredibly hard labor appears to be going on inside the cab, some rearrangement of heavy things. The man's neck reddens and ripples like a weight lifter's, and finally, with his arms braced on the open door and the frame of the cab, his shoulders, then his chest emerge. It has taken him three or four minutes to achieve this, and no more of him comes out for a time.

"Who *is* that, Joe?"

"Oh, that's Kermit Van Gelder. You know. He's got that awful muscle disease. I can't remember if I ever knew what it's called. His mom had it, and finally died of it. You remember. But he's gotten so bad now he barely gets around at all. And he refuses to use a walker or crutches. Too proud to accept it, I guess, but golly, you'd think he'd sure have an easier time of it if he used something, wouldn't you?"

More of Van Gelder is outside the truck now, enough for me to see that I'd have recognized him.

I remember. There was word that he'd inherited an early crippling death. Everyone knew that, but no more, and there were no signs of it at all, when I was in school and Van Gelder, a few years older, sat in a booth at Snub's Please 'U' and snickered about the latest simplicity of Adolph Schultze. It was as if someone had simply hypothesized a fate: a three-car collision on route 6 at the age of twenty-three; a heart attack at a basketball game at twenty-eight; a muscular disease, already working, that would begin to show its damage at thirty-two, thirty-three.

Van Gelder finally has all his body out of the cab, by an effort of such slow and continuous pain that I can't separate its parts. He is coming out; he is, somehow, out. All I've seen is amorphous pain. He leans against his truck, his legs radically bent so that they touch at the knees and then angle away again. He peers around, and I realize what he was searching for when he first looked out of his cab—surfaces, waist high or nearly so, that can serve him from his truck to the office door. Van Gelder, refusing crutches, refusing a walker, views the world as a network of railings. He must have every step accounted for before he takes it, like plotting a walk from rock to rock, in a low, running creek. But with unimaginable pain.

"You see," Joe says as we watch. "He gets as close to the door as possible with his truck. He does that everywhere. You watch. He always eats at Freda's, they say, because there's no curb or anything in front of the place and he can drive right up to the door and use the truck to hold on to till he can get hold of the doorknob."

Van Gelder begins, takes one dead leg in his arms and places it ahead of him, then moves the other leg forward, evening them. The rest of him flaps about epileptically with the effort.

"It's a sad, sad thing," Joe says. "Goll, I can hardly stand to watch him, but I'm sure people would like to give him a hand, like now across the street, instead of having their yards torn up. You know? I'll bet you anything they're watching him right now inside the office and wanting to come out and help him, but he doesn't want that, see? It's hard not to reach out and give the poor guy a hand, but he doesn't want to be treated any differently."

At last Van Gelder reaches the door, and, with one hand still braced against the pickup's hood, works it open. He slides his legs forward, drags them up onto the small front step, a cliff wall. Again, I can't see anything specifically, his progress is too slow. I know only that he's in the doorway, then inside. And that the door shuts.

Joe and I exhale long tension-letting breaths, and I imagine the same simultaneous sighs in the houses around the dentist's office. What we've seen compares to any episode I've watched on New York streets; is worse, in fact, because his is the only affliction here. But for Van Gelder, it's perhaps a slightly better fate to be here in Prairie City, where everyone knows him, and has seen his illness previously. Here he can keep a kind of mobility. A city's crowded impatience would already have made him a complete invalid. But his neighbors have allowed him to make his own convenient routes, using the same walker they use, a pickup truck, where he can sit in his cab as they do, can stay behind the glass until the last moment. Prairie City watches Van Gelder from its picture windows, and has the grace to ignore his public pain.

WINTER

The cold gathers and breaks like a tide; winter shown, winter withdrawn. Farmers stand on the sidewalks, sit in the shops, stare out at the allusive skies and wait for absolution. They rise just as early in winter as any other time, put on the same dress. Some of them come to town at five thirty for coffee at Don and Opal's, on 163. From there they drive to coffee shops all around the county, to Pat and Mel's in Colfax, to places in Mitchellville, Baxter, Monroe, Newton, Pella, Pleasantville. The company and the gossip of Prairie City are not enough; in winter, they greatly expand their territory, driving seventy and eighty miles on narrow country blacktop every day, drinking twenty, thirty cups of coffee. And at every place, they repeat their mannered entrance, a slow and cautious easing into a restaurant booth, as if their backs were badly wrenched. Settled in the booths, nearly smiling, they push their cap bills back. After they've stared out the window for a long moment, arms folded, hunched over their coffee as if to get its heat, they shift slightly toward the middle of the table, bring their heads slowly around and say: "Well, what's goin' on in Colfax . . . Mitchellville . . . Newton . . . today?"

This same kind of gathering takes place in other parts of the country, other regions, especially in the South, but there's none of the Southern oral tradition here. These men do not come together to compete with their finest stories. Escape, diversion, the drawing in of others are inherent in the art of the Southern lie. But these Midwestern farmers seem to have exactly the opposite motive. They practice an inquiring journalism, compared with the Southerners' flowing fiction, gathering facts about the methods of labor, the movement of land, not looking to escape their working lives but, rather, getting even nearer to them.

And they want no author's credit. The Midwesterner gives his information, then backs away from it, backs and covers:

"The way *I* get it, Max's gonna make himself about ten thousand dollars by saying no yesterday and yes today."

"You mean Bidwell raised his price on that piece a land ten thousand from yesterday?"

"Yep." Then quickly: "But now, that's just the way I got it. Don't misunderstand, this is just what I heard."

By late morning, the local men are back in Prairie City, having bartered the region's news. Deaths. Auctions. Acres gained and acres sold. Stories of fate and cunning from throughout Jasper County and beyond, sorted by noon of every winter day. What's the news? Gotta run. Zoom. Monroe to Baxter. Halpern sold his cattle? What'd he get? Slurp. Catch ya later. Baxter to Colfax. Halpern sold his cattle. Lost his ass. Davidson held out? Be damned. Wylie died? The hell he did, uh, no more for me, honey, I gotta get home. Zoom. Colfax to farm on 117. I'll just stop in for a second. You hear Willie Wilson dropped dead? Dead as dung. Yesterday. Better get home. Zoom. Little wonder a small town's weekly paper has no chance to print news.

A dusty wind blows through town, exerting new weather that has taken some of what's worst of all the seasons. The dust blows uncontested through town, more seriously in the country. Its source is the fields, those fall-plowed fields that have received no covering snows and are literally being lifted and scattered to the air. The late-autumn obsession to work at something, anything, as the weather remained so brutally fine, has come back as crisis. The topsoil is flowing up until it is air and the effect, as one looks out at the countryside, is a smudging of the horizon. Of all things upon which one can no longer rely, who'd have thought the very horizon might ultimately fail? Even when the earth was a cube, people's ultimate faith was in the horizon; it told them when to turn. It was out there, clean and inviolate. Now the line has been smeared and if you look to the edge, focus on the startling indistinction, it can cause you almost to sway and stumble.

In fact, Iowa has lost almost half its topsoil in the past one hundred years and now, where it had once run fifteen, twenty feet deep, there remains over the state only six to eight inches, and some of that is at the moment evaporating like steam.

When the topsoil leaves, the veinous reservoir of subsoil moisture leaves with it. There's no truly accurate way to gauge the depth of subsoil moisture. Conditions activate it, call it up, but it's clear that there's dangerously little of it left, and that there'll be less still if its lid continues to blow away on winter wind.

Of course, the farmer can choose not to work his soil so fully. But he's something of a victim of his cultural concern for appearance. From the road, his farm must look trimmed and tended. Black, black earth exactly striped with living green. At least as clean as his neighbors'; cleaner, if possible. His meticulousness resists a new farming concept that's come down from the scientists in agricultural schools, Iowa State University and others, and from equipment developers. It's called no-till farming, and one of its goals is the preservation of soil. With new equipment, new chemicals, a new philosophy applied, the farmer can virtually drill his spring seeds into the ground, shoot them on a strong stream of air down through ground that has not been significantly moved since it thawed. There's no plowing, no disking, no real turning at all. An elaborate historic rhythm of preparation is rendered merely aesthetic; no-tilled fields look after planting nearly as they looked before any machinery moved over them. Corn and soybeans lie beneath a hard crust snarled and matted with last year's stalks and vines. Then fertilizers and weed killers are applied, exactly over the plants, clearing slender growth paths, leaving the rest of the field in a state of firm, entwined neglect. The crust, strengthened further by root systems, holds against wind, keeps topsoil in place.

The scientists insist that farmers must, more than ever, envision their fields cubically. How long is this field? How wide? And now, most critically, how deep? But no-till farming has two strong disadvantages slowing its acceptance. It is ugly. And it is easy. Recently, in a radio interview, an Iowa State agronomist admitted his informal research shows many Iowa farmers were reluctant to try no-till farming not only because they feared their fields would look like the fields of lazy men but because they were at heart uncomfortable with its simplicity. They were resisting the obsolescence of methods that acquire with time an individual grace, a man's signature on his work. They were dubious of a process that seemed to take from their work a good deal of its craft, much of its memory, some of its soul.

Younger farmers, naturally, have been more accepting,

the agronomist said. They see that no-till farming, fast and minimal, makes it possible to plant a huge number of acres during the very brief germinating season. No matter how much land one must plant, the work ideally must get done within two weeks in late April or early May, when the soil temperature has ideally risen. Some new farmers, fresh from their texts, recite a litany of exact haste: For every day after May 15 you've not finished planting, you lose one bushel per acre per day. So any farmer with a taste for further acquisition of land looks eagerly to no-till methods. Others are caught between satisfying habit and the hard evidence for change, evidence that's not easy to ignore in this freezing dust, when a farmer inhales his mistakes.

In his men's shop, on the north side of the square, Dick Vroom sits among his mistakes. Last summer, he ordered an optimistically large stock of winter goods. Snow has not come. He surveys his inventory, coats, slacks, boots and overshoes, especially boots and overshoes, and curses the mild winter. This is his sixth year at D and L Clothing, and his worst.

"You need about three hard snows between November fifteenth and December fifteenth to make your season. Especially your overshoe season. If you don't sell 'em before December fifteenth, you got 'em. People figure they can wait out the winter, can't be too much more coming, or they can make what they got last another month or so."

He sits at his desk at the back of the store, arms folded, rubbing his biceps, his Cardinal barstool posture. Paralyzed ease. You almost expect him to slide an empty Budweiser bottle forward, reaching at the same time into his billfold for a neatly creased dollar bill, folded *exactly* in half. "'Nother one here." He sits at his desk in defiance of accusations he's come to expect from some of his customers. "Nothing burns me more'n some union guy earnin' nine dollars an hour, come in and say, 'By God, you sure as hell got it made. Must be nice to sit there on your ass all day.'" If there's one thing he dislikes more than merchandise returned, more than tennis-shoe weather in the month of overshoes, it is unions. When he talks about unions, he rubs the biceps as if he were preparing to polish it. "If they're that stupid, let 'em be." Bastards. Rub. Damn dumb weather.

"What happens, weather like this, people drive to Des Moines or Newton to shop. Worse the weather, better it is for your local businessman. He hasn't got a chance in weather like this. You count on winter, cold, roads get bad, people stay home. This year, out of town to shop *every* night. I watch 'em heading out of town. Highway's packed. Or they *stay* in Des Moines if they work there." He looks around his store, piles of clothes new-shipment tall, most of his season still in stacks. This was a men's store before Vroom bought it, but he's so radically remodeled that it's hard to believe he owns the same space. For years, Bert Van Haalen owned it. He sold to Vroom in 1969, retired, died a few years ago. For all the years Bert ran his business, he disturbed the interior as little as possible, and the long dark room gave off a woolen mustiness. It had a high ceiling and a bare wooden floor that creaked and gave like a sponge in spots. At the back was a wood-burning stove and beside it a hard wooden bench where Bert's shoe customers sat, and where Bert napped when there were no customers. He often left the store to play cards in the back of Shorty Vanderzyl's feed store, or at the Odd Fellows hall. But business went on. People entered, waited for their eyes to dilate and called: "Bert, you here?" If silence was returned, they went to the counters and the drawers, rummaged for what they needed, left Bert money and a note, made change from the cash register. There was no time lost if they helped themselves; the rest of the town knew Bert's inventory method as well as he did. They knew there was no method.

That's not quite true. In fact, his method of stocking was merchandising eloquence, ultimate efficiency. He waited for his wholesaler to unload a delivery, then built a crate around the pile wherever it had been left.

If Bert was in his store and helped with a sale, he'd wrap whatever was purchased—shoes, shirts, coats, regardless of shape and size—with brown paper from a big roll. He tied it all up in heavy white cord, which he whipped expertly around the goods, and finished it all with a tight knot. He sighed, "Ah," as he pulled the knot and clipped the cord. Bert's goods as they left his store looked like packaged meat from John the Butcher. Local shoppers with bundles in their hands may have been carrying, for all one could tell, a pair of shoes or five pounds of ground round.

When Dick Vroom bought the store, he changed every measurement but its length. He lowered the ceiling drastically, took down the ceiling fan lights, installed fluorescent tubes front to back. He papered and paneled, carpeted, literally built a new, smaller, bright and modern rectangle within the impractical dimensions of Bert's musty alley. That is to say, he ruined the store.

"Bad year up and down the street," Vroom says. "Trav, Charls. Same thing." Cryptic mumbles. Don't need a sentence; phrase'll do. "New people in town? Don't help the local man. Thing is, Prairie City's in a bad spot. Des Moines on one side of it, Newton on the other. Now, you put Prairie City up in northern Iowa, town this size'd be a business center. Nothing big around it. Here, it's a little town stuck between two big ones." He looks out at the damnable sky, high and clear and blue, only a soiled edge at the bottom. "Can't sell seventy-dollar insulated boots in this weather."

Before he became a clothier, Vroom lived here and worked for the Hormel meat company in its Des Moines office, "bookkeeping and accounting work." He was called one morning to a meeting with his boss and was told that Hormel was leaving Des Moines, tha he had a job if he wished it at the company's plant in suburban Minneapolis. He had the remaining days of the week in which to decide. Vroom went home, told his wife, and for three days they talked. At one point, they gave their decision to a dime. Heads, Minneapolis. Tails, Prairie City. After one hundred flips, they'd left for Minnesota fifty-one times, stayed forty-nine and decided a dime gave unreliable advice.

Vroom had always been uncomfortable with a supervisor at his shoulder and the time seemed appropriate to look for some business of his own. He bought Van Haalen's Men's Clothing. He had only himself to employ, so there was little chance his work force would unionize.

Bert Van Haalen's orientation lecture was brief and practical. He reduced the sum of his wisdom from a long life in retailing to a recognition of two pre-eminent needs. He passed them on to Vroom, with the tools he'd used to meet them. "Here's the tin can," Bert said, "when you need to take a piss. And," nodding to the wooden bench by the stove, "here's the pillow."

Vroom believed that his business would grow as the town grew. He looked to the surrounding farms and constructed a private demography. He saw farmers who were sixty and seventy years old, would soon retire, move to town or die, and he believed that much of their land would then be released from its history. Some of it would open up, let the town out, and Prairie City would spread, its population growing in time to perhaps twenty-five hundred. Enough people to keep local shops prosperous.'

But his prophecy has stalled. The encircling farmers have remained healthy; their land has remained fields. There's little to do now but wait. Vroom still believes his vision valid, even if stubborn good health has slowed it. It seems that nearly everything has acquired for him a deeper implication of money gained or lost. He looks to the skies for overshoes, looks to the farms and imagines an actuarial flow. There also seems in his attitude the expectation of a return on his invested loyalty. He deliberately chose this place, not a city job with the Hormel packing company, and Prairie City has an obligation to repay him. "Can't get over these local people who've never set foot in this place. Or if they do, it's for some small item. They call you up at five fifteen when their kids need a new pair of tennis shoes for the game that night. But for their big items, like your leisure suit, they go to Des Moines. When people want something good, they figure the local man doesn't have it. Makes it more special, I guess, to go to Des Moines for your new coat than to get it here." He rubs his arm to a high gloss.

Bright lights outline Rip and Hazel Perry's low, white house, formalizing Christmas. The Perrys have strung rows of red and green lights across their rooftop, down its sides, along its overhanging lip, have trimmed their doors and their windows and the corners of their house. Lights blaze like vine rows of some garish winter fruit. The Perrys are not always the first to decorate for Christmas, but they decorate with absolutely no restraint. Lights and wreaths and candles and climbing electric script. Every year their house seems certain to collapse under the weight of their spectacular excess.

A few days after the Perrys', other houses bloom, and some businesses. A huge red star shines from the bank's marquee. On the square, a few of the merchants' windows are trimmed in small, twinkling lights, and some of them have placed decorations inside their stores. In the Please 'U', Snub or Pam has made pine-needle wreaths that look like tiny birds' nests, dropped half a candy cane inside each one, and placed a wreath atop every napkin dispenser on the horseshoe counter. ("Damn, Snub, you went all out on your decorations this year." "I'da done more," Snub says, "but I been so damn busy I ain't been able to decide which ashtray to empty first.")

Next Saturday morning, Santa Claus will come to the center of the park with Christmas sacks—peanuts and apples and hard candy. The town's volunteer firemen spend a long night stuffing the sacks in the fire station, passing around insults and beer. Last year, there were complaints heard in the park that Santa had visited Prairie City in an austere mood, that his sacks contained little more than "peanuts, with once in a while an old apple." Some of the firemen, hearing the complaint and knowing well the quantity of beer that had been needed to keep them warm, said that the children were just damn lucky that Santa hadn't accidentally left empty beer cans in their Christmas sacks.

Several Christmas parties have been scheduled for the private rooms at the Cardinal Inn: the bank staff, the employees at Kent Feeds, Bert Breen's construction crews. Jim Billingsley has already hosted one party, for the faculty and staff of the school, the first time an administration has sanctioned any party in a local place where only one wall separates teachers from liquor. Jim was surprised and pleased when the superintendent called and he quietly informed Betty that the teachers' Christmas party would be served flawlessly, and it was. These parties are for Jim a form of personal reply. He says, "I'll lose money on a party just to show people I can do one."

There were nearly sixty people, too many for a party room, so Jim rearranged his place, kept his regular beer drinkers in the small room on the west side of the building, gave te teachers the main bar and dining area.

"They were brought in through a side door, so they wouldn't even have to see the beer cases and the kegs," Jim explained. All the bar signs were turned off, all the lights but the dimmed, low-hanging Old Milwaukee Tiffany-patterned lights. Tables were placed end to end and set intermittently with Christmas candles and with Betty's favorite Bicentennial place mats and napkins. Everyone remarked at how lovely the long tables looked, how intimate the room felt.

"We didn't push any drinks on 'em," Jim said. "Half of them didn't even notice the bar, since it was all dark, and if they wanted a drink, they had to come to the bar and ask for it."

As if to provide an antidote to parties at the Cardinal, the Faith Baptist Church has scheduled a week of evangelism. Brother Buel Limey, direct from nights of celebrated faith with congregations in Rochester, Indiana, has come to preach. Among the congregations of Prairie City, the Baptists are its perennial students. They carry to their small white church Bibles heavily underscored and annotated. Brother Limey travels a circuit of small towns, like a pioneer preacher of the Old West. He wears on his feet high-heeled cowboy boots, vines of dazzling color winding up their sides. Brother Limey's boots have been prescribed by his doctor to support a surgically weakened back. Nevertheless, he's not about to ignore a prop:

"When Jesus calls those of us who have been saved, the Bible tells us that he will say, 'Ride with me to heaven. Ride on white horses!'" Brother Limey, smiling, bends to slowly raise his pants leg. "Beloved," he says, "I am ready to *ride!*" Vines of salvation climb nearly to his knees.

Hoop Timmons has begun his hibernation. He has thoroughly cleaned his silos, swept and shoveled, brought down in the elevator buckets of concrete scraps. He sits in his four-by-eight-by-six plywood box, a man at deserved rest after a long season of sloppy house guests. He peers out at the cold, quiet streets, so recently chaotic with lines of grain. "Not much bein' sold," Hoop says. "Farmers are holdin' on, waitin' for higher markets. I look for some activity after the first of the year." He is not completely idle. As if to get a head start, he's begun to mourn next season's failure. "Won't be no harvest next year. No rain. Lookit the air right now. Soil'll just keep blowin', blow worse in the spring. I predict a famine. It's just a matter of your cycles. We're due. Common sense. Like ol' Tom Paine wrote: *Common Sense*, right? The *Farmer's Almanac* says next year's gonna be the grand-daddy of 'em all. Europe caught it this year. It's comin' over. We'da had it last year if we hadn't got those two rains at just the *exact* right time." His library shelf holds more than the *Farmer's Almanac*. He reaches for a paperback, *The Boys of Summer*, biographies of Brooklyn Dodgers who played in the 1950s and nearly always lost in autumn to Hoop's beloved New York Yankees. Except for 1955, when the Dodgers beat the Yankees in a classic World Series. "I took that loss awful hard," Hoop says, grimacing as if he'd just watched the final pitch. He has obsessively loved the Yankees nearly all his life, began to follow them when Gehrig was in decline. Now, with a winter on his hands, he reads avidly of one of the few years when they lost.

A few days ago, Wilbur Van Engen, standing with a customer in his grocery store, dropped to his knees with a pain he believed to be the knife edge of a heart attack. He raised up, gray as dusk, and walked from his store unaided. It was not, tests showed, a heart attack but something building up in his blood, something less immediately threatening, more permanently trouble. As if, Prairie City said, Van hadn't trouble enough. Nearing Christmas, signs of surrender are in his grocery store. Newly stocked shelves look as if they'd been picked by vandals. Word has spread that Jim Billingsley visited Van with words of sympathy and an offer to buy.

Some of the other businesses are abbreviating their hours, not to economize but because it gets dark early. McKlveen Lumber and others with work requiring sunlight quit in winter at five o'clock, back a black half hour from five thirty.

At the cement plant, Hank Ostlin has imposed his more severe reductions. He can pour no concrete when the air quickly freezes it, so Hank pares his work force, retaining only his office staff and his senior foremen until the ground thaws and the temperature warms. He pays the men he must lay off the difference between their salaries and the unemployment check they seasonally collect.

As a wealthy businessman due some rest and sun, Hank will leave for Arizona in three weeks. As mayor, he has made his first appointment. For city clerk, Ken Birkenholtz, a young lawyer, a native, practicing privately from an office at the northwest corner of the square. Dick Vroom had investigated the city clerk's job, but withdrew when he heard that Birkenholtz had applied. "I figured that's all there was to that. Ken's dad is Lyle. Lyle works for Hank. That about wraps it up. Real neat and tidy."

Many have wondered why Birkenholtz would choose to start here in his small home town. The rule that says one takes professional matters to another town assumes even more strength when the local man is, will always remain in memory, a boy fresh from high school: Kennie Birkenholtz, son of Lyle, south of town. So Ken's work has been as he'd expected: slow and narrow. A few deeds, some tax returns; plenty of coffee at the Please 'U'. But now he'll pay the city's bills, send its monthly utility statements, handwritten on carbon forms; keep the pink slip, send back the white. Personally delivered in rubber-banded stacks to Joe Sparks in the post office, two doors north.

Joe has seen his private sign of the season, his Christmas robin. Russ Danley's booze has come and been ritualistically passed, postmaster to box holder. Russ Danley's booze comes every year, a Christmas gift from a distant relative, brightly wrapped in its unmistakably shaped box: tall, slender, shining and not what it appears. It is not liquor at all, but a gift packaged in a discarded liquor box. In his first Christmas season as postmaster, Joe gave Russ the package, smiled, said, "Here's your booze, Russ."

Danley took the line. "Thanks, Joe, I've been waiting." Others, eavesdropping, took the line, too, out the door, and soon Russ Danley, deacon of the Christian Church, was reported to be receiving liquor through the mails.

People still send Christmas cards here, so Joe and Bob Bowen sift and sort like Las Vegas tellers for three weeks. Stacks of cards drop through the PRAIRIE CITY mail slot. On Joe Sparks's side, a cardboard box catches the mail. Plop. For three weeks in December, Joe needs a bigger box. "Joe, I think I put the wrong box number on Frank and Erma's card. Could you check?"

Joe bends to the box, sifts for Frank and Erma. "Yeah. Should be seventy-five. Wanna change it?" He hands it back. There. Seventy-five. And back through the slot, officially remailed. Plop.

Bright plastic stars and Santa Claus faces hang from wires that run to the center of the park. They swing pendulously in the wind, ornaments and weather vanes. People are seen less and less on the streets, scurrying from door to door like figures on a Swiss clock. The air hurts terribly now, cuts like a poisonous smoke in the lungs. In the absence of snow, a crystalline frost, a fur, covers almost every surface, not only the roofs and the black branches, the streets and light poles but, microscopically, blades of grass, pebbles, runneled vines.

Jim closes the Cardinal early on Christmas Eve. He pours drinks through the hours after work, through dinner, through early evening, offering the men in town a place to come "and get out of Momma's way while she's cookin' for Christmas." But at nine o'clock, December 24, he moves to his door with his ring of keys, crowded as a charm bracelet; each key a charm; each charm a building. "Comin' home on Christmas Eve drunked up; there's not much worse a man can do to his family," he says. "If a fella wants to get drunk, he's gonna. But it won't be in my place. I send nobody home drunk on Christmas Eve."

By seven, nearly everyone is gone. Leaving, in a resonant quiet, Vern, from the factory, and Jack, a construction man who travels all week, comes home Friday nights to his trailer in the north end, but comes first to the Cardinal and drinks vodka as if the idea had come to him about a hundred miles up the road.

Leaving Larry, whose wife, more than eight months pregnant, has not for some time been able to ease his urges; urges whose only relief has been "to just keep movin' around and not touch anything even half soft."

Leaving Jim, and Betty, and leaving me behind the bar.

I've asked Jim for a night of work and he's obliged me. Since October, when Hoop and I shared the harvest, I've wanted to take an active part again in Prairie City. Jim, without hesitation, invited me behind his bar, showed me the landscape, turned me loose. In truth, his is an easy bar to serve, because his customers' preferences rarely run beyond two ingredients in one glass at the same time, and most often, only one: beer. Bud, cold, in a can, "you can keep your glass." So tending calls for little more than remembering the order in which various labels lie, like stockpiled ammunition, in the long, low cooler butt-high behind me: Olympia, Pabst, Schlitz, Budweiser, Old Milwaukee. In another cooler, a few cans of the residual flavors: Hamm's, Miller's, Falstaff, and an Iowa beer, sweet and heavy, Pickett's of Dubuque.

Today I've watched the place progress through its distinctive hours, from late afternoon to this moment: three men spaced along the bar, and the room's accompanying quiet.

Larry stands to leave, drains his Old Milwaukee. He looks sullen as he pays me, speaks from the cellar of a bad cold: "You drivin' east tonight? 'Cause if you are, watch out for the patrol. I seen about six of 'em between here and Newton on the way home from work."

I thank him, wish him health.

"And I see our local cop hidin' in the weeds at the edge of town, too." He shakes his head scornfully. "So be careful." And he leaves.

Earlier, I'd faced a solid line that ran, left to right: factory worker, factory worker, farmer, feed salesman, auto-body repairman, farmer, farmer, Saint Bernard. Lyle Birkenholtz had brought his son's dog with him, and the Saint Bernard stood, paws on counter, claiming no more space than was due him, blinking from the smoke. From my vantage, he fit into the row of drinkers. A little quieter and more respectful than the others, perhaps; more hair, a really extraordinary tongue.

"Damn dog just stood there like he was waitin' on a pizza to go," Jim says from the kitchen. He laughs.

"There's a dog in here?" asks Jack.

"Berkie's Saint Bernard. Stood right there two stools from where you are."

"What'd he do?" asks Jack.

"What'd he do? He watched Berkie drink his drink is what he did. I wish some others that come in here had his manners."

"Hell, I should go get *my* dog," Jack says. "He's out in the pickup." Jack waits, as if for permission, and from the kitchen comes a reverberant silence. Permission denied. Jack tips his hard hat back on his head, his face below it lined as the palm of a hand. He's a small, wiry man, and looks as hard as the stone he moves for wages. "One more here," he says. "My dog's about the smartest thing I've ever seen. Smarter than my damn *kid*. I'll tell you that, by God." He chases the comparison with a shot of vodka. "That dog'll do anything you tell him. He just sits there in the seat with me, lookin' out, lookin' over at me. He'll do anything. Come. Go get this. Go get that. He's out there in the pickup now, just waitin' for me. Probably asleep." Jack drinks. His round eyes grow with pride.

Vern, three stools away, has just begun to listen. "Is that a person you're talkin' about?" he says, "and if it is, is it a *woman?* If it *is* a woman, I'd like right here and now to put down a deposit on it. Sounds like hell on square wheels to me."

"No, hell, my *dog*," Jack says, "I'm talkin' about my dog. He's out in the pickup, waitin' for me, and he's the smartest damn thing I know. Smarter than my kid, for sure." Vodka chaser.

"You got a dog smarter than your kid?" Vern asks.

"For sure," Jack says.

Vern shakes his head. "Well, in that case, I'd say you better git your dog an agent or your kid off the streets. One or the other."

"By God, you hit it *exactly!*" Jack shouts and pounds the counter with his palm. "That's the whole damn thing. My kid's out runnin' around somewhere and I ain't got a *clue* where. He don't listen to a thing I tell him. You can *hit* him, you can knock him on his ass, and he'll just *look* at ya, not say a damn word. He won't talk back or nothing. Just looks at ya. Then he goes out, stays out all hours, never know where he is. That's why I say: My dog's smarter than he is. Look at tonight. It's cold as hell. He's out somewhere, walkin' around, and my dog's asleep in my pickup cab with the heat on. Now, I ask you: Who's smarter?"

Vern had assumed Jack's humor was light; now he sees otherwise.

"Hey," he says, "I'm sorry. I didn't mean to make fun, really."

This seems to embarrass Jack. Vodka. Vodka. Ice dregs. "One more here." He adjusts his hard hat. "No. That's all right. Shit, I guess I can't expect my kid to have any brains. I ain't much for brains myself . . . I could have gone to college, too. They offered me baseball scholarships. Several of 'em did. But what the hell would I do with that? I didn't want to go to college. . . . I was purty good in history, and all that, but I couldn't get that math. Or English. Or speech." Vern nods in time to Jack's despairing hymn.

Jack says, "I remember when we had to read *Hamlet* in high school. Lord in heaven. I never met a soul in my life could make a damn bit of sense of that *Hamlet*. Any of that Shakespeare. And that math. . . . I don't think they make you take that stuff in college now." Vodka. "But at *least*, god damn it," and he slams his hand down hard, his frustration as close as skin, "at *least* I got sense enough to stay in the house when it's fuckin' freezing." Vodka. Vodka.

Jack is silent for a time. Vern continues to stare at him with a fixed sympathy. Jack turns suddenly to me. "How about you? You as smart as *your* dad is?" he says.

I'm not sure what Jack means, but before I can say anything, he adds, "You know, your dad's one of the smartest men in this town. I've heard 'em talking in here about him working at the factory. They say he's the one that makes it work. They could fire all the rest of 'em and keep him. That's what I've heard 'em say."

Vern works in the factory and any talk of sweeping dismissals, even empty whiskey talk, straightens him up. Yet he feels he must agree, for my sake, and offers tempering praise: "Hey," he says, "your dad's a good man. He's on top of it, no question. I'll kiss a fat man's ass if he ain't."

Jack tosses his drink to the back of his throat, wipes his mouth with the back of his hand. He burps silently. He gets up, waves, and says anomalously, "Merry Christmas."

Leaving Vern, and the room. "Tarbender," Vern says and pushes his beer glass, opaque with his fingerprints, forward. Behind him, through the Cardinal's windows, is Christmas Eve. Although it's early, Vern has been able to get in four hours of Schlitz and is threatening Jim's holiday policy. He takes the glass, lifts it to his lips and when he puckers, the seams in his face appear to flow toward the glass.

"Well," he says, "I plan to wake up tomorrow morning, burn me an egg, cremate some bacon. Go back to bed. Get up in the afternoon and do it all over again." He drinks, and Camel smoke furls about him. "I'll tell ya," he says. "Listenin' to that ol' boy just now talk about his kid—hey, it's tough. I remember."

I assume he's recalling his own hard childhood. He's not.

"I had five kids, myself, when I left. Good kids. Tough as boiled hell. They *were*, anyway. What I mean is, they were good the last I seen 'em."

This sounds like an invitation. So I ask, "When was that?"

"Five years ago. I left five years ago . . . and I'll tell ya, like the fella says, 'I been blue, I been due, I been lost in Waterloo, but I never been much sorry I been gone.'"

"Does that fella work at the factory?" I ask, smiling at the lyricist across the bar. Vern laughs. He looks quickly over his shoulder. He drinks and his seams run into the foam.

"No, seriously," he says, "I stuck it out for eighteen years. I was married eighteen years. Well, what I mean, I suppose I still *am* married, if you come right down to the technicals of it, but what I mean, I was *with* her eighteen years. And I never drank at all around her, what I mean, not a drop. And she was always naggin' me about no money. We ain't makin' it. We got no money. We got nothin' for the kids. Shit! I was workin' my *ass* off. I mean, I was workin' like a nigger for neck bones, but she never was satisfied.

"So, one night, I said, 'Ah, the hell with it,' and I went out and got drunk. And you know what? I liked it. I liked it a lot. It made me feel a whole lot better than sitting in the kitchen, sippin' coffee, while she ticked off a list of my recent failures. I'll tell ya that. So I did it some more. She was real religious, see, and when I started drinkin', she lit into me till sideways from Tuesday." He pushes his glass to me.

"So you never think about going back?"

"Naw." And softly, "I'd just get mad." He swings around on his stool and stares for several seconds beyond the room, through the window. He says, "My oldest boy, damn, he was a scrapper like *my* father. You'd knock my boy down, hell, you could col'cock the kid and he'd get up and just stare back at ya. Kid had more guts than a government mule." Vern laughs, full of pride. "I'd like to see 'em, with their mom, in the house. . . . Wish I had a picture."

I imagine a family posed: mother, seated centrally, children around her. "You'd like a picture of them?" I ask. "Sure, I can understand that."

"No—" Vern says, "of the *house*. I wisht I had a picture of my house. I had a fine house. Had a basement, a full basement. It had ten-inch-thick walls."

In the kitchen, Betty scrapes the grill. Jim stocks the huge storage coolers for a full day of business on the 26th.

Vern says, "Tarbender." Then, "You know anybody wants to buy a camper?"

"What camper—yours? You want to sell it now?"

A few months ago, Vern had planned to repair it for the ride away from this town. Now he wants to sell his horse.

"I got a letter from my brother the other day," Vern says. He leans toward me, speaking so low that I lean forward to hear him. We look like bookends. "He figures if we can get a little cash between us, we can get down to Oklahoma, to the oil fields down there, and we can buy into a drillin' operation. I guess they got a lot of wildcatters down there still looking for a quick bunch of money, so they give out shares, what I mean, shares, in return for usin' your money to drill. And if it comes through for ya, hey. Hey, it sure beats sweatin' for the beauty of it over there." He tosses his head toward the factory across the highway. "So, let me know. You hear anybody wants to buy a camper, let me know."

"I'll let you know."

He nods firmly, as if we've completed business.

Not only his language and his denim but almost everything else about him seems to come out of an earnest fidelity to the Old West—prospecting, wildcatting for oil—a kind of self-destructive outlaw independence; an esteem for hand-to-hand violence.

Vern's genealogy, too, could have been written by Louis L'Amour. His paternal grandfather, he says, was a Kansas farmer, better with land than with people. One day Vern's grandfather looked up from his work and saw dust, then horses, coming out of the sun. Minutes later, he'd been charged by a posse with horse stealing, had been tried, convicted and sentenced to hang from the elm that bordered his field. Vern's father, sixteen years old, watched the sentence carried out, and later, after the posse had left, he cut the dangling body from the branch. Vern's father had listened for names, and he remembered faces. Within two weeks of the hanging he had shot and killed all three members of the posse. He fled Kansas, never returned, and lived for years in the Oklahoma Indian nation. He married an Indian, fathered several children, half-brothers and half-sisters Vern has never seen, and when his Indian wife died, he left and roamed Oklahoma, working several jobs under several names. In a small border town near the Texas line, he met and married a second wife, Vern's mother, and for the rest of his life, many years and miles from Kansas, he more or less settled down. In time, when he looked up from his work to see rolling dust clouds, it came to mean merely poverty approaching.

Vern speaks of his father with pride and fondness. He admires most of all the methodical revenge, sometimes moves a step back from the Cardinal's bar, looks at the stools with white hate and kills three of them, drawing from his hip as he imagines his father did. The father was a big, large-boned man, Vern says, hard but fair, and if you pleased him, he'd smile fleetingly and say, "You ain't got the balls of a house cat." If you displeased him, he'd knock you down.

"Tarbender." I reach for his glass. "No," he says, "I think I'll have a shot of Southern Comfort."

Vern is ready for bed. At the end of a drinking evening, he often orders a shot of Southern Comfort, sweet, viscous and, for Vern, a chemist of long experience, unfailingly sedative after beer. It's become nearly ritual: Vern, Schlitz-filled, orders a shot of Southern Comfort. Jim pours and slides it forward, saying, "Good night, Vern." Within fifteen minutes, Vern's head begins slowly to fall like a curtain.

Vern knocks back the Southern Comfort.

"Good night, Vern."

"Merry Christmas," Vern says. "Merry Christmas. . . . Mer-ry Christ-mas." His eyes have begun to blink like an owl's; one, then the other, the lid held for several seconds. "Now, this is probably—you may not even believe this and I wouldn't blame ya if ya didn't, but there was a time in my life when I was thinkin' about being a minister. And I still *do* know something about the Bible." His eyes close for what seems a full minute. In repose, his face shows more animation than the faces of most people when they're actively conversing, every tic a long tributarial journey.

His eyes closed, he says, "It's like, you can lose the faith, but the faith don't lose track a' you."

He opens his eyes as wide as he can and says suddenly, "He divided the sea, and caused them to pass through; and He made the waters to stand as a *heap*. In the daytime, He led them with a cloud and all the night with a light of fire." His voice is very soft and he says, quoting more loosely now, "But they still doubted God, and they spoke against Him. So you know what God did?" Vern returns to the sobriety of verse, "He destroyed their vines with hail, and their sycamores with frost. He gave up their cattle also to the hail, and their flocks to hot thunderbolts." Vern nods. "He nailed 'em good. He always nails ya good. He'll col'cock ya." Vern smiles proudly. His Lord is tough as boiled hell. His Lord has got more guts than a government mule.

Vern gets to his feet to leave and his arms are spread, pulpit width, on the bar. Jim comes from the kitchen with the benediction: "Gonna be closin' it up, Vern."

"On my way, Jim." To me, he says, "So, it's for sure He's hailed on my vines. Hail. Hell. Go to hell. Well, that's all right. I'd rather go to hell than to heaven, anyway." An owl's wink. "At least they got plenty of hot fire in hell so you can heat your frozen pizzas." Vern waves to Jim and Betty, holds his arm in the air. "You take care," he says to me.

"Merry Christmas, Vern."

"Hey. Merry Christmas, back at ya." Vern lives no more than three or four minutes from here, has perhaps six or seven minutes left. Time enough so that he's perfectly ambulatory and losing quickly his coordination. The front door gives him a moment of trouble. He pulls, but it fails to open. Jim comes up and unlocks it, but Vern doesn't notice the keys jangling, the quick clockwise turn. He pulls a second time, steps through, waves again. He doesn't seem to notice the temperature or the night.

Merry Christmas.

I lie for several minutes with last night in my head and a retailer's aching in my feet. It's nearly nine o'clock and I wonder if Vern has risen for his first cremated meal, if he feels this morning as if his Lord has col'cocked him.

Through the thin strip of Christmas between my shade and sill, I can see the weather—gray, cold, gusty. There are loose, hard bits of snow, wind-scattered, making broad white streaks on the ground.

I'll drive soon to the farm to eat breakfast and exchange gifts. Later, aunts, uncles, and cousins will come from Colfax and Newton for more gifts and dinner. There won't be as many people as there were when I was small and we drove on Christmas Eve to Colfax and slept— didn't sleep—in my Grandmother Evans' unheated upstairs bedrooms. We lay awake, all the cousins, listening through the night to grown-up voices coming up from the register in the middle of the floor.

"How does this railroad fit together?"

"Kenneth, you forgot a piece of the frontier fort."

Santa's elves, pushed to frenzy by their deadline.

We descended the stairs at dawn for a brief, agonizing wait in the kitchen while a family quorum gathered. Then were turned loose on the living room, where the presents waited. In minutes, pillage.

Now the day has moved to the farm; my mother has become the pivot of her family. Christmas begins at a later hour, is smaller, quieter, but there remains a firm resolve to keep its form and as much of its substance as possible. These days, that requires a will; my mother must work to preserve what had seemed in the past to have its own familial momentum.

Last night's clothes are piled on a chair in a corner of the room. From the pile, I smell the Cardinal, as if it's hidden beneath my clothes. Its cigarette smoke is woven like thread into the fabric of my shirt; its sweet fermented beer smell, stains on my jeans. My clothes smell like an old and filthy bar. I think: Snub as something deep-fried.

His brother, Boone, as meat. Leo B. as tractor grease. Me and beer and tavern smoke. I have a Prairie City work smell.

We need two tables just to hold the food, the kitchen table and a large square folding table in the dining room. Plates of turkey, slices of white meat coming off the carcass like thick pages; dark meat in hunks. Mashed potatoes, sweet potatoes in butter and brown sugar, dark-brown gravy, huge bowls of turkey dressing, dark, rich. Baked beans covered by slabs of bacon, plates of raw vegetables, several shades of olives, dishes of Mother's "bread-and-butter pickles," sweet as sin, with onion strands mixed in. Gelatin salads in pastel colors. Rolls from the Newton bakery, hot and vaporously fresh, fine for dinner, even better later tonight, with cold turkey slices in them. Cherry pies. Pumpkin pies.

With plates on trays, we all walk the cornucopia, settle around the dining-room table and on chairs in the den, the "TV room." The set plays football Muzak.

I'm certain that as Christmas has gotten smaller, the amount of food has grown, as if to fill family holes, and maintain the sense of a crowd. In fact, a recent history of the Evanses, all its mortal transitions, lies in the bounty surrounding us. Grandma Evans historically cooked the turkey, made gravy. Now Mother does, and much more. Aunt Mabel, Mother's only sister in a family of eight, has always made pies, her touch with cinnamon in pumpkin pie unduplicably precise. Her daughter, Judy, has made these, and if you'd never known her mother's, you'd think them unsurpassable. Aunt Mabel sits now at the end of the table, brought down for the day from a nursing home in Des Moines; she's thin and weak, mumbling inaudibly through the phlegm of long sickness. Her eyes bulge from a sunken face like a newly born bird's. I meet them, and smile, and they look at me from a place of pure clarity unblemished by the predicaments of speech.

"Everything is delicious," says Uncle Bob at my side.

"Fabulous!" says Aunt Pat, across the table.

"I can see I took too much, as usual," says my cousin Delmar.

Aunt Mabel's eyes dart wildly about, following the conversation. Her hair, chopped short, sticks straight out in places. Her hand shakes from the weight of food on her fork.

"I believe this is the best turkey we've ever had," Uncle Bob says. "I know I say that every year, but this is just delicious."

"Even the white meat. Usually, white meat's so dry, but this is *moist*."

"Say, these beans are good. Who brought the beans?"

Mabel has been the family's comic spirit, quick, sarcastic, warmly cynical, and acted as a court of final test. If someone new in the family passed Mabel's scrutinizing eye, there was a sense of verdict. On those frantic Christmas mornings in Grandma Evans' living room, she was Santa Claus, placing herself strategically near the tree, handing the presents around with a strict equanimity: "Quit grabbing, Nancy, or Santa will knock you in the head."

"Say, Mabe's doin' real good. Look at her clean her plate."

"She sure is. My, she was *hungry*."

"Doin' *real* good."

"Mmmmm," Aunt Mabel manages. "Deelishush." But I imagine her mind's words, something matching better her fiercely blinking eyes: "Don't use that patronizing baby talk with me, like I'm some deaf infant with chronic gas. Why *shouldn't* I be hungry? And I can still hear, and my mind is working today at least at half capacity, which makes me the equal of anybody I see at this table."

The day moves cautiously around her. For a moment, at the end of dinner, she's suddenly alone, as everyone rises, goes off to wash dishes, to nap, to let the food have its way in swollen stomachs. Still in her chair at the end of the table, weak from nourishment, she watches small nieces and nephews race past her, veering from a collision at the last instant. Her brothers, her in-laws, step gingerly past her, squeezing her shoulder, as if trying to knead into her some of their health. She continues to define the center of our Christmas, as we choreograph ourselves around her.

Her daughter, Judy, comes into the dining room, leans over. "Where would you like to be, Mom? In the kitchen with the girls? In the TV room?"

"The kitchen."

She's wheeled out, sits in a corner, in a new Christmas dress and pink slippers, her swollen ankles growing out of them. Late in the day, against halfhearted protests from the women, she mischievously gnaws at a popcorn ball.

"I hope you don't get sick!"

"That's awful hard for you to digest, Mabe."

All I'm able to say to her for the rest of Christmas is a strong and smiling, "Goodbye, Mabe. You take care, now," as she's lifted, wrapped in blankets, into the car for the ride back to Des Moines.

The house is quiet by eight. Dad sits in his huge leather recliner, feet up, head back, small as a child in its generous cushions. He looks as tired as he has a right to be. Mother, awake and working since four this morning, works still in the kitchen, stacking dishes, wrapping in foil food enough for a month of lunches.

"I hear things about you, Pop," I say, smiling.

"Oh, I suppose," he says. "Must be a pretty slow time for gossip around town if *my* name's floating. You know, they say anything gets around Prairie City in half an hour. . . . Didn't use to take that long when Les DeVilbis had his hardware store." He laughs, then says, "What'd you hear now?"

"I hear you could run the factory all by yourself."

"Ha!" He closes his eyes as he laughs, shakes his head, rubs it slowly against the leather cushions, like a dog enjoyably scratching. This is an ancestral itch. My Grandpa Bauer had nearly the same gesture, though his seemed more feline. "Well," Dad says, "I'll tell you, no more work than we've got over there right now, that's not sayin' a whole lot. I told a guy the other day, 'You know, we farm with a hoe here,' and Lord, they do. Scratch it out. I'd go about half nuts if it wasn't for the entertainment. But I get a kick out of just listening to those guys yap. I tell ya, they all got a story. It's like a soap opera over there every day." He closes his eyes again, rubs his head against the cushions, stretches in the chair. "That's what's so nice about the place, actually," he says, "after spending all spring in the fields . . . just being around some people."

Mother has always said that Dad could draw conversation from anyone, that he liked nothing more than to sit with men and float with the eddying talk. I've seen his gift, in the coffee shops, on the streets, and have seen how valuably it serves him. There's a constant responsibility, in a place this size, simply to converse. Everywhere a person pauses—grocery line, dentist's office, gas pump—there are people who have, most often, a shallow familiarity, an acquaintance, with his life. So nearly every encounter falls somewhere between the natural ease of friendship and the city freedom of silence. It requires conversation at a level of aimless interest. There's a delicacy in this: Too much interest, you're snooping; too little, you're rude, even moody. (There's no sympathy for moodiness. Especially in the personalities of merchants. I've heard, about a retailer who failed, and his wife: "I liked her, but he was awful moody sometimes.")

So the small-town personality speaks ideally with a tone stronger than duty, softer than inquiry. My father's personality. He says, "There just aren't too many places left a fella can go to *have* conversations unless it's at work. Hell, in the old days, it was Rosie's or the station during the day, and then, when Everett and Katherine ran the Tower, we'd all go there after Lions Club on Thursday night."

Rosie's was a tiny café, run by a small, gregarious man named Howard Rose. Don Sparks' Phillips 66 stood next door, the most socially popular filling station in town and known, consequently, simply as "the station," as though all the gasoline in Prairie City ran from Sparky's pumps. Both places are now corners of the Co-op gas station.

"Down at the Tower, we had everybody," he says wistfully. "Stevens, myself, Clarence Rowe, Schlosser. . . ." His closest friends in Prairie City, Keith Stevens and Bill Schlosser, have been dead for some time, and it occurs to me, as I think of him watching with amusement the transient factory men, that at the youthful age of fifty-six, he has no close male friends left here. "We'd fill the Tower up so you couldn't hear yourself. Some guys'd be playin' cards, shouting back and forth. Then Everett and Katherine'd get going behind the bar. He'd start telling some wild tale and she'd be over by the cooler. Somebody'd sure as hell start egging him on, telling him, 'Oh,

Everett, now I know you're lyin' to me,' and he'd get all huffed up and say, 'No, by God, I'm *not*. Ain't that right, Katherine?' 'Right, Everett,' she'd say. 'Right, Katherine?' 'Right, Everett.' Back and forth all night. 'Right, Katherine?' 'Right, Everett.' So we—Stevens and some of us—we'd see each other somewhere and say, 'Right, Katherine?' 'Right, Everett.'"

He chuckles. I imagine him fifteen, twenty years ago, sitting with his friends over bottles of beer, sharing private codes, and feel a sense of the boyishness that was still his then. In his voice just now was the airy tone of an athlete reminiscing.

Half his age, I must *return* to the places of my nostalgia. I have, it seems, lived in episodic blocks. In each block, a beginning, middle, end. I picture each short stretch and the whole takes a form, a tidy row of rectangles: Prairie City, College, First Work, Second Work, Prairie City. Each block self-contained and tightly thematic, each one rooted in a different place. Hardly nomadic, but each change accompanied by a relocation. Even this return has had from the beginning a certain closure built into the planning of it. And my memory, roaming freely through town, has been asked to work, gather all it can hold, and leave; a mercenary.

My father's life has been almost exclusively here, and he has chronologically stacked his episodes in the tight life box of Jasper County, Iowa. After high school, he stayed in Colfax, worked in a gas station, helped his father farm. A few years later, he bought a station from his future brother-in-law, and quickly became known as a businessman who'd accept as payment one's solemn promise to return soon with money. The time was the late 1930's. He drew the town's poorest citizens, and its lounging high school boys. The station foundered.

He worked as a rural mail carrier, drove the hills west

and north of Colfax. On dry days, in a 1938 Chevy. When it rained, the roads a brown paste, in a 1925 Model A, the mud car. 23.7 miles, 167 mailboxes. Delivering not only mail but food and messages from house to house. People stood in the morning by their boxes, waiting for him to come. He gave them mail. They gave him errands. Show this pheasant tail to Oleander. Ain't it something? Tell me tomorrow what he says about it.

He lived on his own route, and on Christmas Day 1942, thirty-three years ago, he sorted for himself a piece of mail he'd been expecting. "Greetings," it began. He delivered his draft notice to himself.

He returned from Fort Laramie, Wyoming, and joined his father at the Prairie City farm. Farming "was the easiest thing." He'd thought of working with airplanes: "There was a time in my life when I'd've *paid* to be around airplanes." And for a long while, the fascination held him, but it began to ease as the science of flight progressed from propellers to jets, and all the cadences of an airplane engine were reduced to the uninteresting purity of air taken in, air blown out. He'd always seen flight as the applicable limit of the conventional gasoline engine, the supremacy of levers and gears. The simple genius of the jet, on the other hand, "took all the fun out of it" for him. He saw no way to get a wrench on a plain stream of air.

And all of that happened, or was dreamed, within fifty square miles. He can trace nearly thirty years of his life along eight blocks of a two-lane highway as he drives from the farm to the factory. There's a depth, a dimension, in that frame of mind I had never understood. Many people here see their histories daily, have their pasts as neighbors; pass them; sit with them. I always regarded that kind of life as unadventurous, if not cowardly. Now I wonder where the greater courage lies, as I see my row of boxes and sense, in comparison, the weight of permanence.

Dad shifts in his huge chair. Leather squeaks beneath him. He says, "That's something else I've just never been able to get used to."

"What?"

"With farming. Being by myself all day. I get lonely as hell out there with no one to talk to. I guess a lot of farmers do. You know what they say, a farmer'll beat a rain to town.

"Now, Dad, *my* dad, was different. He loved to be out there by himself so he wouldn't have to talk to anybody. 'Course, he was so terribly shy. I take after your grandma, I guess. Lord, she'd rattle your head with her jabber."

He talks more of his work, and it takes me longer than it should to hear in my father's descriptions the harshest qualities of my own work. Isolation, patience, planting with no assurance of a crop. And as he talks, another voice comes through. I am sitting in the living room of the poet Wendell Berry. I've come to Port Royal, Kentucky, Berry's home, to interview him for a magazine piece I've been assigned.

Berry's part of Kentucky is breath-taking, gently mountainous and arboreally green in summer. Tobacco and cornfields. Detrital roads. The muddy Kentucky River running slowly just below Berry's white-frame house.

He's a tall, thin man. His face has a fixed, pinched look, as though he's squinted for years into the glare of something harsh and sustenant. Perhaps, among other things, the sun, for Berry also farms, and his poems and novels and essays celebrate the work and its privileged burdens.

We drink coffee from thick mugs. Below us, motorboats violate the sleepy river. Berry slouches in a chair, one long leg draped over its arm like a sleeping snake. And I pose a question, one I have formed on the drive out from Louisville, a smart-journalist kind of question that I am pleased with.

"Do you think of yourself," I ask, "as a writer who farms or as a farmer who writes?"

He takes a sip of coffee and looks out his window to the river, as if seeking the patience of its current. At last, he says, "Well, farming was the work I knew first. But, frankly, I'm not really interested in the distinction." Then, a more charitable gesture than he'll ever know, he smiles.

Dad says, "Buck Walker asked me the other day if I'd be interested in renting the farm. He stopped me on the street."

Buck Walker works at the lumberyard, has never farmed, as far as I know. "I didn't know Buck wanted to farm," I say.

"Not for himself," Dad says. "He was asking for young Thompson. They're big friends, you know. I guess he's looking—what's his name? Emmett. Emmett Thompson—I guess he's looking for some more land."

This news, offered casually, irritates me. I imagine every young farmer in the country eying the farm predatorily, see Buck Walker serving as liaison, making the cool, diplomatic probe. Prairie City has grown just large enough to justify mediation. Young Thompson doesn't know my father well enough to stop him on the street and say, "Hey, listen, Ken. Want to rent your farm?" He sends instead a middleman.

"What'd you tell him?" I know, on the other hand, that there's a certain validity, perhaps from Dad's view even a desirability, in the broker's question. For he has been publicly indecisive, has pondered aloud in groups of men what he might do with the half of farm now legally his:

buy his sister's half? Buy a small piece of hers, giving him that neat and even eighty? Sell his own? Rent it all? Certainly, any farmer still making his decision lays himself open to the farmer who's reached one—"All the land I can find and gather."

He says, "I told him I'd probably leave things for now. Go on, this year, at least, like it's been." He stretches in his chair, rubs his head against the cushions, seems to get smaller in them. Neither of us speaks for a few minutes, and that is all the time he needs to fall asleep. His head drops back and to one side, the light from the lamp casting white wax across his forehead and his cheeks.

O f the two highways, 117, north and south through town, is more the resident. For the distance it inhabits Prairie City, it has a local name—State Street. Highway 163, east and west, does not, has been historically "the highway," an important state road connecting the relatively large towns to the east of Prairie City—Pella, Oskaloosa—with the sprawl of Des Moines to the west. 117 has led nowhere but south toward the meager hill farms, north over bluffs to the edge of Colfax. Now, the proximity of Interstate 80 attracts more assorted traffic, but it remains in comparison a local road bearing local parades.

From my windows, I've learned to identify its various rhythms. Early-morning tractors, shifting through their power. Afternoon school buses, scattered to the corners of the district. A few times weekly, the echoing horn blasts of Verlin DeRaad's semi cab, as he returns from a cross-country haul and signals to his wife in their small brown-shingled house near the highway, like a pilot flamboyantly dipping his wings to loved ones on the ground. And, several times a week, it seems, shortly before or shortly after the lunch hour, a string of cars moving at the speed of mourning, following Travis Walters' hearse north to the cemetery. They pass like a train, crossing my window as:

. . . grief; grief; grief; grief; grief grief. . . .

Then, jarringly, a final car with no grief in it at all, a car simply caught in slow traffic, perhaps on its way to a livestock sale at the Colfax auction barn:

. . . grief; grief; grief; let's move it; who was it died?

I've ridden highway 117 twice as a mourning grandson. But there is a stronger memory of something else. We drove the road every Sunday, returning at night from a day at Grandma Evans' in Colfax. As we passed the old grade school and approached the railroad tracks, my mother, father and I would all turn reflexively to the right, but not to look for trains. One block away stood Travis Walters' white funeral home, moon spotted under dense trees. We could see it for only a few seconds, but one of us would always say aloud, "Wonder if Trav's light is on." Trav's light, on the east side of the house, was the kind that lights porch steps. But Trav's was more than a hospitable light. He turned it on to tell the town that someone had that day died.
"Trav's light is on," Mother might say.
"Wonder who it is."
"Leonard Vanderwyck has been awful sick, I hear."
"So has Hattie Green."
The town would have details in the morning, but we drove to the farm with *word*, at least, of death.

Two nights ago, Trav's light was on. Howard Van Wyngarden, clearing trees from a pasture on his farm, had been killed in ironically brutal fashion. Van Wyngarden was nearly sixty and known in Prairie City for his apparently insatiable need to do hard physical work. This day he had been pulling stumps, pruning, burning in a sizable pile dead limbs and rotten girth. The day was crisp and clear, the ground covered by arid winter, and he worked easily into the afternoon. Earlier, before he'd sent his grandchildren off so he could finish, Van Wyngarden had played softball with them in the fields. Alone, he built his flames, working, as later speculation ran, to turn still another acre into land that he could plant; working mostly for the sake of working.

His son-in-law, Donald Rozenboom, found him in the smoldering fire. He lay among the limbs, arranged with an eerie efficiency, as if he'd been placed for fuel. His son-in-law's eyes could take him in only piece by piece, his legs, then his arms, slowly putting together a form amidst the piled timber. Rozenboom first thought the head was gone, then saw that it was hidden by a limb. As the ambulance driver for Travis Walters and the town of Prairie City, Rozenboom has gotten accustomed to composing anatomically the victims of accidents.

Rozenboom had come into the field with his neighbor, John De Vries, and once the two men realized what was before them, De Vries led Rozenboom away, placed him a distance from the pile. As De Vries disassembled the accident, lifting limbs away, lifting Van Wyngarden out, its sequence became clear. He'd been struck on the skull by a limb and had fallen with it into the pile. The limb that killed him had been silently, internally afire, burning undetectably above his head. Raking and tending, dragging and building, Van Wyngarden was precisely in the line of fall at the instant fire released it. The limb lay with

Van Wyngarden like a companion. He was horribly burned, but De Vries, Rozenboom and others who saw him took comfort from a long wide break in his skull, evidence that the blow had immediately killed him.

Van Wyngarden's death, accidental and grotesque, is of the kind that needs no night light to announce it. Its details had spread by evening. He was widely known, had lived here all his life, and was killed by horrible circumstances in the course of labor. Any of these elements speeds the flow of death news; all three gave it flight.

Travis Walters' experience has shown him that if one wishes a big funeral in a small town, death should come early or tragically. Either draws inordinately. This day, the cars move fast down 117 in a seemingly infinite row, past Adolph Schultze's tall gray home, and past the Clearview Manor nursing home. Its huge lobby window is filled with faces, arranged all about the glass surface like hanging plants. A funeral procession sends signals to these residents, draws them wordlessly to the window. They sit and stand at the window for as long as the service lasts. They watch the full length of the train turn left into the cemetery, snake slowly up its auto paths, watch people gather beneath the canvas tent, circling the open grave in rings of self-assigned intimacy—family on chairs, under canvas, casual friends standing at the rim of respect. The nursing-home residents wait in their own place of attendance, loyal to the life of the ceremony. When the residents see people walking from the tent, they begin to leave the window, move back to their rooms and for the rest of the day, the halls and the foyers are filled with a silence extraordinary even in this place of monasterial quiet.

"There is a special interest in death in a small town," says Travis Walters. "I suppose it has something to do

with the fact you know everybody, so news of somebody's death hits everybody a little closer. I suppose, too,
somebody said to me once, that it's because there's not a
lot of other things going on and funerals are, oh, *events*, I
guess you might say. I know there used to be a group of
old ladies who came to every funeral in town. Sat
together. Not only did they come to every one but they
were the first to arrive. You could count on it. . . . They're
all gone now."

Travis' hearse and his grave digger's truck are all that
are left at the cemetery. Always, for large funerals, there's
bountiful consolation, cut and arranged. Flowers are
carried to the hearse. What the family doesn't want to
keep will be delivered, in one of the town's more
insensitive attempts at good will, to the lobby of the
nursing home.

"We have the grave ready early in the morning,"
Walters explains. "Mr. Stover, who lives over in Monroe,
is fully responsible for all that. The state says you have to
have three feet of dirt over the top. He does a fine job.
Dependable, like any person in that job would have to
be." As Howard Van Wyngarden was during the time he
dug graves for Travis Walters—proof, some said, that
Howard Van Wyngarden was eager to do most any kind
of work.

T ravis Walters' new long living room looks like a model
grouping in a furniture showroom. Paintings, tables,
chairs all picking up one another's hues. It's a comfortable
room, in any event, quiet and soft as Walters himself.
He's a small, slight man, wears glasses, has a sharp silver
V of hair combed straight back. He has an abrupt, soaring

laugh. All that's remotely an undertaker is his voice, a melismatic whine. Slow and nasal, he somehow manages to make it sound not unpleasant. His personality cuts it. He explains his professions—funeral director and furniture dealer. I've known this combination in other small towns and in the literature of them. Gopher Prairie, Minnesota, for example. I'd heard it had to do with the undertakers' needs, long ago, for fine custom furniture made quickly and on the shortest notice. He confirms this.

"In the old days, the individual was measured, and they'd proceed to build a casket. So the man who built cabinets and furniture for a living was the most natural person in town to do both, and that's how it got started. I came to Prairie City, my family moved here, in 1928, and I followed my father into the business. What's changed, of course, is that concrete is as cheap or cheaper now than wood, so it's used for the burial receptacle most often these days."

Softening euphemisms sprinkle his vocabulary—"the individual," "funeral director," "burial receptacle." He owns a funeral home in Colfax now as well, and recently has taken a young partner. And he owns one third of a company that sells funeral homes, travels the Midwest to find suitably stately real estate.

"It's true, I suppose, that there is a special *re-spon-si-bility* in a small town—I wouldn't call it a pressure—to do the very best you possibly can on the individual. Everybody in a small town knew what he looked like, so well, they immediately see if you've done a bad job. That's why it's such a compliment—the highest I can ever receive—when a family decides to have a closed service, then changes its mind after seeing the individual."

People tend to grow and work and die in small towns, and people from larger towns retire to them. A small town seems like a place where a funeral home would prosper.

"Yes," says Walters, a merchant assessing a market. "That's true. If you select the *right* small town. An older town is good, but a *new* town, a place like Altoona, right outside Des Moines, that town just shot up overnight and is filled with young people. A small town like that is bad. At least at first."

The spacing and the frequency of his services have become reliable. He holds about 100 funerals a year. Rarely do two weeks pass without one. They usually come in clusters of three, four, five. But he's felt recent changes in the temperament of local deaths. Walters is accustomed to death that follows a conventionally lingering disease, or a sudden tragedy such as Howard Van Wyngarden's death. When older people die, there is, with the sadness, a certain sense of lives that have conformed calendrically to the time we're allowed. More and more in the past ten years, Walters has witnessed a different kind of tragedy, accidents of the kind small towns had assumed belonged in cities. Liquor-inspired auto crashes. A motorcycle death that seemed a hit-and-run revenge. Last year, a twenty-year-old Vietnam veteran, unable and finally unwilling to come home, committed suicide. Such incidents remain rare, but not *as* rare, and the young suicide made mordant history in this area. Walters has yet to see anything like murder or death by overdose but senses a narrowing gap between urban barbarities and the sane sorrow he's accustomed to.

"It's hard," says Travis Walters, in his big living-room chair, feet up, head back, the position my father assumes. "It's hard in a small town, because you can never get completely away from it. You know all the people, you've known them for so long, see them every day. They come into your store to buy a piece of furniture. I'll pass someone on the street and find myself thinking, Gee, his color's bad. It won't be too long before I'll be taking care of him. I know, after all this time, when somebody's sick even before they know it themselves. It's almost like you develop an extra sense.

"I suppose," he says, "I sup-pose it's that I'm realizing, after all these years, working with the families, taking great satisfaction from the help we try to pro-vide in bad times, that I'm realizing that it's get-ting close to home. . . . I buried an old poker-playing buddy not too long ago, and that was really one of the hardest things I ever done." He raises his hand from the arm of the chair—stop!—as if to hold in place any thoughts that seem to be going unnecessarily bleak. To make sure, he whoops: "Ha!" and trails behind it a loose, bouncing nasal giggle. Not too close; not yet.

In Prairie City, nothing is more manifest than the designated steps toward death. Squares on a game board: first home, small and rented. Children. New home, long, new, bedrooms for the future. In town, in the country. Smaller home. Nursing home. Funeral home. My grandmother's life exactly. All the squares within a few miles, a couple of blocks, arranged with a clarity not at all benevolent.

L, widowed, sells her Prairie City home, builds a new one, and views from her picture window the house where she lived her married life, directly across the street. S, alone for many years, begins casually to see M. M lives next door, a gravel drive between them. They drive to dances in Newton. M prepares their meals. It is warm and fine. She daily picks up S's mail and places it on his kitchen table. She finds him one day on his kitchen floor, gone. Now she summons from somewhere the strength to continue living there, crossing the gravel driveway to the post office.

But even as one must settle in with memory, one can see just as clearly the exact fashion of his future. A man visits his mother at Clearview Manor and knows that he'll be visited there. He'll lean forward, mean with pain, in the same beige lobby and strain to *his* son's cheery litanies. Most of us will end this way, in a clean beige room, dutifully visited, but mercifully, we don't know its precise address. Many Prairie City people do know; sometimes they even preview the time they'll spend there. Mrs. P visited her husband for two years. Now, when she's able to return to call on others, the residents rush to her, cling like orphans. "Where have you been? We don't see you like we used to." More than duty brings her. She finds she misses these people. It's as if she began, with her husband's days here, the company of her own.

T has decided to set his own pace rather than follow nature's. Strong, keen, self-sufficient, T has moved up his time. His wife has been at Clearview Manor for several months, her arthritis stiffening to a brittleness T has just fleetingly begun to feel. Why wait for it? T has joined his wife. They share a room like a couple at a residential hotel. T would rather live at Clearview with his wife than wait at home under the lonely sentence of health.

R, neat and dapper, has been at Clearview for a year. He is short, thin. He wears a line of mustache, trig as a gigolo's. A clear rivulet runs from the corner of his mouth, hardens to a white crust at the edge of his lip, like dripping water of a high lime content. R missed his wife's time here. He clung to the farm as long as he could.. His son and daughter-in-law are there now, "on the place." He sits with E on the "back porch" of Clearview, a small vestibule where two hallways perpendicularly meet, and they look out at the fields, watch the vaporous soil, "row" the beginning beans. R and E have known each other since they were twelve and have lived remarkably similar lives, never more than a few miles from each other. They've worked manually in fields and workshops. Now R's hands move tremulously, like idling motors. E's cannot close around tool handles, and feel like twigs inside a rough sack. His skin is dry as old wallpaper and has peeled in long strips from his arms, in the places where the aides hold him in their grip.

"What will I do when you're gone?" R asked E. "You're the only friend I have here." A few mornings later, R rose, dressed, walked quickly to the front door. He told aides he was walking to the bank, withdrawing his money, would spend what was needed for passage to Wyoming.

"Wyoming?" asked the aides. Delirium, they nodded. But not at all. R had seen Wyoming as a young man. He remembered its mountains. He wanted once more to see land that magisterially rose and fell, land as exotically opposite as he could imagine from the subtle planes and hummocks that surround Clearview Manor, that have surrounded his life like a moat. Having done that, he would return satisfied, could sit again with E and watch the fields fall away from the porch in new crops. But he could not articulate his need when asked, "Wyoming?" There was increased concern for his self-sufficiency and R wept.

The windows in City Hall's council room give west, across an empty lot, to the square. A fitting view. From their chairs, the town councilmen can refer through panes to the scenery they legislate. If the language of an ordinance ("Lot 2A, in subdivision of South one half of

Government Lot 6 of Section 2, Township 78 . . .")
obscures its location, one can walk to the windows,
overlay language on geography, and once more be set
straight: "Oh. *That* lot. Behind Louie Beener's."

It's also true, of course, that as the councilmen can see
the town, so the town can see the councilmen. And some
do look curiously into the windows as they drive past:
one way of keeping an eye on government. But few
people, as Erlene Veverka complained during her candidacy, go inside to hear the words. Tonight, besides
myself, only one person is voluntarily present. Everyone
else has a reason. Paul Elrod, city engineer, short, slight,.
a Budweiser beer hat pulled to his brows, is here. Terry
Massick, police chief, is here. His black boots have been
meeting-polished. He wears brown knit pants, brown
shirt with Prairie City Police Department sleeve patches of
his own design, a black down-filled vest. A local busi-
nesswoman, Esther Krohn, is here. She fidgets on her
folding chair and is pale with purpose. Erlene Veverka is
not here.

Tom McKlveen, mayor pro tem, sits at the end of the
long council table. City Clerk Ken Birkenholtz and Duane
"Punk" Jennings—who is nicknamed Punk in the way
that short, fat men are nicknamed Stretch—are on his
right. The two newly elected council members, Doug
Jansz and Curt Charter, and Councilman Art Stremfel, on
his left. The presence of Mayor Henry Ostlin, currently in
Arizona, is overhead. Birkenholtz, as city clerk, has no
vote. Neither, constitutionally, does the spirit of Ostlin.

"Hank is expecting to be back for the next meeting,"
McKlveen explains. He is young, handsome, with age in
his voice and manner. "I'm in touch with him once a
week, or Ken is. He keeps asking about all the flu that's
going around up here and wants to wait for it to die down
a bit before he comes back."

McKlveen, twenty-eight, is the youngest councilman. If there is, in a literary sense, a rich and central family in the plot of this town, it is the McKlveens. They own lumberyards, here and in other small Jasper County towns. Tom's two older brothers have become a doctor and a lawyer. His younger sister has a Ph.D. in psychology. Unlike them, and unlike his parents, Tom did not attend Grinnell College, but graduated, with honors, from Brown University. He was a Coast Guard officer and lived and worked for a time in Boston. Although he traveled farthest, he is the one who's returned and joined the business. He says he always assumed he would. He enjoyed the East, and received from an Ivy League education all he'd expected. But he came to feel during his years there that the East "had had its day," and clearly the East did not deeply influence him. He speaks with the raw twang of this place, as he did when he left it. And if there can be such a thing as a twang in one's movements—paralleling the sharp, aggressive gestures of the East, the languid postures of the South—then McKlveen moves with a certain plains hardness, moves with a Midwest twang.

As a businessman in Prairie City, he soon felt the obligation to serve the community and, not caring for clubs or lodges, ran for election. Sooner than he'd have liked, he says; sooner, too, than some in town would have liked. "Just 'cause he's a McKlveen, he thinks he can get on the council right away." That theme, with variations, surfaced when he ran. A Kennedy syndrome of sorts. And with Kennedy results: Some people, McKlveen says, have urged him already to run in two years for mayor.

He begins the meeting. "First we have Mattie Howell's petition for property-tax exemption."

"How's that?" asks Charter, new to government.

"It's a form that she fills out every year. She hasn't got any income, is unable to contribute, as an 'infirm citizen,' to 'the public revenue.'"

The council receives Mattie Howell's poverty. Charter, smiling, reaches for her letter. "What do you have to claim to get that kind of deal?" he asks. The council laughs.

The city has, in fact, a great deal of public revenue at the moment. So much that Ken Birkenholtz feels a duty to report it.

"We've got eighty-eight thousand in checking," he says. "Last month, I disbursed eleven thousand. So I think we can afford to invest some. Just having it lay around is costing us, I figure, roughly about three hundred a month."

"I think we should have no more than sixty days' cash on hand, and put the rest in some interest-bearing account," Curt Charter says.

A resolution unanimously passes. In the spirit of thrift, McKlveen adds, "Ken. When you write up the minutes for the *News*, just put 'unanimous' after the 'ayes' instead of listing our names. He's charging us nineteen cents a line and maybe we can save a few."

An early sign of spring: "We're gonna have to find somebody else to mow the cemetery. The Jaycees have said they're no longer interested."

"They've lost members on account of their having to mow it," Charter says. "You try to recruit a new member and then tell him he's gonna have to mow the cemetery for six months . . . it's rough."

Punk Jennings says, "I can't help but think we won't have any trouble finding somebody." He deliberately rubs his chin. If McKlveen moves with a twang, Punk embodies a full prairie drawl. He shakes his head as if he were cautiously testing a cramp in his neck. He was a fine athlete in the middle 1950s, and is still hard-muscled, physically intimidating.

Curt Charter says, "Hell, why don't we contract *all* our lawns? I bet we'd be money ahead."

"We've got a four-thousand-dollar tractor and a thousand-dollar mower," McKlveen says.

"*Sell* the damn things," Charter suggests. "I read there was a town in New York that contracts everything. Garbage, everything."

"New York City?" Punk Jennings asks. The council laughs.

"No. Not New York City," says Charter. "One of the solvent ones."

McKlveen pauses to write things down. What began as a minor point has leaped to a full-scale liquidation of machinery.

The men work convivially down the agenda. Birkenholtz brings out sweet rolls. Coffee is poured from a twelve-cup pot on his desk behind the table. Through the windows, the square's west-side façade seems a fortress wall that marks the geographical edge of reasonable concern.

McKlveen says, "Last night, I got a call from the Krohns that bothered me quite a lot. So I suggested that the best way to handle it was for them to come to the meeting and say to all of us what I heard over the phone. Esther is here, so," he looks up from his papers, "Esther, why don't you tell us what you came here to say?"

Through the first two hours of the meeting, Esther's silence has been tympanic. She has moved on her chair as if her mission were jumping around inside her and might at any moment spring out into the room. Now she shakes from nerves and adjusts her thick glasses.

"I had to come to make a complaint," she begins. No one at the table appears to have assumed something else.

Esther is short and stocky, and her face, behind the glasses, looks as if she had spent her life trying to draw a frayed thread through a needle's eye.

"I's getting pretty fed up with the way our police chief has been actin'." She speaks of Massick, who is separated from her by the width of a folding chair, as if he were not in the room. "I thought it only right to come here, as a citizen, as a *tax*payer, really is what I mean, to come here and tell what's been goin' on. For weeks now, oh, months, golly, I've been hearing him on the C.B. at night, talking to this Country Girl. She drives through town ever' night on her way home from work, I guess. It's late when she comes through, midnight or so. One, maybe. You hear 'em talkin': 'Country Girl, this is the Brown Bear.' Brown Bear and Country Girl back and forth. Well, that ain't so bad, although it seems to me Brown Bear oughta have somethin' better to do on duty than yap on the C.B."

If he knows what is coming, Massick gives not the slightest sign of a man sitting at his own ambush. He inspects with interest the sheen of his boots.

"Then it got to be more'n that," Esther says, her narrative opening out. "One night, they set up a meeting outside town. Brown Bear says to Country Girl, 'I be meetin' ya in a few minutes.' And Country Girl says, 'I waitin'.'" Her manner has grown now to something prosecutorial.

Esther says that the Brown Bear and Country Girl met on back roads. Esther heard them and her C.B. receiver needle showed the strength of their voices, indicating their locations until, at last sound—"Good evening, ma'am"—it showed them car to car.

"You'd hear 'em talkin'. Brown Bear says, 'I'll see ya by the anhydrous tanks.' Then Country Girl says, 'Ten-four. I'm at your twenty, Brown Bear.' Then you don't hear nothin'. And then you hear a long while later, Brown Bear gets back on and says, 'You take 'em easy, Country Girl. We be seein' ya tomorrow.'

"Now, it ain't no business of mine what Brown Bear does on his own time. But here he's supposed to be a peace officer watchin' the town, and he's out in the country half the night and on taxpayers' money." Esther has moved up to the edge of her chair, her momentum carrying her into a summary. "Now, that ain't right and I think it's about time the council knew what was goin' on with their employees that's getting good wages—I know, we all know, we see the money wages in the paper ever' month when he gets paid—and carryin' on like that." She nods sharply.

The room is quiet. Finally, McKlveen says, "Well . . . Terry. What do you say?" Massick is big, blond; leaning forward, elbows on thighs, he looks enormous and nearly round. At the moment, his face is lit from within.

"Seems to me it's a pretty lousy thing when a person's got nothing better to do than sit around all night and listen in on the C.B. and make up a buncha lies from it." He chews the inside of his mouth. "Thing was, my friend Bill Wells wanted to meet Country Girl. I ain't denyin' we talked. We talk when she drives through town. Just like I talk to truckers. I talk to Big Foot most every night. I talk to the Screamin' Axle. And I talk to her. But this other stuff Esther's claimin', that—"

"You denyin' you followed her outa town?"

"Why don't you let me finish, Esther, okay? No, I ain't denyin' that, either. Like I say, Billy wanted to meet Country Girl, so one night when she drove through and Billy was with me, I said to her, 'Let's meet up,' and we did and she and Billy talked. And that's all there was about it."

• 230 •

All color leaves Esther's face. Her lips smack like a suction cup coming off porcelain. "Land. He's lyin'. He's lyin'. I never heard nothin' mentioned about Bill Wells. And it didn't happen just the once. Since it started, it's *been* happenin'."

"Watch it, Esther. I ain't a liar."

"All right, now," McKlveen says.

"Well," Esther says, "but he *is* lyin'. And I can prove it. I got a tape in the car. Leave me get it and I'll play it for you."

The councilmen sit up in their chairs: This has suddenly become highly complicated. McKlveen asks, for all of them, "You have a *tape?* You mean you taped from your C.B.?"

"It's out in the glove compartment," Esther says again. "Leave me go get it." She starts to stand.

"Uh, wait, wait, Esther," McKlveen quickly stops her. "I'm not sure about this." He pans the room for help. "What do the rest of you fellas think?"

"It's the only way you're gonna know who's tellin' the truth," Esther insists. "Otherwise, it's just his words against mine."

Massick's eyes have returned to his boots. Somehow, his presence is the least felt of any in the room.

Punk Jennings says, "I doan know. I'm just not sure it's the thing to do, to play a tape to the council."

"I'm not, either," says McKlveen.

"How you gonna know?" Esther asks.

"I, I just . . ." says Punk Jennings.

"I'm . . . yeah," says Art Stremfel.

"I'm goin' out to get it," Esther declares. She stands and moves toward the door.

"Hold it, Esther! Hold on. Just a second, now," McKlveen says, talking her back to her chair. "I don't know about the rest of you guys, but I don't think I want to hear Esther's tape. I don't think it would be proper to do that in front of the council."

"I can't think but what you're right," Punk says.

Esther pops her lips again and seems to tense in her chair with something pugilistic in mind.

"Leave me play it," she says frantically. "He's callin' me a liar and how'm I gonna show it's he that's lyin' and not me unless you hear it what really happened on the tape?"

Every councilman agrees that a tape has no right before the council. For a moment, Esther seems ready to make a run for the tape and dash back in, recorder running, but she only clears her throat and makes a final statement. "Well, I just got one thing to say. I'm tired of what's goin' on. I'm tired of the way our police department is runnin' around when he's supposed to be at work. And you oughta know this. It ain't just me that knows what's goin' on right under your noses. Half the town anyway has heard them on the C.B. and everybody's just about had it. I'm tired of it."

She stands up, seems to halt as if from the habit of being called back down by McKlveen, then walks out. If her preintroductory silence was tympanic, her absence now is cymbals, bass, and kettle as well.

"I'm certain it was the right thing to do," Punk says.

"I didn't want to hear her tape," McKlveen adds. "She didn't tell me she had a tape."

In turn, each councilman speaks to Massick.

"I don't know what the trouble is between you two, but it's got no place here."

"You have no business using the C.B. for personal conversations."

"I know it gets awfully boring on duty, but you can't be driving all over the country."

"Use your head, man. You should know half the town listens in on the C.B."

"I've had people stop me on the street to tell me what you've been up to the night before."

Massick accepts all this with an obedience of one who's pleased to be taking the lighter of punishments. No one, whatever his curiosity, asks, "Now, what *about* you and this Country Girl?" Instead, returning the meeting to the dignity of city sums, they ask Massick for his monthly report.

"I drove two thousand, four hundred forty-five miles, for an average of sixty miles a night, used two hundred eighty-four point two gallons of gas. I performed eleven motorist assists, four C.B. assists, issued twenty-eight tickets, twenty-three for speeding, one O.M.V.I.I., one pedestrian intoxication. Collected somewhere between six hundred and six hundred and fifty in city revenues. I haven't got it quite figured totally."

Ken Birkenholtz reads the bills he's paid. Near midnight, the meeting adjourns. At the door, one of the councilmen says, "It just seems like there's somethin' with Terry all the time."

"Terry's ideas are too police-officer oriented for Prairie City," says another. "But I don't think we can, or should, discourage him."

"Yeah, but first he wants to get to police school. Then he wants an auxiliary force. I don't know, he's got awful big ideas. Now this."

"This thing tonight, though. Could you believe she made a damn *tape* off her C.B.?"

"No, I couldn't. I couldn't believe she made a tape off her C.B."

"I couldn't believe she actually made a damn tape."

The local C.B.-radio dealer, Tim Trier, believes that there are C.B. radios in a quarter of Prairie City's households—in cars, in homes, in both. Terry Massick believes the number much higher, believes as much as sixty percent of Prairie City owns a set in one of its forms. Regardless of the count, the presence of citizen's-band radio seems enveloping. Aerials wave from cars and pickups. Receivers sit on shelves in many places of business, sending static. The Cardinal has no telephone, but does have a formidable C.B. base—a Tram, Cadillac of receivers, hangs in the kitchen. When a voice breaks the muzzled noise, Jim or Betty or someone else puts an ear to the receiver, once in a while asking identities: "Who's the Spruce Goose?" "Uh . . . Jake Schuttinga." "Right." More infrequently still, one of them will prepare to make a call by consulting the directory of their customers' collective memory: "What's Otto Churchill's handle?" "Uh, let's see. Farm Fresh, is it?" "Right."

There are channels specifying locations and generation. Channel nineteen, the national band, can be used away from town. And Massick turns to nineteen when he wants to hear the highway. Channel seven is the local frequency, the space of air that Prairie City generally uses. But more specifically, channel ten excludes the countryside, has become the private space of the town, block to block. Students in cars, roaming through the maze, use channel five.

From its original appeal—as a way of cheating a federal speed limit most of these people find contrary to everything they believe about the purpose and worth of the automobile—citizen's-band radios have recently moved into the home. Bases—in home C.B.s—have become more popular than the automobile style, and the dealer is also selling to many farmers who install them in tractors and in distant farm buildings, for communication with the bases in their kitchens. C.B.s, their idiom founded in truck slang, are still primarily for travel, but they are becoming more and more settled in. Part of the reason is the design limitations of the radios themselves. They are a weak species, the most powerful of them able to send signals a few miles. This has clear advantages on the dashboard of a moving car, keeping reception tight and close. At home, however, the radio loses its engine, can carry just those same few miles, and becomes an incredibly local piece of equipment, little more than a walkie-talkie housed in knobs and cabinetry. You can speak, field to field, farm to farm, and, in town, north end to south. The resident who purchases a C.B., takes it home, hooks it up, tunes to ten, may be admitting in a way that his life is locally public, no matter what he does, so he may as well conduct it on the radio, have some fun, and receive the amplified lives of neighbors he'd otherwise have to spend time, doughnut money and some inquiring effort in Snub's to keep up with. But a certain craft has been made obsolete in the process. Modern methods have replaced the artisanship of gossip.

On the other hand, some seem, with C.B. microphones, to believe that they are having private conversations.

"I's listenin' on the C.B. last night," a man said to another. "Heard ol' Long Hauler tellin' he had half a mind to fire his whole crew. Sounded 'bout half pissed."

"Yeah, I heard that, too," said the other man.

"Oh . . . you did?" said the first.

If Terry Massick has behaved as Esther charges, perhaps he's become at night the Brown Bear, has accomplished a fairly complete personality split. If he has not, if Esther's imagination has run loose, then the point—that C.B. conversation is at least two places from reality—seems clear. And one place more when Esther puts it on plastic, takes it uptown and offers it as evidence.

"Prairie City, this is Twenty-nine. Come in, Prairie City."

"*Squak. Squak.* This is Prairie City. Go ahead, Twenty-nine."

"Roger, Prairie City. We'll be out of the car awhile. Check back with us when we're in communication."

"Roger, Twenty-nine."

"Be about fifteen minutes, anyway, Prairie City."

"Roger, Twenty-nine."

"We're leavin' the car now. We be back in touch. Ten-four, Prairie City."

"Ten-four, Twenty-nine."

Massick leaves and locks the car, fumbling in an icy midnight wind for the lock buttons and the door handles. With his hands, he cups his face, presses it against the window and peers back inside, like a voyeur checking for back-seat love. Two rifles lie on the seat. A revolver in its case. Three rounds of ammunition in preloaded cartridges—eighteen soft-nosed bullets that open upon entrance like blossoming flowers. His dashboard is swollen with two radios, a citizen's-band and a police channel, their wires ensnarled like avid vines.

"All right back there?" Massick asks his weapons and laughs. Against the wind, he wears his down-filled vest. His hands are prominently ungloved; the cold grows them. "Hate to leave all that in there, even locked up," he says. The car is parked, front bumper to front steps, against City Hall. We hasten up the steps, into the hallway that, compared with the air outside, is merely refrigerated. At the top step, Massick again checks his dark-brown Chevrolet. The car's tone blends with the dark, a perfect shade for a radar watch, Massick says. "It's the first police car I feel like's really mine. I got to order it and all. I cooked an engine in the other one they had, just after I got here." Satisfied, he closes the front door and, as he explained to his young wife on the radio—he calls her Prairie City, she calls him Twenty-nine—begins for a while "to be out of touch." She'll monitor the radio in his absence and if she hears anything that Twenty-nine should know, she'll call the City Hall telephone.

In the council room, he opens a metal file drawer and lifts from it a can of coffee. He spoons inexactly into the twelve-cup pot, looking over his shoulder as he does through the tall west windows to the square, his eye cocked for crime.

"Those donkey bastards, they'll start screechin' their tires and tearin' ass sure as hell once they see we're out of the car. Never fails."

In a few seconds, the coffeepot begins to make long tidal groans. Massick walks to the council table and unsnaps the lip of his holster. His gun rings, heavy as cast iron, as he places it on the table. He peers through the windows. The streets of the square are lit by high lamps. Whatever sounds there are outside are covered by the asthmatic coffeepot.

"Donkey bastards," Massick says. He carries boxes of blank cartridges to the table, pulls a chair close, begins to push hard rubber noses into the hollow blanks. He works with quick, assembly-line movements. He arranges the blanks in rows; shiny-armored bodies; dull rubber helmets. All the time, he keeps an eye on the square, which, for the first time this year, is snow-covered.

It fell last week, through a night and a day, casual as settling fog. It stopped traffic and a weekend's meetings. When it finished, the city plow scraped down through it, but the less essential streets remain white-surfaced, the snow in pillowed walls on either side, like a toboggan run for infants—square, flat, harmless, but scenically faithful to the idea. The snow has softened an angular meanness that had been on the town. The square has a high white rim of plowed street snow all around it and, in the middle, a layer nearly fibrous. Dry snow rises with the slightest wind and hangs in the lighted air like glistening dust.

Massick has occupational bias against the snow. All winter, he's had no need to watch for cars spinning and turning on slickened streets, a move called, since the beginning of time, a "cat's ass." Now, as late and heavy as this snow was, he's sure the town's young men will find the streets, the parking lots, the smooth spaciousness of the park, too tempting. He expects that we may see someone try the park at any moment, even though it's clear that the chief of police is watching from the windows.

He quickly assembles a battalion of blanks. Fumbling and dropping rubber caps, I help him as I can. We have come at midnight to City Hall to shoot pistols. It's his coffee break. We'd been riding in the car for a few hours when Massick said, "Let's take a breather. Wanna shoot some rounds?"

"Shoot?" I asked.

"Yeah. Shoot some targets."

"Where?"

"City Hall."

I've never fired a handgun in my life, much less shot a round in Prairie City's City Hall, so the question sounded a little like an invitation to hit golf balls in church. It also had the ring of an adolescent challenge, when some classmate with pure mischief in mind asks you along.

"The last time I shot anything was when I was twelve years old and had a BB gun. I used to miss pigeons sitting on barn beams."

Massick looked at me like a man who suspects he's being hustled.

"Honest," I said. "I've never shot a pistol."

"Well. You wanna?"

"Sure," I said, to make up for all the times in my youth when I'd declined the mischief.

Massick takes a folded poster from the files, opens it to show a frontal silhouette, my height, roughly, its limbs vulnerably spread. It's thoroughly pocked and scabbed and around its heart, blanks have blown a jagged hole. Massick puts cardboard boxes between the poster and the varnished door, tacks the target up. "It's the same target they use on the testing range at Police Academy," he says. "Same target Des Moines coppers shoot at."

The room, closed and unheated on every night of the month but one, has in it that feeling of stored cold, like the air in a meat locker. It's as if the cold air preserves the council meetings from month to month. The memory of the most recent meeting is still in the room, even though we do not speak of it. Massick has let it be known that Esther's story was inspired by old grudges and there's little more he can do than patiently let it die. Of course, since the meeting, I've found myself filled with the same kind of small curiosity that I've always resented Prairie City for displaying, and I see how easily one's vision, trained no farther than the edge of town, can narrow. I've thought, also, that it was wise of the council to refuse Esther's tape. It seems to set moral ordinance, for the present, anyway, in a town that apparently has no objection to bugging itself.

Massick loads his gun, a .45, and takes from a soft cloth sack a .38, smaller, smelling richly lubricated, shining blue as pond ice. "Which ya wanta try?" he asks. "This'n"—lifting the .38— "might be better for you. It's lighter. Fires a little high and to the left, so figure on that."

I take the .38. It fits my hand like a mold.

Massick has been police chief for nearly a year. He came from Knoxville, a city of at least ten thousand, where he worked for its police department. His home town is Tracy, a very small settlement near Knoxville, and his coming fifty miles to Prairie City represented the farthest distance anyone in his family had traveled to live. His mother "threw a fit" when he broke the news.

He found Knoxville, and his first police work, ultimately disillusioning. Politics and rivalry ran through the department; graft sat in its chief's chair, he says. "You couldn't count on your boss backing you up, was what it got down to." There was bribery loose and floating. "I loved that movie, *Serpico*," he told me earlier this evening in the car. "I knew just how he felt. I know just what he was up against. I had the exact same thing. But they learned in Knoxville that you can't bribe the Brown Bear."

Prairie City seemed an answer. He'd be chief of the department, even though he'd also be *all* of it. He'd have only the simple authority of a mayor and a council above him. The salary—printed every month under "Bills paid" in the *News*, a fact that greatly irritates him—was higher than what he earned in Knoxville. I wondered if he found the work here sufficiently diverse and challenging after Knoxville, with its larger population, its status as a county seat, its police station. He said that he has in mind an office and a new jail here, next to the fire station. As for the quality of the work itself, he made this comparison: He drew his gun four times while he worked in Knoxville, six times here. Mostly, to quiet some drunken belligerent passing through on the highway. But a couple of times, he's shown it to young residents who were drunk, or appeared to be passing marijuana in their car. Once, late on Halloween night, hay bales were set fire on the square and dozens of cars roamed the streets, seeming to threaten something more than he and a borrowed county sheriff could control. That night he "Maced a kid."

"You cock the hammer and you'll hear it click," Massick instructs me from the council table. I'm at the opposite end of the room from the target, five feet from the mayor's high-backed chair. "You just line up the notch in the V, like any gun. Like your BB gun, probably. Remember, it shoots high to the left."

I hold the .38 with both hands and sight it. In the frame of vision imposed by the sight, the blown-away heart, the whole body, bobs beyond the barrel like a floating buoy. I'd always thought my nerves admirably steady, and now, as I try to stop the silhouette from floating, I feel palsied. I decide to exhale.

"High and left."

Crack! High and left, with the .38, has nothing in common with any high and left my BB gun might have fired. I've wounded the door. Massick giggles. I've shot city property.

"Bring 'er down a bit," he advises.

Crack! I've struck the air, the white space behind the silhouette. But I'm on the poster.

"Yer getting there." Between my shots, Massick has been loading his gun, his chair turned sideways, so that he has one eye on my ordeal, another on the window.

I fire six shots, and my last three find poster flesh.

"There you go," Massick says. "There you go! You sure you haven't ever shot?"

I take a chair and eagerly load blanks, the idea of gun shots ringing through City Hall already as natural as if I hunted here nightly. While I'm curious to see Massick's accuracy, I'm more impatient for my next turn. I'm also unnerved by the extent to which I like it. Simply, viserally, I like the posture and the process, like most of all the sudden injection of something like liquid weight from the handle through me at that echoing *crack!*

Massick keeps his gun in his holster. He wants to practice shots that begin on his hip. Facing the target, he mirrors it: legs spread, a slightly squatting stance, arms away from his body. He's said that he possesses only passable skill with a pistol, nothing like that of his wife, who can hit a floating milk carton at twenty yards. His weapon is a rifle. His first, when he was twelve, was an old one an uncle allowed him to clean and use. It was stiff and rusted when he took it and Massick cleaned the rifle down to its life. He didn't hunt game but shot regularly all kinds of targets, moving and still. He was feared by every tin can in Tracy. When his uncle died, his parents sold the rifle for ten dollars. "That hurt," he says.

He smoothly lifts the gun and fires. Crack! Crack! . . . Crack! . . . Crack! Crack! Crack! All his shots are through or near the heart, and such a round seems to warrant some kind of frontier gesture; blowing curling smoke from the end of the barrel. "Guess I'd qualify for coppin' in Des Moines, all right," Massick nods.

He'd like to be a member of a SWAT team or a chase squad, the latter combining his need "to cop"—It's just something that's in me"—with his love for cars and fast driving. He'd also like to work as an undercover detective, "plainclothes stuff." He believes he'd be little more susceptible to risk than he is now, working the western half of Jasper County, which has a higher crime rate because it touches the Polk County line, gets spillage from Des Moines.

"The figures show most of your lives are lost answering domestic quarrels," he says. "So you just never know. Especially when you're fairly new in town. I got a call once just after I got here. 'Come to 206 Sixth Street.' Hell,

I didn't know 206 Sixth Street. Is that East Sixth or West? If he'd just told me the name who they lived next to, I'da been better off. In the old days, they'd just say, 'Come to my house.'

"But you never know for sure. Some nights I'm getting ready for work and I think, Is this my time? Or you get a feeling, like when you stop a car for speeding. There've been times when I'd get out of the car and think, This might be it, and I'll unbuckle my gun case while I'm walking up to it."

He walks to the windows and, cupping his face on the pane, looks out. "Wonder what the little angels are up to? Wonder where they are?" Above the square, the moon is brilliantly opaque, as if it's been thinly applied.

"Full moon," Massick notes, not happily. "God damn full moon. We could be in for big trouble tonight. If something happens in town, you can just bet there's a full moon. It may sound crazy, but you can count on it."

For half an hour, we trade turns. I manage to reduce the number of my wild shots, but I remain inconsistent, the silhouette always threatening to bob and escape the notch at the last instant. The atmosphere in the room has grown more serious. We shoot, academically assess the round, return to our chairs to make bullets, quiet over our chore, like women at a table shelling peas. Massick looks at his watch. "We're gonna have to go back to work in a minute. I get worried when I'm out of touch like this. I'm thinking of putting speakers in this room, so I'll be able to hear the radio in here." He shakes his head. "What I worry about most is the B and E's. B and E's. I go to bed and dream of B and E's."

"B and E's?" I ask.

"Breakin' and entering," he explains. "I'm tellin' you, a group of professionals could pick this town clean in half an hour. I just imagine me goin' off duty at three and getting a call an hour later from the council saying, 'Where the hell were you this time? Ever' store's been hit.' Makes you old thinkin' about it. I didn't smoke, drink or nothin' before I started coppin'. But there's not a hell of a lot you can do when it gets in your blood like it is. Pay's lousy. Divorce rates are the highest of any job. Did you know that?" He pauses. Rubber blank-heads snap into place, the only sound for several seconds the rhythmic clicking of assemblage. He says, "It's hard being a cop's wife, though. For sure. It wears the woman down." He's twenty-six. He was married once before, a fact that he speaks of as a confirmation: I wear a uniform. I am bedecked with firearms. I've been divorced.

In Knoxville, he worked a variety of jobs before he joined the police. He spent summers at the Knoxville Speedway, a dirt track for stock cars and one of the Midwest's most famous. He was its voice and its diarist. He convinced a local radio station that he knew the sport and the drivers and the reasons some of them repeatedly won. "I just walked into the station and started spielin' off what I knew. I knew all the guys by heart. I'd been watchin' them all my life. And I'd done a fair bit of racing myself on little tracks till I busted my toe and it threw my timing off." On Sundays, after Saturday night's race, he took a typewriter and paper down to the Des Moines River and filed from its banks dispatches for *Speed Sports News*. "Those were good days," he says. "I'd get to the track hours before the race, walk through the pits, talkin' to the drivers. Ernie Derr. Ramo Stott. All of 'em.

"Now my radio voice is shot after all these years and all the cigarettes."

We fire last rounds. I try to end memorably and approach each shot with tournament care. Applying the night's instruction to each shot, I hit the target twice. But if the area around the doorknob is vital to its life, I've left it spectacularly dead.

Massick finishes with a flourish, firing as he sits on the floor, knees up under his elbows. "This is one of the positions they test you out at in Police Academy." Seated, tucked in, he once more looks round, as he did at the council meeting, and very large, a brown cloth boulder on the floor. A lock of blond hair hangs across his forehead like a rooster's comb.

Crack! Crack! Crack! Crack! Crack! Crack! Purposely swift. Four of six.

"Well, we best get back to work," he says from the floor. We return the room to the seat of government. Massick takes down the target and files it. I shake blanks from the cardboard boxes, sweep, and together we box the blanks. In a few minutes, the room once again looks solemn enough to host a discussion of mill rates.

"Ready?" He flips the light switch. I fumble in the dark for the knob and feel what seem a dozen deep ravines in the wood. Outside, Massick starts the car and eases it slowly away from the curb. He picks up one of his microphones.

"Prairie City, this is Twenty-nine. Come in, Prairie City."

"Come in, Twenty-nine."

"We're back in the car. Everything okay?"

"Roger, Twenty-nine. I didn't hear anything to speak of."

"Okay, Roger. We be talkin' to ya."

"Ten-four."

"Ten-four."

He drives the town in quadrants. When he's not parked in radar shadow on the highway, Massick drives the streets and alleys continuously. Small as Prairie City may seem to anyone driving through it, for Massick it runs sixty miles from beginning to end. As he drives, he watches the town settle down, knows which lights will be the last. Prairie City darkens, as it does everything else, routinely, like someone moving habitually from room to room and shutting off lights in preparation for bed. The Cardinal closes. Jim and Betty drive their inspection road home. In the south end, Ralph Dykstra turns his kitchen lights off. Less than half an hour later, Dr. Veverka's house, at the north edge, goes dark. From a second-floor apartment in Prairie House, Bill VerMeer descends the steps with Joan Sampson tucked close and smiling, Massick says, "from her nightly servicing." Meanwhile, the young men slowly give up on the maze and wind like thinning smoke into the countryside. By one o'clock, certainly by two, Prairie City is black and still and Massick, having supervised it all, drives, crosshatching.

He turns into the alley behind the north-side stores and aims a searchlight toward the backs of the shops. The powerful light strips the block, lighting up the alley's neglect—rust, warped cellar doors, the conventional decay. Massick reaches the end of the alley, having lit no crimes. He turns off the searchlight and his headlights and drives slowly toward the square, hoping to catch a pickup at play in the park.

"This is the worst season for a peace officer," he says. "Summer's the best, because the trees are full and you can hide. I know every spot in town where I can park and sort of look through the spaces between houses and trees and alleys and check out what's going on a block over. But after the leaves fall, your hiding places are shot."

At the corner, he sees nothing but the white park.

"Shit," he says. "Wonder where all the little buckwheats are tonight. I know they're around. I can hear 'em at the edge of town."

He turns on his lights, turns away from the square. "Another thing. This town's laid out all wrong for coppin'. Flat. There ain't a place anywhere where you can look down on it. Fella can see a hell of a lot more if he can get *above* it."

We drive Prairie City, slowly and methodically. The scenery in the headlights appears mounted on the bumper of the car.

"There's really only about two dozen kids I gotta worry about. A few real bums; the druggies."

"Are there a lot of drugs here?" I ask.

"Bet your ass. There's marijuana all over this town. I had me ten drug busts last year. Goin' for a dozen this year."

"You raided houses?"

"No. Most of 'em was out-of-towners I picked up on the highway. Trouble is, the law today is written for the outlaw. I can stake out a place where I know the druggies live, but by the time I see somethin', drive to Newton to get a search warrant and get back here, chances are they've broken up the party. I missed a raid last weekend 'cause of that. Pissed me off somethin' royal."

"Have you found more than marijuana?"

"Just marijuana. We got it all in a big plastic bag, all the stuff I confiscated, up in City Hall. Must be two thousand dollars' worth of it in the files."

"What are you doing with it?"

"Nothing. I mix a little of it with my dog's meat so he'll get the idea of it. I'm training him good. Sometimes I mix up some freshly killed rabbit, blood and gun powder in his food. Makes him mean as hell."

We meet the square and drive around it. City Hall stands dark and innocent. Massick begins to talk about books and writing. I've shown an interest in his work. He returns one in mine. "That Wambaugh really fell into it, didn't he? I've read all his books. Sucker's richer'n hell now, ain't he?"

"Richer than that," I say.

"Yeah. I used to do some writin'. When I was on the Knoxville P.D., I wrote an article on a high-speed chase I had. I mailed it to the *Reader's Digest*, but they sent it back. Not enough blood and guts in it for them, I guess.

"I eat up cop stories, though. And movies. Clint Eastwood. We got to see *Magnum Force* on a fancy screen in Kansas City. Big, wide sucker. Eastwood pointed that magnum and it like to come out of the screen at you. I love him. And John Wayne: *'Well, whatdoya think you're doin' there, fella?'*"

He does a very recognizable Wayne.

"Oh, and *American Graffiti*. There you go. *American Graffiti*. I saw it eight times. Laugh! God, I loved that movie."

I recall the memorable scene from *American Graffiti*: The town's young men plot against the patrolling police car, tying down its axle, then teasing the policemen into a chase so the car's body flies off its chassis. Perhaps Massick loves shooting pistols in City Hall for the same reasons I did.

"When I was a kid, I read World War Two histories. I was nuts on it. I remember"—and he laughs—"I remember once I read this book about some flier and I spotted some mistakes in it. Some of the information about the planes was wrong. So I wrote the author a letter. Ha! I did, sure as hell. And he wrote back to me. I wish I could remember his name, I can't, and he thanked me. Damn, I wish I could remember that sucker's name."

"Did you keep the letter?"

"Nah. My mom saw it and raised the roof. When my dad got home, she said, 'Look what your son's been up to now. Writin' letters to some author in New York!' The ol' man raised hell, too."

"Why?"

"Thought I was actin' a little too big for my britches or somethin', I guess. He said, 'Who you think you are, bothering with that stuff?'"

We've pulled into an alley southeast of the square, Travis Walters' funeral home directly across the street. Our lights are dark. So are his. The railroad tracks that equatorially split the town are twenty yards north. Massick's radios are open and if there's an audible distinction between the static of work and of hobby, I cannot hear it. Somewhere in the county, a sheriff is giving chase to a speeding car, is calling each turn of the back roads he drives, like a public-address man at a speedway microphone. Massick knows the sheriff and tries to tune in the chase more clearly.

"Ol' Deek's got him one," Massick says, and as he listens, he begins unconsciously to move his feet from brake to accelerator, playing the car like an organ. He catches himself and laughs.

"Actually," he says, "I drive with two feet. Most people get taught otherwise, but I keep one on the brake, one on the accelerator, to cut down the time. When you're in a high-speed chase, ever' fraction of a second counts and I learned the technique when I was hanging around the race drivers. This is how they drive."

The sheriff's voice fades as the chase drops off the edge of reception. We hear static and wait wordlessly for several minutes while the square does nothing at all. It seems to be staring back at us.

From the northeast corner, a pickup moves slowly into the light of the square. Massick straightens in his seat. "It's young Wilson," he says, "and he's sure as hell gonna turn some cat's asses."

The pickup moves very slowly into the street, drives its length, U-turns, drives back. On its return, having found

as it passed the spot of lubricant ice, it suddenly acceler-
ates and spins, revolves on an axis of freed momentum.
Twice around, marking rings on the ice with the measured grace of a blade. A perfectly executed cat's ass.

"Let's go get him," Massick says, and drives out of the
alley. The pickup, seeing, catches and jerks immediately
and proceeds forward with law-abiding caution. Massick
meets it, rolls down his window. Young Wilson does the
same.

"Evening, Darrell," Massick says, musical sarcasm in
his voice. "What ya doin'?"

Young Wilson is red-haired, gnomish behind the
wheel. He decides a lie will do him no good. "Man," he
says, "geeeze. I just couldn't resist it. Geeze, that was
fun." His voice is high and hoarse. "Oh, man."

"Uhhhuh."

"Man, it's so slick! I just had to try it once." He giggles.

"Yeah, well I think you best be going home now, don't
you? You had your fun."

"Yeah."

"Yeah."

"Yeah, okay. Thanks."

"Okay, Darrell. Good night, now."

"Okay."

The pickup moves away.

"I coulda given him a ticket, and he knows it. So maybe
he'll remember he owes me one. Strange kid, though.
Don't smoke, don't drink, don't date. Nothin'. But
orneryer'n hell. Just loves to drive that truck. Drives it
into town every night and just cruises around and
around."

And that's it. A mild reprimand. Massick's vigilance
has made me expect more. Perhaps, as one who's called
stock-car races, given high-speed chase, done "a fair bit of
racing" in his day, he simply defers to talent when he
sees it.

That would not have mattered to the One-Armed Bandit. He had no patience with talent, and certainly no bond with the teenagers—when I was one of them—that the town hired him to watch. Then, the city council saw no need for anything so ornamental as a police car, uniform, or even a title. The One-Armed Bandit was not called Prairie City's police chief but simply and informally its "night watchman," and that phrase defined his work precisely. He sat at the southwest corner of the square, the hood of his rusty old beige Ford poking out of the Co-op office's shadows, and watched the night. Through the hours of his shift, he probably drove no more than three or four miles, but the simple knowledge that he was sitting there kept an efficient peace.

His name was Orville Pressman. He farmed a bit, I believe, and sometimes worked a shift at the Maytag plant in Newton. That's all I ever knew about him. His left arm ended in a knob above the elbow, and there were several stories explaining it—a farm accident, a bullet wound, the end of a drunken brawl. It was all extremely indefinite, like everything else about him, for he some-how managed to live around here in a kind of looming mystery, a really remarkable feat in a place so small. He existed as he worked, in shadow.

True to the pattern of my upright youth, and to the fact that I couldn't turn a competent cat's ass to save me, I had only one incidental conversation with him, the memory of which comes back full after witnessing Massick's hand-ling of young Wilson. The spot, the season, the hour were all the same, but I had done nothing more than park my father's 1960 Dodge Dart on the square in front of Snub's and ride aimlessly about town with my best friend, Hardnose Walker, the two of us sharing the terror of being high school seniors who were just beginning to see the form and height of the precipice. After several hours, Hardnose drove me to my car and as we sat in the front seat of his Plymouth, the beam from a flashlight hit us full face and held. I jumped from the Plymouth in a simple attempt to get away from the light, leaping out as if a rattlesnake had raised up suddenly in the car. Outside, I saw the One-Armed Bandit in his car. He held the flashlight in the pit of his arm and rested it on the ledge of the rolled-down window, sighting it.

He got out, the flashlight still in the V of his half-arm and his body. By minimally turning, he could direct its beam with a marksman's accuracy, learned movement fluid as instinct. He shone the light on Hardnose, held it, then turned it onto my chest and said, "Get out of town." He was of medium height, and had a small paunch. He wore the work clothes of a layman—khaki shirt and trousers, plaid jacket. He had a stubbled face that seemed to have slipped in a flesh slide to the lower right corner of his jaw. He added, "Now." It was clearly the last word he intended to use on us.

With that light beam on me, I wanted only to get out of town. Then. And we did, Hardnose in his Plymouth, me in the Dart, moving away from the square as if we were a cortege.

There was violence in the One-Armed Bandit's light, conducted through the barrel and suspended like particles in its glare. Violence was near his surface in a certain raw and careless form, seemed to flow from the base of his half-arm. A flashlight, under his arm, it was a weapon.

The fact that he wore farmer's clothes and drove his own rusted car made him seem more, not less, fearsome. There's a certain implicit responsibility that goes with the paraphernalia—uniform, siren-lighted car—an assumption that whatever abuse might occur, it will be orderly and professional. But the Bandit seemed a vigilante deputized at nightfall, with a temper and no one to answer to. Furthermore, if legend serves, he carried a shotgun, strapped to the inside of his door and brushing his left leg as he drove. Nothing official or Police Academy recommended; just a shotgun, familiar as family, kept perhaps in his barn during the day, strapped to his door at night, the sort of gun with which he might casually drop stray dogs running his horizon.

I've no idea what became of him, but he's the law I'll always associate with this place. It strikes me, as I glance into the back seat at Massick's rifles, hear his radios, that the town, by costuming its enforcement to meet modern crimes, has unintentionally weakened it a bit. I'm not sure what might happen if Massick, with all his accessories loaded and willing, drives some night into a corner that really frightens him. That's the scenario that turns an irony dark. I do know that I could more comfortably shoot pistols in the council room with Massick than shine flashlights in the same room with the Bandit.

Massick drives to the highway, pulls in behind the Tower Cafe, swings around past Vern's camper, inanimatedly dark in the way of vehicles that are not simply parked, comes to a stop next to the Tower's east wall. "Time to run some radar," he says. He places the radar base on his dashboard. It looks like a large digital clock. He frees from tangled wires the detector, shaped like a megaphone. "Some of the council don't like me doing this so much. They don't want no one to think of their precious little town as a speed trap. They none of them complained, though, about the revenue I've brought in."

The highway at early morning is nearly as still as a side street. In the space of an hour, three semis move past us, west to east, coming loud and lawless around DeRaad's corner a mile out, then gearing down to a diesel pianissimo through the eight quick blocks of town, modulation that shows *someone* thinks of this precious little town as a speed trap.

The radios are empty. We seem the only law awake in Jasper County. The car's dashboard, swollen with melodrama and salutation earlier this evening, seems to contract in the quiet. A light snow begins to fall, the only movement, and each flake seems to strike the highway percussively.

We hear a car approaching from the west, an event after three trucks in fifty minutes, and Massick aims his megaphone at the noise. Out of the dark, a local car, a car he recognizes, moves past us. As it crosses his line of sight, the driver honks and can be seen in silhouette broadly waving at our hiding place.

"Horse nuts," Massick says, putting the megaphone down. He laughs and honks in return.

The snow paves Prairie City with alternatives to the maze. Its ditches and fields are filled and smooth, like newly opened roads, and from all over town comes the raw reverberating ignition of snowmobile engines. In comparison, the noisiest cars move as quietly as if they were under sail. Idle through a dry winter, snowmobiles fly through the streets like a militia come out of hiding. They race in long files along field fences and through ditches to neighboring towns.

The snow fell too late for Dick Vroom. Deep as it lay, it might as well have come in July for all the help it has been to him. His store enjoyed a small run of business near

Christmas but not enough to change his mind or his fiscal year and Vroom has closed his business. For the past weeks, he's held a final sale, clearing nearly all his merchandise. Everything but boots and shoes, and for them, he has a wholesaler. A truck will drive from Des Moines to load 347 pairs. He's consoled by the sale and embittered by the customers it's drawn. "My best customers over the years have come in once, maybe twice," he says. "But all the freeloaders lookin' for something for nothing, they been in every other day. Never set foot in the place once till now. Suddenly, we're big buddies. 'Hey, sure sorry you're selling out. Where you gonna go? What you gonna do?' Concerned as can be." A small-town merchant, selling out, has the conflicting emotions of a pastor at his Easter service. He's requisitely grateful to the people attending for the first time, and resents just a bit their nerve.

Vroom says that he will go to work again for the Hormel Company, at its new plant in Ottumwa, fifty miles southeast of here, for the same man and in the same department he left six years ago. "I'm glad of that," he says. "I know I can get along with him. And the benefits are good. Free health insurance, eighteen thousand dollars' life insurance, three weeks' vacation after five years—I took exactly three days off the past five—and every day off the union gets. Only reason we get benefits like that is because of the unions. Company wants to make sure we get everything they get."

He's sold his store to a young woman who's run a plants-and-crafts shop in a smaller space down the street. Ferns will rise from the slacks shelves, macramé hang where double knit has hung. It's difficult to imagine Vroom passing over to her Bert's pillow and the large tin can.

Van's Grocery has also closed. His health has not

returned. While he looks for a buyer, DeWit's once again is Prairie City's grocery. "I hope he finds somebody," Don DeWit says. "We got more than we can handle. The town can use a second store, for sure." All that's surprising about Van's closing is that it didn't happen months ago. The grocery, bakery, and coffee shop—most of Prairie City's west side—are dark and, expected or not, the closing gives the square an inordinate span of recession.

Jim Billingsley still believes a man could profitably run the grocery. "I'd first thing hire a good check-out lady, a good baker, and a good meat cutter," Jim says. "Then I'd shop Des Moines for wholesale specials, not just one warehouse like Van did, but all over town. Shop one day a week for different leader items, not just your standard leaders." Customers at the Cardinal nod with Jim's pronouncements. Opinion has gone from surmise to certainty that he will buy the grocery.

Jim's parties filled December, and much of January. The teachers were so pleased with their evening they have asked already to return. "That's real nice," Jim says, "but I'll believe it when they walk through the door." He's thinking of opening the Tower again, of segregating firmly the men who want to drink beer until they're full from the family diners who inhibit them from doing so. "I been getting complaints from some of the boys. They say they can't relax in here. They just want a place where they can raise hell, break glasses and pull each other's pants down." Angry as this makes him, he sees the merit of bars with separate personalities. "I got half a mind to just hire somebody big and good to run the Tower, sweep out the place once, and turn 'em loose in it." Last week, a few of his better customers found, at the Knoxville Legion Hall, the talent they'd like him to hire. "They came back here, a bunch of 'em, telling me about this lady bartender at the Legion with 38-inch knockers. They're saying they want me to hire her, but only on nights when no wives would come in. They's *serious.* Dead serious. They's drunk, but they's serious. 'So what am I supposed to do?' I ask 'em. 'Have an extra bartender waiting in the kitchen, so's if one of your wives walks in, I can run the lady out the back door and run him in?' Well, they wasn't sure how that'd work."

If he gives his plainest drinkers the Tower, he'd like to turn the Cardinal into a true "supper club" and wants to hire a cook who can administer a grill filled with steaks. He's asked informally around town but has been hampered by the allegiance to the nuclear family in Prairie City. "All the women in this town are married with kids and don't want to give up their nights. I'm thinking of running an ad in the Pleasantville paper. Everybody runs around in Pleasantville. Town's full of divorcees."

At the Co-op elevators, Hoop Timmons has been out of his winter box more often than in the past. He's been filling long semi trailers with corn. "Prices are up a bit, so some of 'em have sold a little." He's happy to be sending off his corn to river barges, happy for the space it leaves him. "Makes a fella nervous sitting here with ever'thing full up. Ya wonder where they think it's all gonna go if they don't sell nothin' all winter and drive in here with next year's crop in the fall." For Hoop, that's an optimistic statement—the admission that there may, indeed, be a crop next fall. But he remains more comfortable with the prospect of a bleached and useless spring. "This winter just sealed it, far as I can see. Soil blowing all over, not a bit of moisture till this snow, which don't amount to beans." On the radio in his shack, he's heard a lot of university agronomists discussing the topic. To raise a crop to the standards of Iowa abundance, the state will need three months of ideal weather. "When's it ever been *ideal?"* Hoop asks. "In the best years, it ain't ideal."

In the face of the belated winter, one can sense an impatience in the farmers to get at the fields once again. Entering Snub's or the Cardinal, one smells grease and oil immediately. Throughout the countryside, tractors and the tools they pull are being given shakedown lubrications.

As a kind of valedictory, the men who drive each morning about the county conspired on a rumor of tabloid proportions. At Snub's, word was passed, seemingly offhandedly, across the counter to one of the waitresses that she was about to have a new neighbor. The way they heard it, old L had bought the house next door to hers. Old L is renowned through Jasper County for the disorder of his farm. His lawns resemble a junk yard that cannot move its inventory. The way the men got it, L had sold his farm, purchased the house that meets the waitress's, and was moving his life's scattered parts to town. The waitress went home that night frightened but skeptical, the skepticism all waitresses grow like a skin. She awoke the next morning to see her worst fears on the lawn. Next door sat a cluster of old cars, their bodies loose and spilling out of themselves. The men at Snub's needed two full days to calm her. She hadn't believed their original story; now she refused for days to believe their explanation—late at night, they had dragged cars from Louie Beener's auto-body shop onto her neighboring lawn.

There've been no further complaints to the council that Police Chief Massick has used his citizen's-band radio for romance. Or for any task other than routine. Sometimes, the channel bears messages to Prairie City from the world. Or at least those in Prairie City not otherwise hooked up. Vern has no telephone, and no known friends with one. So, as a bearer of interstate news, Massick drove to Vern's basement apartment to tell him that word from Kansas had arrived on the radio. Police had arrested a man who had shot and killed Vern's brother in a fight in a Kansas bar.

SPRING

For the first time in many days, the lights are on, the doors unlocked, the cash register ringing at Van's. The inside of his store is brighter than this Saturday-morning sky, for the latest rain, in a series that has been ideal in its interval and strength, has created a ten-A.M. dusk. Some cars have their lights on as they circle for a parking place, and the normal Saturday pace of the square has quickened considerably with a morning of business at Van's.

Van stands near the front windows by the door. He is tall, even though his posture has bent nearly into a parenthesis. He has thick silver hair and a narrow, chiseled face. He should be the dominant figure in a crowd, but people are entering the store and walking past Van without noticing him. There is a translucence to him, as if health were what gave a body its mass, and the chroma of the morning shines through him. More than that, he stands in his store as if he were visiting it, while the men and women of the town walk through it with a proprietary stride. Incongruously, Van plays host, giving off, as he stands on one foot and then the other, the particular shyness of failure.

He's watching the auction of his remaining goods—groceries, fixtures, carts, shelves, all he was not able to sell at reductions that started at ten percent, went to twenty, then thirty during the store's final week. Now this space is almost a shell. The items to be auctioned have been moved to one end, where they sit in boxes and piles, like basement miscellany. All the shelves have been dismantled; now they themselves will be sold. Without the shelves, there are no aisles. People walk about a bit aimlessly, as if looking for the streets. The wooden floor groans underfoot, echoes running the length of the store.

Auctions are commonplace here, so much so that they have become a social form, people coming to watch the bidding on the goods that are a man's compiled biography. Every week, handbills are posted in all the shops, advertisements run in the *News*, explaining the terms and items of sale. Land is auctioned. Buildings. Machinery and equipment. Household goods, used and contemporary. At some point in almost everyone's time here, there comes a day of auction. It may be the day, like a horizon point at the end of a field row, that a working life has aimed for. Or it may be, like this one, a public surrender. But, regardless of what feelings the seller may bring to an auction, everyone else brings festivity.

Near the front window, there's a mattress on the floor and next to it an old maroon couch, swaybacked. Rip and Hazel Perry are sitting on the couch, at ease in its hollows, chatting and smiling and waving to passers-by visible through the front window as if it were a pane in their living room.

"Whatcha gonna buy, Rip?" asks a man who's come to sit on the arm of the couch.

"Ah, I don't think I'm gonna buy," Rip says. "I was thinking maybe I could sneak her"—he points to Hazel, small and round—"into a pile and somebody'd bid on *her!* Ha!"

"Ha!" says the man.

"Tssk! Ohhh, *Rip!*" Hazel says. "Don't listen to him."

"Ha," says Rip.

Van smiles at the Perrys. He's wearing a red windbreaker that hangs on him like the past. He stands, with his arms folded, at the front of his store while the auction goes on at the back. He says, "I told him to bid it down. Don't mess around. I told him to get the stuff out of here in a hurry." He nods toward the auctioneer, a man from Altoona who's getting local help. The auctioneer stands on steps, looks over the crowd, while below him Van's sons and a few other men are bringing in the boxes and holding up the numbered items. Nothing has been deemed too trivial for sale. Cases of Jell-O, starch, rice, jelly have been officially numbered and stand for bid.

Perhaps forty people surround the sale. Cement-plant workers, farmers, some town wives, a few couples, a huge man named Potsy Clark standing like a Douglas fir amidst shrubbery.

"I'll give ya a dime for the lot of it," someone shouts.

"I'll give *you* a dime to go home."

"Ha, ha."

Van smiles at a couple as they leave with cardboard cartons.

"I told him the sooner the better," he says. "I told him, 'Get it outa here.'"

Only half a dozen or so are seriously shopping. The rest of the crowd watch and laugh and ride the auctioneer's syncopated narrative. Except for the half dozen, people seem to be listening more for momentum than for facts, taking an energy from his beat in the way that music moves the blood.

"What we got here, what we got, we got a box of Campbell's soup, twenty-four cans, what kinda soup we got here, John?"

"Red!" yells someone in the crowd.

"Ha! A case a red soup. You can eat it or paint your rust spots with it."

"Whata we bid on a case a soup, Campbell's tomato soup? Do I hear a dollar, whata ya say a dollar?"

"Christ, you imagine eatin' tomato soup for lunch ever' day? You'd spend the afternoon with a magazine in your hand, wouldn't ya?"

"Grow vines after a while, wouldn't ya?"

"What'mI bid?"

"Half a dollar," says a cement-plant worker at the edge of the crowd.

"Jesus, Big Bucks, you still holdin' on to your Christmas bonus? Whata you gonna do with tomato soup? Pour it in your beer?"

Van says that he hasn't any idea what will happen to this space, nor any interest. He tried to find a buyer, came close a few times, but no one had enough capital to open up or to obtain a loan. Lately, a young man with experience in large Des Moines groceries has been interested. In Des Moines, big groceries stay open seven days a week and sell beer, so speculation has risen that if he buys the store, he'll bring with him both the hours and the beer.

Van says he doesn't know how Prairie City would respond. "You figure this town wouldn't go for that," he says quietly. "Beer and such. You carry beer out of a tavern, you can do it in the dark and in front of people who are there for the same reason. You carry beer out of a grocery store, you might have to stand in line with somebody buying a week's worth of food who'll be looking you up and down and up again." He rubs his chin distractedly. "But you never know. This town'll do things nobody can figure."

He says that all he plans to do for now is rest. He walks to a low railing near the door and squats carefully on it.

"Better get ya a bargain, Rip," says a man leaving the store, walking past the Perrys on the couch, past Van on the railing.

"They sellin' any horse feed?" Rip asks. "I could feed it to the horses in the day and she get to nibble some at night."

"Ha!" says the man.

"Oh, Rip!" says Hazel.

"Ha!" laughs Rip.

Van's family has already moved to Pella. After the auction, he'll make a final inventory, sweep the auctioneer's debris, and on Monday morning lock the door. He may have a cup of coffee at Snub's before he leaves for Pella, giving Snub another fifteen cents of business. (Snub has gained fifteen to twenty noon meals from the closing of Van's lunch counter. He said the other day that he's pleased to have anyone come through his door, but not at the expense of another man's misfortune.)

"What'mI bid? What we got here, John? What's that say? Hold it up here and let—oh, okay, whatamI bid for a box of Stayfree Mini-Pads? Twenty-four boxes in the carton here, what am I bid?"

"You could use those, couldn't ya, John?" someone shouts to the local man holding the carton. Adolescent snickers run through the crowd.

"Okay, let's have a bid," says the auctioneer.

"Know you can find a use around the house for 'em, John."

The crowd laughs.

"No, all my mice got saddles," John says, and a larger laugh spreads to the edges.

"Okay, folks, let's get a bid here. What'mI bid for the Mini-Pads?"

From his place on the railing, Van says softly, "Bid it down."

Across the street, on the north side of the square, the plants-and-crafts shop is holding its grand opening. It's drawing a steady flow of ten, twelve people. Prices are reduced, small plants by fifty percent. The merchandising of openings and closings are the same—half price starting up; half price selling out—but the day in this shop belongs to its owner; across the street, to the crowd.

"Very nice," says a woman in the shop.

"Good luck," says her friend.

"Have a cookie, and some coffee. Cream?" says the young woman, the owner. She is short, beginning to grow fat, and with her she has her young child, who'll occupy during the shop's hours a crib at the back of the store.

"Prairie City can use a bigger shop like yours. I'm glad you moved."

"It'll be a lot handier."

"It will."

"Come back." Her child lifts a toy and wails happily.

"We will."

"We will."

Outside, the sky has begun to lift. The rest of the square's population is attending neither opening nor closing, but is going about its prosaic Saturday business. Cars and people move through a day of variegated gray.

"Hey, there." My father, from his car, waves and pulls to the curb. He leans across the front seat, says to me, "Let's go down to the office and see if we can catch Cookie."

I step from the sidewalk, open the door of the '67 Dodge, metallic gold, maiden clean. We start away from the square.

"You see him down there?" I ask.

"No," my father says, "but it's Saturday morning. He's not home and he's not at his shop." He laughs and we exchange reductive nods: Cookie's "at the office," at the Cardinal.

"I got a strip of chrome for the side of this car," Dad explains, "so I thought I'd better see if I can twist Cookie's arm to put it on for me." My father preserves his cars with a curator's care. Consequently, for all the years he's lived here, he's been a friend and client of Cookie's.

We drive past Van's, past the Co-op silos, and cross the tracks. Dad says, "He'll probably give me all kinds of excuses why he can't get to the car." He smiles. "I'll have to bribe him a little."

Cookie has not worked full time at his auto-body shop since he began to receive Social Security checks last year, but retirement has not greatly changed the reliability of his hours. Always, he has seemed determined to elude work that was looking for him; a truant. Perhaps that's been because he's obsessive about the work he does, and wished to postpone such depth of effort for as long as possible. In any event, he has divided his life between two poles—intense labor and none. Some say he has worked as hard at hiding from work as at the work itself.

There's a story told of a man named Maynard, who lived in a small Alaskan settlement. He was the only electrician within hundreds of miles and he followed periods of hard work with equilibriums of whiskey. He was alternately devoted, so that if someone wished electrical work done, one went to the bar, stuck his head in the door and inquired, "Is Maynard drinkin' or workin'?" That is Cookie's pattern and, surprisingly, it's accepted in Prairie City by a greater share of the people than might be expected. Something, perhaps his honesty, touches the best instincts here. It would be nearly impossible, strategically, to hide a thirst as habitual as his, but others who've lived here have tried, have driven to the state's southern border towns to drink, or have taken their bottles out to the narrowest country roads. But Cookie has always spoken openly, without apologizing, of what he needs to do. And he's accepted in the way of Maynard the Alaskan electrician: When you're ready, Cookie, whenever you're ready.

Which says a great deal about his work. There are other auto-body men in town who get considerable business, quite a lot of it reflecting the new schools of form and technique—transplants, hybrids, fronts of Chevrolets melted to backs of Fords. Within those trends, Cookie has held to original intentions, his work pure inside the narrower freedoms of restoration. And as far as my father and many others are concerned, that is an attitude worth their patience.

Shortly after I'd returned to Prairie City, I was at work one afternoon at my desk. Outside, Dad mowed my yard. He'd been able to find no work at home. The fields needed nothing. The factory was closed that day. So he drove to town with his lawn mower and, without knocking on my door, simply started over grass that was by his standards the height of pasture. I looked up and was watching him through my window, when a white 1965 Chevrolet passed slowly on the highway. Dad instantly let go of the mower and raced to his car as if summoned to a fire. He sped off in the gold '67, returned half an hour later, and I met him at the door.

"What was *that* all about?"

"I saw Cookie's Chevy drive by," he explained. "I had to chase him down to ask him about some paint. I've been trying to corner him for weeks." Cookie was loose; everything else could wait.

Since then, I've watched the same scene all over town: Cookie's Chevrolet moving past; someone dropping work or conversation to run for his car.

We pull into the Cardinal's gravel lot, half filled at

eleven A.M. Simultaneously, we spot the Chevrolet. It is dirty and around its wheels, its lights, its fenders are the speckled trimmings of rust. Seeing the car, I think of similar anomalies, people at odds with the idea of their work. I've never seen a tailor whose pants did not hang on him like drapery.

"Looks like everyone's present," Dad says. Saturday's early crowd. The hour, the day, act like filters, and the men who are here now are as reliably here as if they held a membership.

The Cardinal is absolutely a tavern at this hour. No one working his way through a steak; no women ordering "ice-cream drinks." The line at the bar is tight and congenially composed. The men seem to fit together, the pointed elbow of one slipped unconsciously into the angled torso of another. Their noise is equally homogeneous. Talk and weaving gestures run up and down, not so much a solid length of conversation as of spirit. All these men might not be friends, but they are unanimously friendly to the reason they are here.

Cookie sits near the end, to the bartender's left. He has one foot on the stool rest, the other on the floor. He's wearing loose gray-cotton pants, a plaid shirt, old high-topped sneakers he's given some thought to tying. Metallic paint spots his clothes like a rash.

My father puts a hand on his shoulder, causing Cookie to jump. He swings around on his stool.

"Well, hello, son," he laughs, then, seeing me, "and son, *junior*. To what do I owe the honor?" He's an extremely handsome man, as elegant as a silent-film star. His hair is straight and silver, and so is his thin mustache, neat as a line of pinstriping. He wears glasses with black, narrow frames, accidentally stylish. In other clothes, in another setting, he would look like a Fairbanks.

He says to me, "You condescend to spend a little time

on *this* side of the bar?" I've gotten to know him, bartender to customer, working Wednesday nights at the ·Cardinal.

"Just tagging along, Cookie," I say, nodding at my father, who's ordering for Cookie a shot of Black Velvet and a short beer. Dad motions like a host for the drink, points to Cookie, all of it orchestrated behind Cookie's back. Whiskey and beer, the parts of the bribe, are placed before him.

Some years ago, Cookie drank screwdrivers, which he sipped delicately through a stirring straw. He says that he suffered hangovers during that time but never, as far as he can remember, a cold. He drinks boilermakers now, and, very rarely, drinks dessert—blackberry brandy— when all the whiskeys taste raw on his tongue. He drank Early Times bourbon for so long and so predictably that Jim confidently ordered an unusually large stock of it. Immediately, without knowing of the supply, Cookie moved experimentally down the shelf, came to Black Velvet, found it the smoothest liquor in the row. Jim reorders Black Velvet more cautiously, a bottle gone, a bottle replaced.

"Here you go, Cook," Dad says. "Happy birthday." Cookie swings back to face the bar.

"If it always was my birthday," he chuckles, "I'd be a thousand and a half." Many people buy Cookie drinks, to preface their requests or simply to wish him well, and he has learned to spread them over a day. Sometimes, offered one, he'll say, "Thanks. I'll get it later," and the order goes down on a piece of paper kept behind the bar. He's the only man in town who has a balance sheet, a running tab of drinks receivable as well as ones he's charged.

He says that he'd always intended to build a new house, but that he's drunk away lumber enough for a subdivision. He says it's too late now "to worry about making a pile." But I cannot hear any significant apology coming through. Cookie gives lip service to the idea that his money would have been better spent on almost anything else, but I sense no repentance. He drinks because he likes the ceremony and the taste of liquor, and likes the companionship.

I once repeated to him what Mark Walker, the man who harvested my father's crops, said: "It's not the liquor I like so much. It's the company."

Cookie nodded at that and said, "I know what he means. A lot of the fun is coming down and lying to some of the boys."

Dad and Cookie made an appointment.

"Not Monday," Cookie says.

"I know, I know," my father replies, having had this conversation before.

"I used to hate like hell to face a Monday," Cookie continues. "And now that I'm retired . . . I don't."

Dad describes the chrome strip and reminds Cookie of the color of paint last used on the Dodge.

"Oh, hell," Cookie says, "didn't you hear, Kenneth? Chrysler stopped making that color years ago. Niggers and farmers were the only ones buying it." He giggles, takes a shot of Black Velvet, washes it, wipes his lip. More seriously, he says, "It'll take some touching up."

"A little bit," Dad agrees.

"I'll be sure to bring some cake pans down from the house to catch the paint that drips."

"How about I drop it off and pick it up after work?"

"Well, let's see," Cookie says, "most jobs, I try to stretch a day into three. But for you, since it's just a farmer's car, won't take me long at all." They laugh, and curse each other. Around them, the Cardinal rudely shouts and jumps. The jukebox has let Merle Haggard loose. Inside the shouting, Dad and Cookie converse. "It's a good thing you're not Dutch, too," Cookie says. "A *Dutch* farmer's car, that doesn't take me an hour. I just pour the paint straight from the can."

We all laugh and Dad orders Cookie another, this one for their friendship.

"Write it down, Jimmy Joe," Cookie says to the bartender, Jim's son. He looks down the bar, a bluish, boisterous line. "I'll see all you good people later," he says, and does a push-up away from the bar. "As the walrus said, I think the time has come." He giggles and squeezes my shoulder. "Why don't you come watch me ruin your ol' man's car?" he asks. "I could stand the company. The shop's kind of off the beaten path. I don't get the loafers like some of the others."

"All right," I say.

"We'll lie to each other some. Come on down."

"I will."

And I do. The following week, late in the morning, seeing the Chevrolet parked in the alley behind the shop, I pull up to a wide overhead door that fronts highway 163. The shop itself, white framed, looks as if its dimensions were drawn by taking the measurements of an average car and adding a foot all around. It appears to be the garage for the big brown house behind it, and, in a sense, it is.

Mrs. William Shearer, widow of the shop's owner, lives in the brown house. Her husband was a fine mechanic who decided late in life that he'd like to run an automobile body shop. He built this one, refused all mechanical work, and began his second career. Shortly afterwards, h~ had a heart attack. He hired Cookie, who'd been working in Newton and Des Moines and had become tired of "carrying a lunch bucket." Cookie ran the shop, Bill Shearer made sure there were paint and parts. Cookie has received as salary over the years a percentage of the work he's brought in.

A small rusted sign—"Shearer's Body Shop"—hangs memorially near the overhead door. Inside, a car and Cookie fill the space. The car is not my father's. Cookie stands in thick shade, liquidly slouched. A small paunch pulls at the front of his shirt. He holds tools, a brass-headed hammer, a chisel, and moves around the car, stalking it. He looks up and smiles. "You're a day late and a dollar short," he says. "Your ol' man's car is done and gone."

"How'd it look?"

"I kept a few wavy lines in it just to keep him humble."

Cans of paint, mixes, cleaning liquid fill a bench along one wall. "If you kept a quart of every kind of paint there is, you'd fill the shop." Above the bench, a collection of wall calendars features women wearing coats of paint. They are sun-faded, vintage sexy, Betty Grable metallic brown. Air hoses, lariat-coiled, are on the floor. A ventilating fan arhythmically starts and hums.

"Help me a second," Cookie says, and motions me toward a rear door of the brown Ford he's disassembling. Chrome strips from the Ford lie like its jewelry about the shop. "I learned my lesson a few years ago," he says. "Tried to lift a door by myself. The glass fell and, like an idiot, I just on instinct let go the door to catch twenty-five dollars' worth of glass. The door fell on my toe and broke it all to hell. I was off work a month and mad every minute." We carry the door to the side of the shop. "Now I wait for some loafer to show up and help me lift them. Sometimes half a day goes by before anybody does. So the door just waits half a day." He laughs, wipes his brow. After a morning of work, he looks freshly bathed, in spite of his speckled clothes. I think of Hoop, spotless in the heaviest dust.

With his hammer and chisel, Cookie lightly taps and probes the crevices of the Ford and its panels peel smoothly away. He taps the pressure points of assembly, can feel in the dark its strategic tensions. Using tools that would seem to require a certain brutality—crow bar, sledge hammer, chisels—he applies instead an intelligent delicacy. Tapping, prying at the cracks of a car, Cookie seems a man solving a safe's lock, using principally the sensitivity of his fingertips.

He has, in fact, spoken proudly of his hands. When he worked full time, his work included manual sanding, scraping, taking several inches of rust from steel fenders. Skin came off with the rust, and Cookie describes squeezing blood, at the end of the day, from the raw ends of his fingers. He talks of the cuts and punctures his hands have endured. But they've survived and Cookie regards that as an act of loyalty. In the Cardinal, he sometimes thoroughly inspects them, holding them at a distance rather like a woman assessing a coat of nail polish. They are long, thin, skeletally undulant from wrist to fingertips. In conversation, they seem to flutter on their own back and forth through his words, describe arcs that cross in front of his face, bank at his shoulders.

I've watched many other men take an unusual interest in their hands—studying them, absently fondling them in conversation. In a televised conversation, Robert Penn Warren spoke of the virtual extinction of such hands. He said, "A man on the American continent in the 18th Century was valuable. Hands were valuable. There were things for hands to do. And so the whole sense of the human value changed . . . beginning with the value of hands, what they could do, . . . Human dignity [was raised] because the hands meant something. They were not just things owned by somebody else. They belonged to that man."

Watching Cookie, I think of my grandfather, his eyes closed, gently drawing his huge, calloused, work-cracked hands across his face as if they were made of fur. Snuggling them.

Tap. Tap. A door panel from the Ford loosens slightly. Tap.

"I'd think you'd be tempted to rare back and pound it, Cookie."

He laughs. "Patience. Bill Shearer always said, 'Patience and sweet oil. That's what a body man needs.'" He waits for me to form the question, then adds, "I have no idea what 'sweet oil' is." Tap. Tap. "But it's for sure a body man can't get too shook up about anything." The panel slides off as if it had just reached its melting point. Cookie appears to melt with it, drops in a single graceful dip to his knees, and works at the floor of the car in a position, legs under him, vaguely meditative.

"Pretty loose for an old fart, aren't I?" he says, feeling my surprise. "I can still get down when I need to. If a man can't, he won't last in the body business these days. Everything's built so damn low, flat, everything slopes now instead of curving. You spend a couple of days on your knees, no matter what part you're working on."

Tap. He rises up with a piece of Ford in his hands, disgust on his face. He says, "The way cars used to be made, the crowns were high, the fenders were rounded, and when you worked on them, you could hold the definition of a curve. No more. The angles they put in them now don't want to come back. Neither do the metals.

"Listen," he says and taps the panel he'll replace.

"Hear that? Dead as hell. The old metals, tin with some carbon, were thick and strong and wanted to spring back when you hit them. They were fun to work on. You could feel the *life* in them. You could feel them respond to you when you hit them. But these fuckin' things," and he spiritlessly taps, "they use steel now that's stretched so thin there's no spring, nothing in it. All the life's gone out of it. I used to get into a frame of mind when I was working, where I was thinking that I was working on a living object and bringing it back. What it seems like now is like I'm working on corpses. They're dead when they bring 'em in and nothing I can do will put any life in them." Tap. "Punkin skins. That's what I call them. Like hitting a punkin skin."

Tap. After his explanation, the sound is dull and unsatisfying, like a chisel sinking through packed dirt. A strip of chrome clatters to the floor. "Those old cars, they'd come in smashed flat. I'd crawl through whatever space there was, get inside, and then judiciously tap, tap, tap all around the perimeter of the top until it popped out, like a crushed hat. Now a car in the same shape is totaled. Totaled. Used to be, 'totaled' was what you were about ten-thirty on a good night. Right?" He laughs, the high, flutelike giggle, and continues to move up and down, above and under the Ford, with an extraordinary nimbleness.

It was in large part his nimbleness that drew him to the work. He grew up in Newton and after school, on weekends, helped one of his relatives varnish wooden washtubs. He says the man's wife, "ambitious, a climber, wanted fancy houses and all that crap," insisted upon the latest varnishing tool—a sprayer. Once they'd begun spray-varnishing, they expanded the business to repainting, in all shades of black, the fenders and hoods of cars and trucks. Cookie, young, thin, lithe, was assigned the crevices—underneath, in the back, into the accordion folds at the top.

He says, "That was nearly fifty years ago and I was just too dumb to ever get out of the business." He worked for Chevrolet dealers in various central Iowa towns, apprenticing. He married a Prairie City girl, moved to town when Bill Shearer asked him. He works on one highway, lives on the other, two blocks north of my place, in a house so tiny it looks as if it could come right through the overhead door and fit inside this shop.

He begins to put the Ford together again, fitting the new panel, rehanging the door, taping paper over the windows as he prepares to paint, all the while working with an exaggerated expression of disdain.

"This doggy bastard," he says of the Ford. "When they drive one in, I make up my mind how much I'm going to put into it. If it comes in doggy, it goes out doggy." He believes that a person's interest, in his car and in other things, can be found underneath the covered places. How much fermenting mud has collected beneath a low runner of chrome? How do the doors swing? As he takes a car apart, he puts together an opinion, working through a kind of archaeology, excavating down to the owners' personalities.

"Sometimes you get surprised," he says. "Some people in this town, you think they're pretty thorough; neat, tidy, caring, and the surfaces of their cars look it. But when you start to take them apart, get close, you see all kinds of abuse. I'll take a man whose car looks like hell from a hundred feet, but he oils the hinges on his doors."

He absently pokes at a place on the Ford that's normally covered by chrome. A leprous flake falls. "No surprises here, though," he adds and chuckles softly. "Doggy bastard. Doggy in; doggy out. The trouble with this kind of job is it makes me feel like I'm wasting my time. I'd much rather work on a car for some finicky guy like your ol' man than on a doggy thing like this one."

He has worked a full morning, hard and unrelievedly, which is unusual for him these days. He looks at his watch, wipes sweat from his face, and moves his glasses up the bridge of his nose. "Past eleven thirty. Gotta stop and get fired up." He shakes his head. "Trouble is, anymore, I need two or three big drinks before I feel like doing anything. I take one drink and I feel like a new man. Then that new man needs a drink of his own." His voice fades elliptically, leaving to my imagination the infinitely redoubling population he suggests. Eyes glinting, he laughs.

He inspects the Ford once more, windows and chrome taped and covered, the new door panel—substantial as heavy cardboard, flat-black from the factory—hung and fitted and ready to be painted. The door is as tight in its frame as the part of a puzzle.

"God damn thing, it's hanging like a screen door in a high wind," Cookie says. "But I guess it's good enough for a Dutchman's car." He wipes his brow. Patches of sweat are on the back of his gray-cotton shirt and make patterns like a gerrymandered map on its front. He says, "If you want to come back after lunch, I'll be shooting some paint at this thing."

I say, "Okay, I will. If you start without me, don't work too hard."

"Good advice," Cookie says as we leave the shop. "Don't need it."

He's busy at the bench when I return. Next to the Ford stands a lamp of his own design—a bulb in a frame that slides the length of a long metal rod; angular and sculpturally spare. He's stirring the paint he'll spray. His silver hair is combed and wet. A stubble, like a silver mist, covers his chin and cheeks. His belly looks swollen after lunch.

"Ate too damn much," he complains, moving somewhat stiffly. "I figured I'd better eat a lot as antidote to what comes later, right?" He pulls the trigger to test the air pressure of his sprayer and sends a small cloud, metallic-brown cirrus, into the air.

"Don't you wear a mask or anything when you paint?" I ask. I imagine his lungs coated with a brilliant metallic sheen.

In answer, he points to the ceiling, to the ventilating fan, pumping fiercely and inadequately. "Also," he says, "I do have a mask, but I forget the longer I do this to wear it. I guess I figure I've been eating the stuff for fifty years and it hasn't killed me yet." He adds, "Besides, if you eat a little paint, it makes the whiskey taste better! Ha!" As if to demonstrate, he sprays a second cirrus. He giggles. "I tell some of the Dutchmen that just to watch them jiggle and wiggle a little bit."

I ask him, "What's the best flavor to eat with your whiskey?"

Without hesitation, he says, "Metallic blue. But you have to drink the whiskey no more than fifteen minutes after you've eaten the paint. Otherwise, the taste isn't nearly as good." Spray gun in hand, he narrows the area he'll begin on. "You know," he says, "some of these people more'n half believe me when I say that."

He crouches down next to the flat-black panel. "There's no way to match this with the original. No way to match what a manufacturer creates in huge vats according to some formula, and we're sittin' out here in the weeds, stirring paint in a little can."

Several years ago, a man from Colfax was brought into Cookie's shop by two local people. They came to see the car they said all Jasper County was admiring. A new Buick, they had told the Colfax man, a few weeks old, had been badly wrecked and was brought to Cookie as a pile of snarled metal. Cookie had somehow found among the ruin the lines and the forms of the Buick and had remade the car, every detail of its original majesty. The man from Colfax paced before the Buick in silent awe. Finally, he said that while he saw a few small waves imperceptible to most men, the car had nevertheless been miraculously restored. The man said that he'd known Cookie was gifted, but that the Buick was evidence of work beyond anything he'd seen. He left the shop with the local men, leaving Cookie—who had understood a few words into the visit what was going on—alone with a new Buick that one of the men had driven in that morning to have Cookie retouch a scratch the width of a hair.

"You can get five or six different tones from the same paint," Cookie says, studying the door. "By regulating the air pressure, by the way you hold the sprayer. The color depends on how close to the surface you hold it, how quickly you cover it. But the manufacturer just makes them to sell. He doesn't give a shit about us poor bastards out here in the weeds who have to fix 'em."

Years before the man from Colfax came to see the Buick, Cookie was brought a 1941 Ford, as unidentifiably a car as the Buick was supposed to have been. Had it not been a friend's, Cookie would have kept the overhead door locked to the amount of work he knew was needed. Over several weeks, the car was slowly shaped, and when it was complete again, Cookie and his friend drove it to Sully and sold it. The buyer met their price in large part because—his appraising hands on the Ford assured him—the car was clean of accident, had not "seen so much as a scratch."

Cookie releases painted air, "Psssst," and a place on the panel is brown. Quickly, the panel fills, black to brown, as Cookie moves the spray can through the air with the same light sureness his hands imply when they fly alone.

"I'd like to find the guy that first dropped metal into paint," Cookie says from inside his work. "I'd like to cut his nuts off."

"Why?"

"Because metallic paint has complicated my life enormously. With an enamel, you do two or three coats. With metallic, it takes seven, eight coats. The stuff is so damn unpredictably tricky that you have to apply a coat, let it dry. Paint, dry, paint, dry, and keep going back into the color to deepen it." He holds the sprayer with his wrist slightly cocked and drops the color, flicks it with the accuracy of a fisherman expertly fly casting. "You can go back into paint to darken it. Light to dark. But you can't reverse it, can't make it increasingly light."

He casts metallic brown and paint settles, feather light, on the surface. If the paint is sprayed directly, forced on, it will dry inside out. The metallic flakes will be trapped, sealed beneath color, and the coat will reflect dull and dark in the sun. "People think I'm lying to them when I say somebody's put their paint job on inside out, but you have to float it on, then let the metal slowly and evenly rise, so it will dry on top."

Too much moisture bleaches paint; too cool a room quickly dries it, gives it waves. After finishing a coat, Cookie will aim his light bulb at it, bathe it in spotlight to retard its drying.

"Metallic's fairly new, right, Cookie?"

"Oh, hell, no," he says. "It's just been really popular recently, but I remember the 1935 Dodge had metallic paint. It's been around that long. But not too many had it back then and those old cars had features that greatly redeemed them."

He gives the car a final preening sweep and steps back to compare the paint with its origins. The entire room smells metallic brown. I breathe deeply and cough. Cookie sees me, laughs, and raises the spray gun. He fires metallic brown at his walls.

"God damn! I used to every so often shoot this whole fucking place. Wall to wall. Get tired of one color, live with another for a while. It made it a little easier to look at those same four walls every day, I'll tell you that."

He describes the cars of the 1930s and '40s, their restrained touches of pinstriping around windows and doors, punctuating a wheel's wooden spokes. He used a thin camel's-hair brush and stroked away every speck of the brush's lint on newspaper spread all about. He was aided, he claims, "by a few stiff drinks to calm my hands."

"Now they have decal kits for that kind of stuff. Pinstripings. Flames. All that shit." He flips his hand in disgust. "I'm not interested in that shit. I don't even have the curiosity to stop and inspect it when I park next to a car that's got it." He says, "So I don't do it in here, just like I don't do custom bodywork. I always felt like I had *important* work to do."

As he speaks, his eyes move over his work. "Looks like this won't take so many coats as I thought," he says. A band of window light shines over the workbench and onto the car. Cookie looks back and forth, old paint to new, and says distractedly, pointing a thumb toward the window, "You have to look at these jobs in front of this window. Northern light's the purest when you're judging color."

Not until now, as he casually explains the necessity of northern light, have I fully understood that, in Prairie City, the automobile—adorned, raked, tilted, or kept pure—is the aesthetic measure. It is Cookie's medium.

Cookie has been, unique among the people here, interested in my work. Others have been curious, not about how I work but about activity that seems to be not work at all. Cookie has, from the beginning, drawn comparison between his work and mine, asking my habits, wondering how I fight off the diversions. "Do you start fresh every day?" he asked me one night. I said that in order to reach a necessary concentration, I began each day rewriting what I'd done the day before. Cookie nodded and said, "To get a running start. Just like I start with an easy, doggy job if I've been away from it for a while. Gets you back in, gets the cobwebs out."

He's asked me if I like noise in the room while I work. I said, "Some music, low."

Again, he nodded, said, "Just enough to puncture that accursed silence when you're sitting there, struggling." And, of course, he's asked, "You ever take a drink to help the words come?" I needed to be absolutely sober, I told him. "I understand that, all right," Cookie said. "I've learned to know the difference myself."

The first few times I was asked by someone in town, "When you going to work for a living?" I humorlessly replied that my days were in their way almost exclusively work. Then I heard myself talking, and decided to laugh instead.

"You should try it. It beats working," I'd say after a while.

"Damn. I wish I could. Must be nice to have so much

money you can loaf all day." No anger in the chord, but a harmony in three parts: accusation, perplexity, a heavy bass of inquiry. And normally, it ended there, openly inviting me once and for all to explain what the hell I was up to. Work is measured here in bushels, head, acres, miles per day behind a wheel. I didn't expect anyone to understand the muscular worth of writing. But I'd overlooked a great deal, and it was all there to be seen, in the interplay between Cookie and the town. Prairie City would never pronounce his work art, but people sense the separateness and the fragility of what Cookie does. They soften their judgments for the sake of something clearly worth it.

We talk for several minutes as the coat dries to a value that I see as exactly the one he's working to get. I say so. Cookie laughs, not condescendingly. To his eye, there is as much precision in the match after this first coat as if panels of green and red lay contiguously on the car.

"Come here," he says. He's down on his knees, with his cheek pressed to the side of the car. He's sighting across his work, old brown, new brown, old again, in refracted sunshine. "What is it they say, 'The angle of incidence equals the angle of reflection'? I don't know the geometry of it, but look at the paint here." I crouch down beside him and squint my eye. Northern sunlight strikes the car and the fresh metal flakes sparkle like a frost. From this vantage, I believe I see the slightest comparable lightness of the new brown. I recall, as I look, similarly viewing in an exhibition some mounted canvas panels of Ellsworth Kelly's. There were thirteen separate panels, the color scale. I stood at one end, head pressed to the wall, looked along the panels for the color shimmering off the surfaces like fumes, color coming off and out, alchemizing in the separating white space, spilling sequentially down the row. Now, in Cookie's shop, I'm trying to perceive the chromatic chasm between metallic brown fresh from the can, and metallic brown from Henry Ford's room-sized vats. Cookie, the pure colorist, says from his crouch that he will need six more coats to duplicate the value. Ellsworth Kelly and Howard Cook would have something to talk about.

Cookie rises up, looks at his watch. "Nothing to do here for another half an hour. Guess I'll go get fired up." We straighten the shop a bit, carrying some of his tools— a rotary sander, some hammer heads—to a tall cabinet near the overhead door.

I say, "It must make you feel good, Cookie, to see your work all around you, all over town."

He shakes his head. "Not so much that. What I notice more is the shit some of the other butchers turn out. Bad work just jumps out at me. Wavy lines and color that isn't even close and that's been recklessly applied." He's lazily straightening his shop as he talks, dropping brass tools into drawers, moving paint cans in and around one another on his bench. "What makes me happy, really, is seeing the work last. I like to see something I did five years ago still looking good." He says, "Bodywork *should* hold up."

We walk out into the bright afternoon sunlight— northern, southern, eastern, and western. A small breeze, uncompressed, comes from the west. I smell no metal in this air, and take a deep breath of it. Cookie laughs.

"How does metallic brown go with the booze?" I ask.

"Fair," he says, smiling. "Not as good as some. Better than others." He adds, "None of them go badly."

I climb into my car. He opens the door of the Chevy, starts up, heads slowly down the alley behind his shop. A left, a right, two blocks west and into the parking lot of the Cardinal. The time is nearly three.

I asked Cookie several months ago what car he would choose if he could have any one he wanted. He said that he would probably buy a General Motors car, and more probably still, a Chevrolet. He said a General Motors frame was most often tight and sensibly built, had fewer double panels, hidden bars than other makes. He said he would never buy a foreign car. "They aren't made to be wrecked." He added that his Chevy would be spectacularly plain. It would have no second color, no chrome, no exterior panels or any other complicating façades. All of it would be open to the light of day.

Through March and the first days of April, the weather has followed a pattern of rain, enough dry time for the ground to absorb the water, then rain again. The rain has come straight down, easily and steadily. It has fallen, in short, perfectly, something that Hoop Timmons said had never happened in the best of growing years. I wonder what sort of adversity Hoop is certain of.

He is out of hibernation. He's walking his grounds, circling the bases of his silos to check the large rotary fans and the general condition of the silos after winter. His grounds today are mud and networks of parallel canals from the sunken tracks of trucks and tractors. His overalls, loose and striped like an engineer's, skim the mud as he walks toward me and pick up little of it. He waves me inside.

"What you up to?" he asks.

I say, "Just trying to keep on top of things around here."

"I try to do that at home," Hoop says. He drops a low stream of Red Man into his coffee-can spittoon. "But it don't always work out that way." He smiles. He spits, between and around his conversation, a vaudevillian pause in the timing of his lines. The team of Timmons and Red Man.

"What do you make of this weather, Hoopie?" I ask. He shakes his head, winces slightly. "It's all a tease," he says. "It's all a tease. Gets everybody thinkin' things are gonna be great, see. Then they plant every damn seed they can lay their hands on." Spit. "I can just see it: Soon's everything's in the ground, we're gonna see a drouth like few have seen before."

I ask Hoop how he knows.

"Too good. Things are going just too good to mean *some*thing's not up. I've never seen a spring like this. Everything melted off by the middle of March. Temperature turnin'." He squirms on his bench. Reciting the evidence seems to be making him freshly nervous. "Then the rains. Most beautiful damn rains I've ever seen in my life." He shakes his head again. "It's *something*, this weather," he complains. "It's perfect." Spit. "It's eerie, is what it is."

Each season has occurred out of all calendric order. Autumn refused to quit, ran warm far into November, giving farmers more weather than they had work to fill it. Winter was more usual, bone cold and snowless, days of ice dust, but then dropped a late-February snow that stopped the town, created a new topography, planes nearly ascendant. Spring almost immediately followed, and not procedurally. There was no slow rebirth, were no vegetative dawns, nothing for the poets in this spring.

No work benefits from seasonal order more than farming. The calendar is its skeleton. Farmers evolve habits of plowing, disking, planting, weeding that begin, weather allowing, on almost an exact date every year. But if each farmer has developed his own calendar of work, unduplicable, a fingerprint, all farmers use the same historical sequence of seasons. The last week in April may mean one step for B, another step entirely for C, but they associate different steps with the same conditions. They know what the features—temperature (the air's and the earth's), moisture, the consistency of the soil—of the last week in April have been, should be. Not this year. Early November was late September. Late February was mid-December. March is May.

Science, as well as practice, has emphasized the calendar to a degree more exact than anyone farming twenty years ago would have been able to imagine. Hybrid seeds, especially seed corn, have made it possible for a farmer to choose how long he'd like his crop to grow. Put a seed in the ground on the date suggested, it will grow in the time specified, will stand ready for harvest at the moment printed on the package. There are early-crop seeds, late-crop seeds, seeds that follow more traditional germinations. The growing lives available are various and nearly guaranteed. But the balance of it all hangs on the confluent timing of the seed in the ground, with the temperature, with the weather.

These new seeds, and the alternatives they allow, have really written a calendar of their own. A crop is planted, grown, harvested on a much faster schedule: Get it in; grow it; quickly get it out. The longer a crop lies in soil, the higher the risk that it may fail; that too much rain or too little, or hail or wind, will claim it. The best way to beat weather is to offer it as few days as possible to get a crop.

Consequently, farmers who in years past began, at the end of April, early May, to work seriously again in their fields now worry that March is ending and they are terribly behind in their work. They seem to have forgotten the possibility, remote as it may be, that a killing frost may strike after May. Two schedules of climate—the agronomists' at Iowa State and God's—run congruently now, and if a farmer learns to believe in the former, he seems to forget that God's older one may be at work, too.

All this has left an air of imbalance in the town. Another framework has become untrustworthy, and the conversations around town are filled with speculation: If fall was summer, and winter blew the earth away, what now should be planted, and when and how much of it? And spring. Now spring has come, early and all at once.

Late in March, as soon as the fields were thawed, farmers went into them with plows and disks. In graceful striations, the land became immediately black. After a season of harvest skin, and a quick belated snow, one easily forgot the practical color of this place: black, running epidemically. The land's mood is relaxed in autumn and in winter, and seems more accessible. Space opens out as the land in town—in the yards and the empty lots—corresponds in its look and its uselessness with the fields surrounding it. But in spring, when the countryside melts, one is quickly reminded of the difference. The whole landscape turns, comes into use, and in a certain frame of mind, it becomes almost threatening. If farmers are making fields out of railroad beds, dried river bottoms, the floors of cleared timber land, if ninety-five percent of Iowa is used for growing things, what will farmers next see as a perfectly suitable cornfield? One imagines stepping out the door in the morning to find plowed ground, wet, richly black, running to his doorstep. Instead of fearing some developer's turning land into subdivisions, one feels here as he stands in his yard an opposite vulnerability: that his lawn might tomorrow be field.

Many of the field steps were finished unusually early. Planting remained, but the ground was not wet or warm enough, and the farmers once again found themselves staring into a vacuum of work. In conversation, they sought from one another, since the calendar no longer does them any good, a feeling for when it might make sense to go in again.

"I'm about decided I'll start planting. This weather's awful tempting. But, hell, I'm afraid it'll dump a snow on us. It's not that unusual—a big snow this time of year."

"One more rain and I'm goin' to. I'm waiting on one more rain."

"There'll be a lot of spot planting next week if it holds up like this."

"I hear Bill Van Dusseldorp started this week."

"You savvy to that guy rents Mrs. Biddleman's place?"

"East?"

"East, right."

"He's in?"

"He's in two days ago."

"Hell, that's nothing. I seen a field down by Monroe, corn's peekin' up and it's all yellow and rotted. I don't know when a fella must have started, to have corn up now, but it's clear ruined."

"Now, why in hell—what would possess a man to do that, I wonder?"

"Just couldn't stand lookin' at this weather anymore, I guess. I'm about half nuts watchin' it myself."

My father's calendar has stayed nearer tradition. He plants hybrid seeds, of course, but he hasn't the land or the equipment to have several plantings germinating at once. He cannot, as many do each year, tie up a few fields with laboratory work. A few fields are all he has.

"I don't know what everybody's in such a rush about." We're standing in his machine shed, several hundred feet from the house. A white picket fence defines the lawns and separates them from this more open land, roughly mown. It's called the barnyard, from the time when there was a barn standing forty yards from where we are. Now this machine shed, made from corrugated tin, long and narrow and open on the south, a small corncrib, and the chicken house—filled with tools, its roof settled, depressed against the sky—are the buildings in the barnyard. In tall grass, the rusted bones of discarded machinery can be seen. An old harrow, a rotary hoe, scattered femora I can't identify. Also, a two-bottomed plow, too old, too small.

It is cool, raining lightly. From where we stand, the yard runs south, meets a long field that runs to the highway. Fields are on the east and on the west, forming a huge block U. The house and the lawns sit in the open space. The U, the land that he tills, measures one hundred forty-seven acres; a lower-case letter in central Iowa, but drawn and measured in such a way that he has been unable yet to make a decision on its future.

Dad says, "I've about decided for sure to buy six and a half acres from Sis, so I'll have eighty." Initially, he and Mom agreed that they'd keep the eastern half of the farm, but have begun to change their minds. "The west half makes more sense if we'd ever want to build a new house on the place," he says. "The drainage is better. And I think it'd be better for Sis to have the east. In case she wanted to sell it, and Byrdie's land right next to it might also be for sale. That would make a better package for somebody."

He's working on his best tractor, a red Farmall. Rain comes down onto the tin roof, playing it. Its sounds, and the sky—all there is to look at from the shed is the dismal breadth of sky—make the day feel cooler than it is. I'm chilly and my father—in shirt and light sweater—seems underdressed. He's rewiring the Farmall, probing, pulling, reaching in and up, at his recognizable pace—

controlled frenzy. As he circles the Farmall, he looks like a man who's lost the keys to his house and is searching for a place to break in.

"So," he says, his face, grease-streaked, inches from the loops and rods of the side-mounted engine, "I guess that's what we'll do. I still think with what I got now in equipment, I can get about as much out of an eighty, taking good care of it, as I have been off the whole place." With a pocket knife, he cuts away long peelings of rubber insulation on the wires leading from the spark plugs to the distributor caps.

"I could have started any time," Dad says. "I've never had ground in this kind of shape. I was walking it the other day. You can just see, from the way the rain has come so gently, that the ground's gonna break like it's been through a sifter. After it's rained a lot like it has, you need another rain again pretty quick. I don't know why. Ground gets hard and clods, maybe. Anyway, that's the pattern we've had this year."

He makes a final check of the Farmall, tightening, testing. He has always turned nuts onto bolts, wrapped wire onto posts, as if he were tightening them for inspection in the next millennium. He straightens up, nods. Apparently, he's satisfied that the Farmall will roll, humming tightly, into the year 3000.

He says, "Back it out for me, will you? I want to make some room in the shed for the A.C." Leo Brubaker has overhauled the Allis-Chalmers, Dad's second tractor now. Both tractors, his patched armada, are ready for the fields.

I climb up to the Farmall's seat and drop into it, looking for the sequence of the knobs and gauges all around me. It seems to me that the components of ignition have multiplied greatly during the years I've been away from tractors. I see ignition keys, starter knobs, on my left an arrangement of foot pedals, treadle wide. I sit in a well of gadgetry that is—compared with the new machinery I've seen this year—relatively antiquated. I engage the clutch, turn the key, pull the choke, press the button. The Farmall ceremonially crackles, weakens, crackles again and smooths out into a roar of considerable volume. The shed is an echo chamber, and sound caroms off the tin.

From above, I look down at my father and he looks very small, with the day's gray on him. Inevitably, I recall the old red Case tractor that I drove as a child. It was a dull rust red and I remember it as having been elementally made. From its seat, I saw no gadgets, just a smooth wide parabola of its fenders flanking me, the levers (brake, hand clutch) left and right, a vertical bar to measure the speed, a steering wheel. All of it, its body and its philosophy, was a thing of planar simplicity. Best of all, it had a crank start. At first, I was too young to turn it, and Dad would have to start it up for me. But my grandfather, who most often drove it, had a touch with the crank that very often eluded even my father.

So I sat up top, while my grandfather moved to the front with the crank. There was a ritual in this act that I took all the way to melodrama. Lining up his bad hip, Grandpa would carefully insert the crank, move it around inside the Case until he found that familiar point of fluid resistance. Then he would place himself, paying as much attention to his body's angles of leverage as the crank's. Leaning away from the tractor, the hip cocked, he became, if you traced the Euclidean logic from the handle through his stance, a vital extension of the crank. At last, satisfied that the crank and his bones were aligned, he gave what seemed the quickest, most effortless tug, a quarter-turn flick, no more, and the Case exploded to life.

On the Farmall, its engine and its frame shaking winter out, I hold the thought that the design of the Case was not simple but refined. An element of its starting system was my grandfather. He grounded its power, like an antenna. Today, that part of a tractor that was human is probably soldered wire and an intimidating coil of some kind. I'm not at all curious to know.

Clutch depressed, I shift through the gear maze, searching for reverse. After several tries, the stick locks firmly into place. I'm beginning to coordinate the various places of power and importance on the Farmall, and I slowly release the clutch. The Farmall starts back, moves into the yard. Dad hops onto the A.C., steers it into the shed. I follow with the Farmall, shut it off, hop down.

"Well," he says, "see you tomorrow morning, then?"

"Think it will be dry enough?"

"Oh, I think so. This don't make a difference, this stuff today. It's about a dew is all it is. Besides," he adds, pointing to a low-spreading creamy band of sky that in the past quarter hour has stratified the gray, "it's lifting. It'll be all right in the morning, easy, if we don't get any more."

"Okay. Good. I'll see you, then."

He smiles. "Take your time. You don't have to be out too early. I'll have to disk ahead of you for a while, anyway."

By our neighbors' standards, we have always risen to the day's high sun. Dad has been known to sleep, some mornings, until seven. He laughs at the memory of being awakened, at five thirty, six o'clock, after a night of continuous rain clearly widespread enough to include four counties, by a phone call from my grandmother in town, asking, "Did you get any rain out there?"

"All right. But I'll be out as early as I can."

Soon after the spring field work began, I began to hear questions in town about my participation. Several mornings, in the post office, after Joe Sparks and I had traded impressions of the weather, estimated the days remaining before golf and tennis could be played, he said, smiling, "I kinda figured you'd be doing some farming this spring, Doug."

I noticed, too, in the Cardinal, in the stores, that the men's complexions were turning infant-pink, and I began to feel a bit as I had when I sat, conspicuously pale, among classmates.

I told that to Dad, told him that farming and my own work here were now pretty much the same. Faced with those terms, he said he'd let me help, no matter how much I managed to ruin his crop. And so I waited while he preliminarily opened some ground, while the month of April set records for rain. Waited until the dry week came, the drought that let us in.

I drive past our farm, continue for a half mile, turn right onto a narrow gravel road, and after another half mile, pull into a driveway that opens to Byrdie's south field. During the drive from town, I competitively noticed the fields along the highway. How much has Warrick done? Jennings and Verhuel? I recalled the way in which Dad used to narrate that drive almost every time he made it— taking me to school, driving to town for any number of reasons. I recalled his eyes jumping nervously left to right as he passed the fields—"Harold's through planting, looks like. . . . Bill's beans are up. . . . Vanderhart's got some to go." This morning, I understood something of his feelings: Farm work stands exposed; progress and mistakes can't be covered, unlike first-draft pages that can be turned face down at the end of a day.

I wait in my car, in high grass, at the corner of the field. On the right, fifty yards away, Byrdie's house, deserted-gray, rises out of grass as tall as the field's. As a child, I used to imagine that when she died, she would immediately rise up through both stories of the house, pass evanescently through the roof and on into heaven.

Months would pass before anyone discovered her absence and no one would ever be able to explain with any certainty where she'd gone. Now empty, the house emanates an occupancy.

My father must feel something similar about the house. Not long ago, he told me he'd once been caught in Byrdie's field as a sudden rain came up. He ran for the cover of the back porch and had to wait hours for the storm to pass. "It was raining like crazy. It was blowing. The weeds were waving back and forth, so tall I couldn't see over them. I mean to tell you, I stood on that porch and got about half scared."

I hear, then see him. He comes out of a small valley in the field, drives to the field's edge, turns sharply toward me, and drives, disk blades waddling in the air, to where I'm waiting. He brakes, the Farmall coughs implosively as it gets to an idling speed, and he jumps down. He has disked the ends of the field and has begun the field itself. Where the disk has run, the ground has been deeply softened in crude, rigorous rows.

He always starts the season in Byrdie's field; it is the historic etiquette of farmers who farm other places as well as their own. You work first the land you don't own. Then you come home. If catastrophe descends, you can endure a lost year with the clear conscience that you placed your own needs last.

He wears a brown jacket, greased and dust-covered, and a brown cap pulled down to his ears. A thin edge of dirt, held by the moisture from his lips, encircles his mouth like a line of mascara.

We shout above the idling Farmall. "How's it working?" I ask.

He points to the evidence. "Beautiful. There's a few wet spots I'd forget about, but the rest is working up beautiful. No clods to speak of."

I crouch, inspecting the ground as if for precious minerals. Each pass of the disk measures thirteen feet. I try to distinguish individual passes, but Dad drives so precisely that I can't break the pattern up into its parts. The area of field he's worked looks as if it's been broken by a single pass of an enormous disk, the edges of one round blending indistinguishably into the next.

He's had this disk for three springs. The one he replaced measured nine feet across and he sees this piece of equipment, nearly new, as a disk and a half. "It makes a hell of a difference, those extra four feet, every time you cross a field." It would seem, then, that what he would really like is a disk capable of twenty, thirty feet of earth. But he doesn't, and money is not the only reason. Money alone does not place on his ambitions the limits I've come to admire. He understands, as equipment designers do not, that the land has a scale of its own. Although he's grateful for the four feet his new disk gives him, he sees not much beyond that extension a point at which equipment begins to ignore its responsibilities to the land. He's watched a neighbor's newer, larger disk ("Twenty-one feet wide, cost him six thousand dollars"—he always quotes price as a feature of design) and believes it performs a grand, careless sweep. "I've looked at some ground that disk's been over," he told me last week, "and it doesn't break things up like it should. The blades are just too wide-set, and too big to get down in the ground and turn it over carefully."

Opened, particulate, prismatic, the earth breaks infallibly. Breaks in 1976 as it broke in 1926, and in 1876. Its grains were formed thirty-five thousand years ago, when the Wisconsin-period glacier began to melt, warmed through substages whose water carried soil to the Des Moines and the Skunk river bottoms. Winds lifted some of the soil from the bottoms, sifted it, leaving rocks, coarse sand, gravel too heavy to be wind-carried. Only the soil was carried away, set down as loess on this upland ridge between streams. Flour-grained, purified by the winds that brought it, its coarsest component is fine sand. This is the smoothest soil in Iowa, fourteen thousand years old, measuring from the final glacial substage, the most recent.

Prairie grass grew over it and settled, over the centuries, to the texture of a hide. When farmers first broke this ground in the 1850s, they used plows that required four, five yoke of oxen, two oxen to a yoke. The plows were massive, their shares set widely, and they opened the earth in shards, the plowshares too huge to slice it carefully, in any detail.

"You ready to go?" Dad shouts, and smiles.

"You bet. Let's see if I can keep from turning the tractor over before you get back."

"I've been running it pretty high," Dad says. He means the disk is set shallowly, the weather having already done much of the deep, clod-breaking work. "It's also pretty wet not too far down, so I've been dropping it just a few inches. You'll get a feel for it. It'll start to drag you if it's set too deep."

"Okay," I nod, eager to go.

"I'll see you back here with the harrow," he says. He pats my shoulder. I feel like an aviator about to board an untested craft.

He hurries to my car. As he takes the wheel, the assumptions of a tractor driver are still in his hands, and the car rocks roughly out of the field, swaying from his oversteering.

The Farmall rumbles patiently. I mount it, climbing the front frame of the disk as if it were a scaffolding and, seated, look back at it. Its blades, steel-gleaming, polished by their work, look like rows of cymbals. With my eye on the disk, I drop the lever that releases it, experimenting, and the blades clang heavily to the ground. Trying to get a feel for the cooperation between controls and disk, I raise and lower the lever, drop the disk blades several times. The frame creaks and moans. After a few minutes, I'm satisfied that I have some sensitivity for the process, put the Farmall in gear, accelerate, slowly releasing the clutch, and pull at the same time on the lever. The tractor starts forward, takes the great scythe weight of the dropping disk, and I steer up a slight incline and into memory. The disk settles, grabs, and we all ease into the field as the sound of the Farmall drops an octave and its huge rear wheels come out of the ground holding, like paddle wheels, loosened soil in their treads. I raise the disk slightly and the tractor, with less to pull, roars and surges. I drop it farther in. Deeply rooted, it strains and slows. After a hundred yards, maybe more, I settle on a depth that feels suitably resistant and appears, in the shade and texture of the soil, to approximate the finished length beside it. On my left, the unworked field, gray and rough with the surface stitch of last year's bean vines, runs south to a fence line. On my right, Dad's work lies blackly, fresh as hope. Rocking easily up the land, I commence to farm.

The disk churns smoothly through three, four, five rounds. I'm working up and down the field, moving farther south with each pass. Corn will be planted in this field. As most farmers do, other considerations aside, Dad annually alternates corn and beans in his fields, and this year, he'll plant slightly more corn. He's somewhat concerned about this, because agricultural experts from the U.S.D.A. and the universities are forecasting more corn than beans nationwide.

A field that last grew beans, as this one did, turns over more cooperatively than one that held cornstalks. The root system of a soybean, snaking for water widely and shallowly through the soil, keeps loose the ground it runs in. A corn kernel, on the other hand, sends roots more narrowly down, plumbs for moisture, breaking little of the soil around it. Beans, the most generous of grains, leave nitrogen and other minerals for the crop that follows. Corn, entirely selfish, leaves nothing, takes everything.

A few years ago, a farm for sale west of town, beautifully sloped for drainage, its soil compositionally pedigreed, was sold for one thousand two hundred and fifty dollars per acre, a very high price. But everyone agreed that if one wished to buy farm land, there was no better farm land in Jasper County. What everyone didn't know was that the seller had planted corn every year and had put no replenishing chemicals back into the earth. The land was ideally gradient, rated on the basis of its type among the best growing soils in the state. But the corn had exhausted it. Now, after years of restorative work, thousands of dollars spent for fertilizers, its new owners hope that they may this year average eighty-five bushels of corn per acre in this part of Iowa where any yield less than one hundred bushels is considered a failure.

I cut latitudinally through the field, certain of the simplest steps. The repetitiveness of the work enfolds me. The passing of a tractor through a field seems, again, something mystical to me. On the Farmall, I could without boredom drive this disk back and forth, saw-stroking the landscape, working my way to Missouri, getting deeper and deeper into the magic.

If my steps are certain, they are increasingly crooked. I have made only ten turns this morning, and already my father's exact work has begun to slope off with a diagonal drift. By midmorning, the edge of my disking looks like the coastline of California. I find myself determined to clean up the mess before Dad returns with the harrow.

At the age of fifteen, I somehow managed to back the rust-red Case into, upon, and nearly entirely over a rotary hoe. I sat on the Case; the Case—caught perilously in the air, a punctured rear tire spewing water like a geyser—sat on the hoe. A few years earlier, at harvest, I drove the Case, as my father had asked, from our farm to Byrdie's to pick up a wagon. He had told me to drive down the edge of the field, and I was puzzled, as I headed down the edge of a densely grown cornfield, why he had asked me to drive that route. I proceeded slowly, corn stalks toppling like sugar cane in the machete path of the Case, and emerged at the end of the field. My father saw me. His mouth dropped, his features fought briefly between rage and sheer perplexity. Rage won. He had, in fact, asked me to come along the edge of the field. The other edge. The edge that was low scrub pasture.

These and dozens of more minor misdeeds are with me as I pause at the east end of the field and plan corrective strategy. Boys learning to drive a tractor are told to pick a spot on the horizon—a tree, a power-line pole—and, ignoring the immediate needs of the field, to steer for it. I select a tree that lines up with the southernmost point of my coastline, drop the disk and head for the maple. Dips and fence shrubs, rain cracks in the soil, the louvered lines of shade and sunlight on the ground, all try to draw me from this course across the field. I hunch over the steering wheel, staring straight ahead. Everything at the sides of my vision blurs. I arrive at the other end, neatly slicing the far isthmus of my completed work, and swing the Farmall around. Before me is an admirably straight thirteen-foot path, gleaming, just-black, through the ocean of last year's land. I make three passes, doubling back, covering bad work, filling in the spaces.

It is eleven o'clock now, cloudless, and close enough to being warm. Halfway across the field, in a low place, I slow and stop, leaving the disk in. The Farmall obediently quiets in the middle of its run, as if, after the erratic activities of the morning, it's given up trying to guess what's going to happen next. Its sputtering is the only sound. A pair of orioles hop over the disked ground for turned-up food.

I unzip my sweat shirt, unbutton my shirt and, in a single tug, pull both over my shoulders. I'm milk-white in the sun, and the breeze, unnoticed until now, has some April and even a little March still in it. There is no paleness like winter skin in first full sun. I look ghostly and flabby under the inspecting field light. After a few seconds, the sun seems to give more heat, like clothing. I feel the heat, and it seems the signal to get on with it. I put the tractor in gear, the disk rattles in the ground, and we meet the field's ascent, come up into view, bits of earth flying from behind the disk, all elements complete. I stand, out of the seat, driving as my grandfather drove, taking all the sun.

The field runs uneventfully beneath, the morning passing quickly. As long as I am on the tractor, it seems to be all there needs to be. I remember a recent late-night conversation at the Cardinal with a farmer, a man a few years younger than I. He has been farming since the age of twelve and farms at the moment several hundred acres. He plans to own more. He's very good at farming. He feels that, if you're shrewd, and know what needs to be known, you can make money farming when almost everyone around you—knowing less—is losing it.

He told me that he likes not only the liquid money but the feeling of permanent value that the land itself gives. And he said that as much as he likes the financial potential of farming, he also loves it for reasons considerably less prosaic. He said, "Farming gives me a certain power. I feel assured that whatever chaos is current—wars, government's changing, the races at violent odds—no matter what, I'll be a constant factor in the world. As long as humans need to eat, I can sit out here in the middle of nowhere, farm, and ignore if I choose to what's going on in the world. And that seems to me an ultimate power."

I turn around to watch the disk, peeling the ground into turbulent ribbons. Far off, through the field that connects our farm with this one, I see Dad approaching on the A.C., bringing the harrow. A harrow is simply a number of rectangular grilles, connected to make a considerable width, with rows of short, blunt metal fingers that rake the ground, crumbling it more finely after a disk has passed over it. The harrow lies flat against the earth, is hooked to the back of a tractor and pulled—as spare, as basic a process as is left in farming. Over time, as other equipment has evolved to new shapes and skills, all the manufacturers of the harrow have been able to improve is its width. Otherwise, it is the same implement it has been.

Run immediately over disked ground, a harrow will, in effect, seal the earth, seal its moisture, so that, with natural exceptions, planting can take place whether or not a field receives additional rain. Rain is already in the ground, pouched in sod by the passing of the harrow. Dad has said that, after harrowing, he'll be able to plant this field almost anytime. He could wait through two or three weeks of ordinary weather, if for some reason he'd need to, and know that the shallow subsoil will stay nearly as moist as the day it was harrowed.

I complete two more rounds while the A.C. comes closer. Back and forth, back and forth, holding firmly his suggested course: work in progress touching work just done, a three-blade width overlapping, a hem of insurance. I finish the second round as he brings the A.C. and the harrow carefully through the opening in the wire fence and into the field. We lean on our tractor fenders toward each other.

Dad nods in the direction of the work, his eyes taking it all in, gently. The sun, noon bright, lights the field, a bulb of no compassion. He says, "You got a lot done."

"It went fine. Nothing gave me any problem. I stayed away from the low spots you told me about. There're still puddles in a couple of them."

"Yeah," he says. "That's all right. Not enough there to worry about." He has held his gaze on the field, and his eyes, squinting from under the visor of shade his cap bill gives him, change very slightly, their wrinkles moving into a smile. He says, "I'll be damned."

"What?"

"I must have some loose blades on that disk."

"Why?" I ask, confused, thinking I've missed a breakdown of the disk.

"Well, look about halfway over," he says and points to the place in the field where I'd stopped to clean up. "Look at the way the disk cut ground there. Angling off, wobbling back and forth in every direction. That whole disk must be ready to fall apart, making a mess like that."

The drawn work of wandering blades shows beside straight furrows like a patch of altogether different fabric. He laughs above the tractors' noise; and so do I, at my absurdity.

We portion the field. Dad, with the harrow, drives toward the north edge, where the disking began, and I resume my cross sections. The disk dumbly lifts and settles. Opened, the earth receives the heat of the day and has heat to give off. The temperature of the air is in the high seventies. The temperature of the ground is sixty on its surface and fifty-two four inches deep. I received this information this morning from WHO farm radio, Des Moines, "the fifty-thousand-watt, clear-channel voice of the Middle West. The only radio you'll ever need." It gives every day at this time of the year readings for air, surface, subsoil, in the way that California stations give the heat of the Pacific or, for that matter, as Colorado weather reports measure in ski seasons the inches of new powder. Iowa's soil is California's ocean, but its temperature is more significant. Spring planting should occur when the ground is in the fifties. Seed corn and seed beans germinate between fifty and sixty degrees; will lie dormant in cooler ground; will splay, expended, in heat. A field warms through the morning, its temperature crests about three o'clock in the afternoon, falls quickly with the sun.

This ground is two hours from its crest. My skin is another matter. I reach to scratch my back and feel through the shoulders the sting of two hours under high sun. Once again, the Farmall slows, stops, waits for me to dress. Under a shirt, the burn pleasantly hurts. The air is seventy-five, the ground is sixty, down to fifty, and my skin has crested for the day.

Dad, on the A.C., moves along the opposite end, appearing on the open field like a toy. He's a quarter mile away and I feel as if his parallel tilling is touching mine.

I have heard him speak of working with Grandpa, with a fondness in his tone that I never hear in quite the same way when he speaks warmly of other things. They differed greatly in the temperaments of their work. It's as if my father met farming with a finicky urgency in order to be done with it, while Grandpa fit his love for the work into any shape it gave him, trying to prolong it.

One day Dad looked at Grandpa far off in the same field, as I have repeatedly glanced at my father today, and saw his tractor slow and stop. He thought little of it, continued his rounds, assumed Grandpa had merely pulled up to rest. Through two, three of my father's rounds, Grandpa could be seen perched high on the old Case hood, his legs dangling as if from the edge of a dock. If he were in pain, or other trouble, his strategy apparently was to simply wait until it got tired of him. Four rounds, my father's curiosity building. He finished another, lifted his disk, drove toward Grandpa taking sun on his rust-red dock. When he reached him, Grandpa explained, chuckling, that he'd simply run out of gas, in the middle of a field in the middle of a day, and had reasoned that the best solution was to wait. He knew that, eventually, Dad would drive over to investigate. In the meantime, there was work to watch and splendid weather in which to watch it.

Dad, in the same situation, would have jumped down from the tractor, walk-trotted across the field to the gasoline tank in the barnyard. But I can't imagine him ever running out of gas. Grandpa's mistake seems the sort I'd make, and maybe that's why I love the story.

I can only imagine the feeling that matures between two people who divide the day's work for twenty-five years. It seems that such conditions would take the germ of whatever was essentially there—love, hate, or anything between—and develop it, until there were no other feelings, no nuances. Wendell Berry speaks of such emotional honing in his novel *The Memory of Old Jack*. Jack Beechum, and his black hired man, Will Wells, had worked side by side with an astonishing dexterity, as if they were limbs of one anatomy. But their minds held an antagonism, initially unrecognized, that inevitably flushed up in their work. Berry writes, "There began to be a roughening . . . in their teamwork that made them conscious and resentful of their dependence on each other. To Jack this had become a confinement. He began to fret that, having so much land to farm, he could not move except in relation to the other man. . . . In Will this was the result of a failure of interest that had been immanent all along in his knowledge that his labor formalized and preserved no bond between him and the place; he was a man laboring for no more than his existence." The resentment builds until, set free finally by a field accident that is neither man's fault, they fight. Will Wells knocks Jack to the ground and walks away, from the field, from the farm. "And it is final. Their anger was the end of words. . . . They cannot be reconciled, for no real peace ever existed between them, and they are far off in history from the terms and the visions of such a peace."

Whatever feelings, complex, contradictory, Dad felt, as everyone feels, for his father, they must have been cleaned by the work, over all that time, and through dependent days, until at the end, he only loved him.

I'm near the end of this field and Dad has harrowed nearly a quarter of it. I think again of Grandpa, legs swinging leisurely over the side of his Case. He and I come from opposite ends to a joy for farming. He, wanting nothing else in life, could lose himself in it, turn absent-minded in its pleasures. I, knowing nothing, love it out of ignorance, with a child's accepting awe. In both cases, there's a true release from farming's rigorous precision, from the severity that my father feels.

He waves, at the east end of the field, for me to join him. I finish the round, lift the circles free. They drop wet clods, like feces, as they rise up out of the ground. Moving toward him, looking back at the gray strip of uncompleted field, I feel as fine as I have felt.

He nods as I pull alongside. "'Bout got it, huh?"

"Just about."

"Let's finish after lunch. Wanna get a sandwich at Jim's?"

Absolutely. I've been waiting to get some field on me, and can think of nothing better to do with it now than show it in town.

T he Cardinal is between shifts. We are late, by the clock of the town, for lunch, early for beer in earnest. (The white Chevy is not in the lot, and was not parked behind the body shop. "He must be putting in some garden," Dad says.) This is the time of day when a majority of the six or seven customers might actually be strangers, highway travelers mindful of no local civic rhythm.

Jim waves from behind the bar. His brother-in-law, Lloyd, dressed as always in bib overalls and a white T-shirt, is his customer. Lloyd drinks draft Schlitz and speaks of the days he was the sheriff of Baxter. His subject matter is more habitual than his brand. He nods at Dad and me. At a table by the window, four high school senior girls sift the crushed ice in the bottoms of their soft-drink glasses. They are eighteen and in Iowa have a legal right to drink something stronger, yet their presence here—"Let's have lunch at the Cardinal"—momentarily surprises me. The town has moved in subtle ways from the ceremonial sins of The Cloud Room.

We take a table. I stretch out, feeling very nearly content, psychically spreading my color and my dirt as if they were peacock feathers.

Jim smiles and says, "Who you got with you there, Ken? Your new hired man?"

Dad says, "Yeah. He don't work worth a damn, but he claims he doesn't eat much. We'll see about that."

We order cheeseburgers, French fries, 7-Up. Dad takes huge swallows of his soda, orders another.

We discuss the way the work has gone, the fields we'll go into next. The talk, the dissection of Byrdie's farm and our own into their working pieces, brings us again to his plan for dividing, or disposing of, the farm. As much as he wants to keep it, and loves in theory the simplicity of an eighty-acre square for himself, he finds the money he'll have to pay, the debt he'll take, no easier to accept.

"It's just, you think of all the money going into the land," he says, speaking of it as if money were seed, "and for me, the struggle has always been to get the money *out* of it."

Vern walks out of the men's room. I remember Dad saying that Vern had been complaining lately of back trouble and has worked sporadically. He heads for our table, appears angularly distorted, like a child's drawing of a stick figure. He drops heavily onto the chair between us and says that he's in pain.

"Trouble is," he says, winking, feeling the small of his back, "I strained it 'cause I got so much to carry down there, don't you see?"

He tells us that he's needed numbing quantities of liquor to keep the pain tolerably dull and reasonably local, and that his newest girlfriend has nursed him nightly with muscle-warming ointments and lots of fried chicken. "She's a good woman," Vern says. "She makes good chicken, but I had to train her. She useda not know any use for a frying pan but to hit you in the ass with it. She's kinda narrow in the head and broad in the hips, but she's hell on square wheels. Only thing, when she starts the deep-heat rub, she goes right to the root of the problem, then my back hurts all the more 'cause a what I have to lift, if you know what I mean."

Vern asks Dad if he's spent any time recently at the

factory, and says that he hasn't, either, and that he misses the place like a bad case of the hives. "I went in a few days ago, tried to do some light work, what I mean, and the boss got on my ass for no good reason. God *damn*, it made me mad. I looked him in the eye and I read him out good. I told him, 'Hey. You talk like that to me again, I'll play with your nose.' I told him, 'Don't you ever talk like that to me.' He backed off like I'd just let the world-champion fart. I showed the sonuvabitch. And I ain't been back. If that's his gratitude for tryin' to work hurt, the hell with him."

In a few minutes, Jim comes with the cheeseburgers. "I held back on his French fries, Ken," he says, nodding and smiling at me.

"Good," Dad says. "Maybe he'll work a little better this afternoon."

Vern looks at me and seems to see for the first time my sunburn. "Work?" he says, smiling as he's able. "You mean you went out and did some work?"

I say, "I figured it was about time, don't you?"

"Hell, I ain't sure about that. Seemed to me you had the secret of *some*thin' going for you, from what I could see, and now you blow it by goin' out and doin' some work."

"Well," I say, "this guy here threatened to kick me out of town, so I had no choice."

Vern laughs. "Well, just be careful and don't let it get habit-forming. Like the fella says, "I got habits good and bad, I got happy songs and sad, but work's a tune I never learned the words to.' You don't watch out, purty soon you'll be ambitious like your ol' man here."

I say I'll watch out. Dad smiles, shakes his head, chews his lunch. Vern moves very cautiously on his chair into a new position and another humor. "My brother's trial, what I mean, the bastard what shot him, his trial starts Monday and I wanna be there." Again I give him my sympathies, and he thanks me. "He wasn't a saint," Vern says of his brother, "but he was a good man who loved his neighbors." He straightens up through the pain with this elegy and says he'd prefer, instead of a trial, some simpler frontier justice, Old Testament justice: "They're only charging the bastard with second degree, I hear. By God, they oughta just plain hang the fucker. I'll tell you what, they just better not leave him unguarded a single second, is all I got to say, or there's no tellin' what I might do to him. Just no guaranteeing. . . ." He says, "Jim," and thrusts his glass upward, "better have one here." He says to me, "You better have one. It's the best painkiller there is."

"I've got no pain," I say, meaning the words to be light, but Vern, subsiding with his medicine, looks at me and says quietly, "You're damn lucky."

His talk of bus rides to Kansas City, his days of drinking on future pay checks, makes me remember the plans he's had for his camper, parked behind the Tower. I ask him if he's found a buyer.

"No. I decided to keep it," he says. "I'll get it fixed up, so I can have me some wheels when I get my license back. Gotta have something to take my lady out, drive over to Newton once in a while, have a few drinks."

"That doesn't sound like a man who's dying to get out of this town for good," I say.

Vern says, "I've decided it's better for a man to just stay in one place and fight it out. I'll get my camper fixed up, get my license back—and not by goin' to driving school, either. Those bastards ain't gettin' my money, which they put straight into their pockets and don't show nothin' on their income tax. I'll get my license back, what I mean, and I'll have my camper and I'll be all right." He stares straight ahead. Dad and I, on either side of him, chew last bites. Vern surfaces on the other side of his solemnity, brightened by the vision of cruising Jasper County in his camper, with his lady, narrow-headed, broad-hipped, at his side. He smiles through the liquor mask. "Hey," he says, apologizing, "don't pay much attention to me, 'cause I'm really just full of shit. If shit were concrete, I could lay an interstate."

All three of us finish our drinks. Vern and Dad talk about the factory, its creaking inefficiencies, and Dad, without a word of challenge, lets Vern be brave to the boss, here in the safety of whiskey conversation. Vern says that if he and Dad were set free in the place, productivity would soar. He complains of the pace of some of the other workers. "I hope he don't fuck like he works," he says of one of the men, "or somebody's gonna take his wife away from him. Somebody's gonna long-cock him. I think I'm safe in that prediction."

Dad's smile is patience. After a while, he says, "Well, you get filled up, son?" We take long swallows of melted ice, set the glasses finally on the table. "Better get going, then," he says. "It's starting to cloud up, looks like. If we don't get outa here, we'll have to stay and watch it rain."

Vern nods at this idea, cheers it: "C'mon, *rain!*"

Dad walks to the bar to pay and I elaborately stand. Vern tells me not to let my father work me like a nigger. He is near the relief, the contemplative void, that he usually reaches after Southern Comfort. I suggest rest for his back, and as much forbearance as he can bring to his brother's killer's trial.

"When are you going?" I ask.

"Sunday night."

Dad comes back to the table and we walk to the door, farmers returning hurriedly to their fields ahead of a rain.

"Take care, Vern," Dad says and Vern says that he will.

He says, "I's gonna go to Colfax this afternoon, but I'm already supposed to be there and back again. Like the fella says, 'If I'd left an hour ago, I'd be late.' So I think I'll just stay here and root for it to rain." He repeats his travel plan—he'll leave Sunday night, take a bus to Kansas City—and he speaks through the drinks and his survivor's bitterness with an adrenal exultation about the trip. I wonder as I listen to him if he realizes in his excited grief that his brother has at last gotten him out of Prairie City.

The clouds hold no meaningful rain, only a soft shower that wets the windshield on the drive back to the farm and, in the fields, mists against the face like the spray of a wave. I finish the thin edge and take the tractor into the north field to put down its opening marks—north and south, against the east-west fabric of the plot completed. The shower ends unnoticed at some point in the afternoon. A gray-blue cloud bank, moving like vestigial smoke in front of the sun, lasts the afternoon, and the last hour of work, running to sundown, is very nearly clear.

And the next weeks are clear, as well, putting all the farmers on the same schedule. Everyone with business on a tractor works the same shift—early light to light's end—with generally the same work. The countryside seems of an industrious harmony, as if all the farmers were working cooperatively to prepare one enormous field. Those earlier weeks, when men separately interpreted the fitful weather, have given way to a wide agreement, the fusion of sense and instinct. There are no subtleties in the reading of this weather, no confusion in a run of spring heat; you drive to your field and stay there; work as long and as quickly as you can.

At the end of the week, Dad gives me a few days off,

while he disks some ground on our farm so that we'll be able to work without one of us waiting on the other.

It's Monday and, after the engaging routine of the last few weeks, I feel, as completely as if I've been reporting to a factory for a strictly monitored wage, the freedom of a day of vacation. The sky this morning is rapidly filling with a turbulent gray, a rain smoke that promises to give a day off to every farmer within several miles, whether he's put in for it or not.

The retailers are surely pleased to see these clouds. Rain, of course, is the only condition that would explain a farmer's presence in town this time of year. A Two-thirds-off sale in every shop on the square would not as effectively stop the field work. The barber shop, the bank, the lumber yard may get today business that's waited for a rain.

After breakfast, I draw up a list of my own weather-deferred chores and head down 117 to Roberts Brothers hardware. At the stop sign, where the highways cross, I see on the left the baseball diamond, its dirt infield freshly rolled and swept, turned like a grain field to receive the season. I make a right turn onto 163 and immediately take in a sight so surprising as to suggest a prairie mirage. Fifty yards ahead, in place of the dimness I am expecting, a light shines through the windows of Cookie's shop. He normally holds so firmly to his aversion for Mondays that I had come to think of the shop's darkness on that day of the week as some regular diminishing of a natural light, like a sunset. Now I also notice the white Chevrolet parked in the rear driveway. Have I lost a day? Is it actually Tuesday? With free time on my hands, I'd have welcomed the chance to spend some of it with Cookie. But this is an event, one that makes a visit nothing less than requisite.

He's standing by the shelves of paint against the east wall of the shop, staring resignedly at the hood of a blue Pinto, looking very much like a victim, as if the Pinto were holding him hostage here. He looks up, apparently sees the question on my face, and answers it.

"I've had some unusual doctor bills," he says. His wife has been quite ill. "And I've got so damn much work stacked up it was actually making me nervous. So it's a Monday morning and here I am . . . Doesn't mean I *like* it, though." He shrugs: What's a man to do?

"This," he says, pointing to the Pinto. "I agreed in a sober moment to touch up this hood months ago. Every time I saw it go by I'd feel a little guiltier." He giggles. "It's terrible to have your procrastinations circling you all the time."

I laugh. "My boss gave me the day off," I say, explaining myself in return. "So I'll bother you for a while."

"Do," Cookie says. "Grab a brush and throw some paint at the hood if you want. No pride of craftmanship involved in this one. . . . Doggy bastard."

He is filling a dent in the hood with a substance he calls, simply, "mud"—which, in color and texture, is exactly what it resembles. He holds the mud on a wooden palate, dips a knife into it, crouches on his knees and applies it in long, sure strokes.

"Don't you ever hammer out a dent like that?" I ask.

"Not much, anymore," he says. "I'm afraid tin beating has vanished in the way I knew it. I used to pound every dent that came in here. Now they replace panels or pile this shit into the hole."

He places the palate on the floor and stands. "C'mere."

We walk to a tall cabinet near the overhead door and he pulls out a drawer filled with tools arranged in a manner that might generously be described as random. He plucks from the pile a small instrument that looks like a hammer that has grown brass tumors at either end of its head.

"This is one I fashioned for pounding out dents," he says, and demonstrates, flipping the tool in his hand like a timpanist. "Wherever you have a dent, you also have a ridge around the dent. So while you tapped the dent out, you had to be tapping the ridge in at the same time." He lightly pounds the air, then drops the tool back into the drawer. He rummages briefly through other drawers, pulling out more tools no longer needed, the brass-green tint of oxidation on them, that he'd designed for the eccentric angles and chasms of a broken automobile. He drops a tool into its drawer. "I always say, 'Be not the first on which the new is tried. Nor the last to cast the old aside.' How's that for a bit of nickel philosophy?" Reluctantly, he moves back to the Pinto.

We talk through the morning over a wide range of subjects: His early memories of nights when he drove with friends to fields south of town where they passed the night drinking alcohol and near beer, and Cookie sat atop his car playing a mouth harp, a kind of accompaniment beneath the conversation. "You could really get some music out of one of those things, and it'd carry for miles on a night breeze." He continues, "You do that now and they'd throw your ass in jail. We didn't have highway patrol spooks to contend with."

He talks of other instruments—the tuba, the E flat alto, the French horn—that he played with varying skills and enthusiasm in high school. "The damn French horn was a bitch. The teacher always said, 'Imagine you've just sucked a lemon,' to get you to pucker your mouth just so, but I'll defy you to get much music from a horn when they tell you to pretend you're blowin' on a lemon."

He pays renewed attention to his work. I ask which manufacturer most often provides new parts—panels and chrome, circles and strips—that fit the spaces they're made for. He says none of them these days supply replacements worth the effort they require. He expresses, as he has before, his amazement at the loyalty people develop for certain automobiles, finding from the point of view of one who sees the skeletons nothing that deserves devotion. He mentions several men in town and the cars they always choose. His own preference for a Chevrolet, when I'd asked him the hypothetical question some weeks ago, was arrived at through negative deduction and with an audible lack of romance.

He says, "Were you savvy to Wayne Morgan?"

"I knew who he was. I knew his daughter. She and your daughter were good friends."

"Oh, hell yes," Cookie says. "They were. Went everywhere together.

"The reason I mention Wayne, though, I thought of him just now because he always drove late-model Oldsmobiles. That's all he'd drive." Morgan was killed in an automobile crash several years ago. I was grown and gone, but the accident, as I recall my hearing of it, was an especially vivid tragedy. At least one other person was killed, and it occurred at a locally notorious spot where several cars have crashed—Warrick's corner, an absurdly sharp curve of 163 east of town, named for the family whose farm house sits at the lethal apex.

Cookie worked on any of Wayne Morgan's cars that needed repair. "We had our differences," he says, "but he wouldn't let anybody else touch his cars, that's for sure." He'd been working, in fact, on the last one Morgan owned, or was waiting to work on it. Ordered parts had not arrived, and after several weeks, Morgan finally bought, for the interim, an old car that was barely able to run. He and another local man began to tool and tune the old car's engine and very late one night decided to test their work. They drove out of town, east on 163, and lost control of the car at Warrick's corner. The new parts for the Oldsmobile had come to Cookie's shop that day.

"If I'da got those parts in reasonable time, he wouldn't have bought that car," Cookie says. He adds, "It wasn't my fault. I know that. But a fellow thinks about those things." Morgan's family insisted that Cookie complete his work on the car, and he began work the day of the funeral. He says, remembering, "There *may* be an eerier feeling than knowing you're working on a dead man's car."

He moves wordlessly around the Pinto for several minutes. The harsh sound of tools dropping to the floor echoes in the suddenly empty cave of conversation and outside, as if cued, the rain begins or is noticed for the first time. After a while, Cookie, as if feeling a host's responsibility, introduces a lighter subject. "Got your garden in?"

As a matter of fact, I do. Behind my house, an area large enough to feed a family was turned for me by a neighbor using his motor-driven tiller. I've planted several kinds of lettuce, spinach, peas, cucumbers, radishes. I'd never planted a garden, my duties as a youth having been confined to some desultory weeding and picking strawberries from our various beds, grown thick as rugs, which left me with a violent rash around my wrists, like bracelets, where the serrated leaves brushed against them.

But now, living here again, for such special reason, it seemed something like sacrilege to ignore the opportunity. The patch behind my house is a nearly perfect square, a deep black color that intimates an aggressive ripeness in the soil that can hardly be held in. In the first few days of hoeing and planting, I drew rows in the dirt with hard-edged precision, dropped seeds into them at package-directed depth and interval, covered the seeds as if I were drawing a blanket over sleeping children. Working with my father, and watching other fields, I've become so keenly aware of the fertility of this soil that I've imagined my garden, surrounded by residential lawn that runs to other lawns, as a small square hole cut into an imprisoning green skin through which I can reach the dirt's intended purpose.

In fact, gardening is an extremely serious subject in Prairie City. I've heard, in the Cardinal, opinions on timing and strategy discussed with the heat normally reserved for matters of sport or the soul. Tomatoes, especially, and the techniques for planting them, are repetitively argued. Shallow trench advocates debate deep hole theorists, with both schools claiming results that give Iowa an agrarian version of the fish story. The tomato that got away.

Gardens, holes to let the earth out, are in nearly every yard in town. Many are landscapes of astonishing ambition, consuming entire lawns, running in long and variously sized rows, in every shade of green, all God's vegetables seemingly represented. Great pride is at stake. Reputations are sought and fluctuate. People assess the plots from season to season:

Mattie doesn't look to have the garden she did last year.

I believe Wilfred has his biggest garden ever.

Not surprisingly, some of the most impressive gardens are planted by farmers—those who've moved to town and now commute to their fields, and those who've retired. For the farmer who resides in Prairie City, his garden seems to be his work in miniature—all the sweep and size of his field work brought down to the tight, representative scale of a manicured rectangle. A retired farmer's garden is, on the other hand, the remaining release for work that's been instinctive. I think of a retired man's former fields, the scope of his work then, and of the methodical reduction of it, as he's aged, to a manageable lawn of farming. And I think of my father, who's always been a most begrudging gardener, wishing to withdraw from what he has to the easier dimensions of "an eighty."

In all cases, the effort given to a garden seems a kind of uninhibited visual flourish that this culture allows. It's as if the austerity that places such psychological restrictions on any personal flamboyance lets pass a preening delivered in the form of work. Gardens here can be as outrageous as their owners wish, and as they begin to bloom through the season, rows of sweet corn and cabbages opening into outlandish leaf-spreads, and squash in brilliant hues, the gardens take on a sanctioned garishness, a plumage.

Cookie, though without a farming history, has long been known as one of the town's best gardeners. He has a spot, south of his house and larger than, extending almost to the road, where he puts a tremendous variety of seeds into the ground, raising sweet corn, cucumbers, tomatoes (he's had equal luck with both techniques), and several kinds of squash, in such abundance that he habitually gives much of his yield away. His motives, however, are different from those of the farmers and offer release of another kind. He has said, when talking of his garden, "When I like it is after the first few weeks of the *hard* work, after it's been all put in and you've fought off the first round of weeds. Then, after I finish up here in the shop, I have a few drinks and go home and walk around in the garden. Just sorta poke and pretend. I'll see a weed here, see a weed over there, poke at 'em with a hoe while I'm walking through."

I've remembered his description, as I've done exactly that at the end of the day, after writing. And I say to him now, "You're right about the true pleasures of it. It's great relaxation just to play in the dirt after a day of work."

He nods. "Like I told you." He says, "I've been real good this year. Usually I'm the last one in the neighborhood to get mine in. And in the past, I'd come home after a session at the 'office' and I'd be too boozy—get some planted too deep or the rows goin' off in wiggly lines." He giggles. "But this year I've been especially careful."

"But it's a therapeutic kind of care," I say.

"That's right," Cookie replies enthusiastically. "As I've said, the best time is after the first thorough weeding. You can go out, poke around, do a little inspecting. Just lean on your hoe and contemplate your sins." He nods again, then begins to direct his attention once more to the car he's patching. "And what feels good to me," he says, having a last thought before he resumes, "is to spend a couple hours in the garden on a hot day. Really get a sweat up, get some of the booze out of the system. I'll tell you, it's the one sweat I've never resented raising." He crouches once again, eye to hood ornament.

"Cookie," I say, recalling an earlier talk we had, "maybe that's what 'sweet oil' is? A sweat you don't resent."

"Maybe," he says, smiling.

He works, and we talk, until noon. The rain falls with a gathering force that threatens to rinse the week.

In our west field, we exchange implements, disk for harrow. Dad has an afternoon's disking left and will be able to plant the ground after I've been over it. So we simply reverse, from our days at Byrdie's (a week earlier), the assignments and the timing.

I steer the harrow to the end of the field opposite Dad, moving slowly along the fence line, feeling out the much wider span of the harrow. Not only is it wider than a disk but it stays always in the ground; its raking fingers cannot be lifted free, like disk blades, of damage they would do. They will simply do it.

The harrow sweeps, like a janitor's broom, through a quarter turn that lines it up with the edge of the field, comes around and makes a sibilant swish of broom claw through soil. There's no need to confer with Dad about the work. Once he has completed his disking, he'll leave and return with the planter, following my harrow marks with seeds. Planting is the fastidious chore of grain farming. There remains in its machinery some vestige of the pioneer manually dropping seeds—precisely, at measured intervals—into a neat shallow slice in the ground. There are faster planters than the one my father uses. His planter does not force seeds into the ground on a high-pressure column of air. His planter is not even his; it's borrowed from our neighbor, along with the squat gray Ford tractor that pulls it.

After manipulating the Farmall's gearshift for several days, I've found its touch, as one knows the peculiarities of his door key in a temperamental lock. Ahead of me, the disked field is a mass, churned and freshly set. The Farmall races forward, the harrow lurching after it. With no blades to drop, no levers to lower, no metal groaning against ground and gravity, the harrow seems the kind of implement that should be pulled by a horse.

The opened ground, catching the sun, is red, yellow, brown, the spectrum of a well-aerated soil. A subsoil is the color of its iron compounds, and soil that is desirably porous will oxidize, will literally rust in the air that freely circulates through it. Soil that cannot get air is a drab, dead gray. Byrdie's subsoil—better than most—is in comparison to ours asthmatically gray-brown. Iowa soils are graded by university agronomists, and named for the place in the state where they were originally found, named like a species. The soil running beneath me is Tama or Muscatine, both of which are highly desirable for growing corn and beans. Minimally sloped, texturally silty, moderately permeable, slightly erodable, they are rated the best grain-farming soils in the state and, since they are in this state, the best grain-farming soils in the world. Each year, soil like this sells for prices that can simply go no higher, and the next year goes for a price higher than that. The land I am crossing is, according to the state's average, more valuable by thirty-six percent than it was a year ago.

The harrow is working like a comb. I finish a length, loosely spin the wheel for my return. Its width demands a larger turning radius than the disk, a distance I'm not used to. The harrow's end seems so far from the tight core of my controls that it must be someone else's duty to watch it. I can't be held responsible for a piece of metal moving that far away from where I sit. But I am responsible, and I'm watching my responsibility about to meet the wire mesh of the fence where harrow, fence or both will twist, snap, who knows what? I cramp the wheel, stomp and hold the left wheel's brake, and the tractor jerks through a turn that has no space to spare. No place for the other side of the harrow, the pivoting side, to go, and it meets the left rear wheel, grabs its tread, begins to climb the wheel toward me as if in sudden revolt. I brake fully, immediately look to the other side of the field to see if I've been discovered. He's disking away from me. I sit for a moment, covered with a dirt that makes a disk's dust look like talcum, one end of the harrow about to become snarled in fence, the other vertical against a wheel and on a path that would harrow the left side of my body. The heat of the day, a pleasant warmth as long as the tractor is moving, descends on this predicament.

I look around me, and feel marvelous in the company of old friends: the heat; the dirt; the Farmall, idling and unquestioning; and, most of all, my careless farming. For I've managed, not a few times in the years past, to steer a tractor and a harrow into this same situation and decide there's a certain gift, a kind of exact haphazardness, in being able to align machine and nature in such complete conflict.

Even better, not only do I recognize the looks of my mistake, I am certain of its solution. For this is work I know, something I do extremely well. I may have no touch for keeping plow in furrow, but nobody knows better than I do how to reassemble equipment after a mistake.

I jump down from the tractor, walk to the fence, kneel at the harrow. Each rectangular section is loosely connected to the frame by iron loops, like chain links, a simple assemblage I could identify blindfolded. As I jiggle the section, the loops slacken to make the uncoupling easier and, with some effort, the section comes free of the frame, clanging like a prisoner in chains. I move behind the harrow and drag the heavy section safely away from the fence. At the other end, where the section rests against a tire, a few links are open from the harrow's scaling of the tread. The remaining links release with a snap, and I pull the section off the tire. The sections sag as they're pulled, the dead weight of iron being dragged through the dirt. Both ends are off and several feet away. The effort brings a sweat that cuts through the dirt on my chest and arms. I climb up, put the tractor in gear, complete the turn, the half harrow obediently following, then hop down and reconnect the outer sections. Dragging, jangling, hammering the chain loops into place again, all movements certain. I nod, satisfield, and swagger, a field mechanic, back to the tractor and the long road of work.

Up, on, ahead into the sun. The field, whitely lit in this direction, appears the same in shade and texture, left, right, center. In other words, I'm having trouble in the bright sun discerning the ground I've covered from the ground I haven't, and the earth itself is no help. With a disk, the path one makes is clear. A disk leaves a black, rippled strip. But the harrow is a subtler instrument, narrows the ridges the disk created. It also leaves a single line at the edge of its span, a mark that guides the farmer and shows him where his previous round ended.

I cannot at the moment find that mark. When the sun was at my back, its shadows lit the field so I could separate the two browns. But as I drive into the sun, the field appears as a single shade and I must rely on texture, must find the mark, a thin, unbroken cut set among an entire field of thin, unbroken paralleling cuts. It seems like trying to find the one cord set millimetrically out of line in a dark-brown corduroy coat. Standing, squinting, leaning over the steering wheel to get slightly closer to the ground, I look vainly for the mark. Every slice and furrow grows and deepens, becomes a canyon, but the canyon I need could—for all I can tell—be any one of them. So I steer to the left, suspecting I'll overlap ground the harrow has finished. Better a field harrowed twice than not harrowed, a thought that sounds puritan enough to be stitched in yarn on a wheat-colored sampler and hung in someone's kitchen.

A friend of mine, a Southern woman I knew in Chicago, once said that she believed the Midwestern sensibility must surely be the most finely tuned of any region's, because of the landscape that nurtures it. Plain, squarely sectioned, altered only by its season, it has none of the easy majesty of oceans, mountains, forests. A Midwesterner must look hard for his natural variety, must grow an appreciation for the hummocky roll of hillsides, the imperceptibly varying line of land to sky. My friend may very well have had something, or so I'm thinking now as I bend, like a man to a microscope, past the steering wheel, searching among millions of disk and harrow tracks for the one that can tell me where I've been.

I reach the end, sure only that I left no gaps. The end rows are in shadow, and the immediate change from sun to shade is blinding. The engine coughs hollowly as the fence, ditch, the road beyond begin to come into focus, extending the field.

My father also comes into focus, out there. He has finished with the disk, returned on the borrowed Ford with the planter. I'd been hunting so obsessively for the harrow mark that I'd paid no attention to his progress. He sits calmly on the Ford's seat, arms draped over the steering wheel, like a man waiting patiently in line. I make the turn, shift to neutral, step down. The soil receives my weight and reluctantly lets go. I walk to him, lean against the Ford's gray fender. It is a small, pugnacious-looking tractor, so low to the ground that I can rest my arms on the top of its fender and feel the metal, sun-heated.

"Didn't even see you finish," I say.

He looks behind him at the planter. Seed corn has been poured into its four round containers and will be dropped, as the planter moves, into rows thirty inches apart. He told me the other day that he'd heard some farmers were planting rows just sixteen inches wide, incredibly tight and another attempt to extend, within the fixed limits of the land they own, the land they own. "I don't know," he said of the idea, "you plant them that close, you might as well sow 'em."

"How's it going?" he asks.

I laugh. "Pretty well. I nearly drove into the fence at the other end, and I'm having a hell of a time telling where I've harrowed. But I figured it was all right to harrow it close, even if I go over some ground more than once. You don't lose anything that way, do you?"

"Just time," he says. He adds, to assure me, "But we've got plenty of that. Besides, you're sure not hurting the ground any."

"Just so you don't overtake me."

He shakes his head. "You're farther already than I'll get today." I turn back to the tractor, and we wave, as if we were hundreds of yards apart, the sounds of the Ford putting the equivalent of space between us. He moves away, the planter's wheels and conveyors squeaking. It rocks fragilely, moves with slightly more speed into a shallow draw, sways with a feminine grace.

Dad reaches the west edge of the field, sets the planter, drops to the ground a long metal rod that extends several feet. At the end of the rod, a sharp metal disk, like a single thin disk blade, turns in the soil, making a line. Like the harrow, a planter leaves a line as it moves, but a mark that must be followed exactly if the planted rows are to be parallel. He looks around, sees that everything that should be in the ground is ready, starts forward, carrying the year's first seeds.

He will put his seed corn two inches beneath the soil. He remembers his father planting four inches deep. But the hybrid he's dropping sprouts more quickly up, sends down a hard, green spiral, like a corkscrew. And when he plants beans, he will almost literally lay them on the surface. The berry itself comes to the top and its vines spread from the vulnerable pale-yellow seed. A bean will break soil four days, five days after it's been planted.

From the Farmall's seat, I watch him plant and think that, whether it's corn, beans, or anything else a farmer puts into the ground, there is in the act an optimism I'd not understood. As much as farmers show their suspicion of the skies, and speak of weather, government and the world's markets as living adversaries, they also assume each year a virginal faith. They place thousands of dollars in seeds into the ground, thinly cover them, and go away, leaving them unattended and exposed. A trust—more essential than rich land, the best hybrids, or new equipment—is required for farming; an almost organic trust that cities have long lost or perhaps never had.

He comes back toward me, an intricately detailed speck, the planter high and fibrillating behind him, like a poised insect. I can see him, seated very low on the Ford in the eye of heat and dust, appearing to straddle the tractor's working shaft. He squints tightly into the sun, sees without effort the crystalline black line his work has drawn; a free miniaturist in a time of imprisoning scale.

I put the Farmall into gear, take the harrow forward, leaving the end of the field he's approaching, moving toward and away from him. We are once more joined and separated by the breadth of our land, as it has been.